SPIRITUAL, ETHICAL AND PASTORAL ASPECTS OF DEATH AND BEREAVEMENT

Gerry R. Cox and Ronald J. Fundis
Editors

Death, Value and Meaning Series
Series Editor: John D. Morgan

Baywood Publishing Company, Inc.
AMITYVILLE, NEW YORK

Library of Congress Catalog Number: 92-5760
ISBN: 0-89503-101-9 (Paper)
ISBN: 0-89503-100-0 (Cloth)

Library of Congress Cataloging-in-Publication Data

Spiritual, ethical, and pastoral aspects of death and bereavement /
   Gerry R. Cox and Ronald J. Fundis, editors.
      p.   cm. – – (Death, value, and meaning series)
   Includes index.
   ISBN 0-89503-100-0 (cloth), – – ISBN 0-89503-101-9 (pbk.)
   1. Church work with the bereaved.   2. Church work with the
terminally ill.   3. Bereavement– –Religious aspects.   4. Death–
–Religious aspects.   5. Euthanasia– –Religious aspects.   I. Cox,
Gerry R. II. Fundis, Ronald J. III. Series.
BV4330.S6   1992
259'.6– –dc20   92-5760
                                              CIP

Table of Contents

Introduction

Gerry R. Cox and Ronald J. Fundis

As the world continues to age, the technologies improve, and the catastrophic and debilitating diseases persist, ethical dilemmas will most likely multiply for societies in general and for mental, physical and spiritual health providers in particular. While societies struggle encumbered with ethical uncertainties without an apparent sense of urgency, professional practitioners, patients and their family members continue to experience the realities of human suffering, the technological limitations, and almost overwhelming personal and psychological burdens in the absence of societal arrangements and rituals needed to educate, support and comfort them.

This collection of previously unpublished essays addresses a wide range of topics so relevant to the on-going debates regarding dying and death and the subtleties, nuances, and complexities which accompany these phenomena. The authors have attempted to contribute their experiences, insights and research results in such a way as to clarify rather than obfuscate. Topic coverage is broad; however, content depth is not sacrificed. The diversity of authors' backgrounds, both geographical and disciplinary, also serves to make this volume rather unique.

In Part I, David Meagher makes a case for the ethics and necessity of death education. After discussing death education and what it is supposed to do, he describes the research in death education. He then defines ethics and addresses ethical issues. Meagher closes by offering ethical principles relevant to the educational process. The focus of this chapter is limited principly to academic education and does not fully address applications and nonacademic settings.

Ross Gray and Brian Doan begin by discussing the changing attitudes toward cancer and the role of heroes in that change. By developing heroic role models for those who have cancer, society has placed an added burden upon them. The authors view hope—both the causes and the consequences—in the development of cancer. They close with an examination of ethical and clinical issues.

Lynne Martins examines the charismatic movement and its impact on dying and bereavement. She analyzes the pros and cons of the charismatic movement and its impact on dying and bereavement within congregations and parishes. She discusses the paradox of Romans 8:28: what to do when God is silent and with hope as the key element of faith. While some might argue that introducing elements of one's own faith might be too intrusive, ethnocentric, or even unwelcome, Martin eloquently develops the charismatic viewpoint.

In Part II, Delton Glebe focuses upon the uniqueness of pastoral care for aiding the dying and bereaved. He examines the dying process, grieving, and the role of the pastor. He also discusses expectations of the pastor, dilemmas in pastoring, styles of pastoring, and pastoral resources. Although there is not a consensus among pastoral counselors that discovering a client's history of coping with previous "smaller" problems or traumas, Glebe builds a case that this can be a useful and productive strategy.

Jean Crabtree offers an approach for ministering to people with AIDS. While ministering to the dying is difficult, ministering to those with AIDS is even more challenging. She offers an approach for meeting the needs of those dying with AIDS. Using the experience of Women's College Hospital, she makes a case for facing the problem in the manner presented in the Canadian experience. This chapter is, in fact, an impassioned plea to effectively minister to AIDS patients and their families.

Dorothy Southall presents a practical model for clergy and lay people to work together in the grieving process. She develops a model for communications between clergy and lay people; offers methods of communications; develops a model for viewing lay persons in grief; and closes with a plan for clergy and lay people to work together. Issues regarding the role of the laity and the continuum of care are raised by the author.

Lynne Martins closes Part II with a model for adjustment for the dying and bereaved. She suggests that the church is a model for healing grief—psychologically, physically, and spiritually. She develops the concept of corporate mourning and the role of the church. The strength of community that comes from small groups such as Sunday schools, choirs, etc. are also discussed. In addition she incorporates familiar stages of grief with practical aspects of ministering to the dying and bereaved. Martins also develops the role of networking and support systems to aid the dying and the bereaved. She finishes with resources to aid both the lay person and the helping professional.

Part III opens with Paul Sakalauskas' examination of the role of belief systems for the bereaved in a comparative study of Canada and the United States. The impact of spiritual and cultural beliefs is also presented. Case studies are used to illustrate the process. He also discusses immigrants and refugees plus the cultural influence that they brought with them. As a funeral director, Sakalauskas offers an analysis of the caregiver's role and examines relevant studies.

Ted Creen develops a model visualization process for handling grief. Using the example of visualization of Psalm 23, Creen demonstrates the model of visualization to assist in facing grief.

Greg Mogenson examines three approaches to the mourning process. Using the concept of irreplaceable objects, he develops an imaginal approach which he contrasts with Freud's notion of "reality testing." He then uses Shelly's elegy, "Adonais," to further contrast Freud's materialistic account of the grieving process. He finishes with an application of the imaginal approach to the mourning process. An example of a dialogue between an image-oriented therapist and a bereaved patient is developed.

Michael Bull develops a persuasive case for the importance of balance as individuals attempt to cope with lifetime losses. Anticipatory grieving, "what if" thinking, and denial are examined in the context of crisis—not merely as dangerous but as potential opportunity. Balancing lifetime losses enhances not only the grieving process, but also enriches daily lives and relationships.

In Part IV, Connie Guist offers an African perspective of attitudes toward childhood death. Her research presents a case for awareness of cultural heritage for caregivers responding to childhood death. Her analysis of Kenyan attitudes toward dying and bereavement provides an understanding of the role of culture in attitude development.

Carol Irizarry presents a study of Australian children's responses to the death of a grandparent. While few studies exist, Irizarry offers new insights into the grieving of children. She found that parents were often unaware of their children's reactions and responses: children remembered a great deal about their grandparent's death; they felt pressured to get over the death quickly; and the opportunity to help children develop was often missed.

Craig Seaton offers a practical guide for helping dying children cope with their future utilizing guided autobiography with an extensive, detailed appendix for maximizing its potential.

In Part V, Mary Kachoyeanos and Florence Selder attempt to answer the question of whether parental grieving is as definite and orderly as traditional grief theorists suggest, or unending as clinicians who work with the grieving suggest. Using a sample of bereaved parents from a Compassionate Friends group, they offer a view of parental survival of sudden death of a child that focuses on the process based upon a Life Transition theory framework. The chapter demonstrates that parental grieving is long-lasting and offer suggestions for aiding the process and Kachoyeanos and Selder support the Compassionate Friends approach.

Kjell Kallenberg systematically develops the concept of "view of life" and its effects on bereavement and loss. The components of "view of life" are empirically tested using in-depth interviewing techniques on a group of subjects who have experienced a sudden and unexpected death. Four distinct patterns of grief emerged from the research that were correlated with aspects of "view of life." The attitudes of trust/mistrust served as major indicators of distinct grief patterns.

Tadini Bacigalupi examines the historical foundations of Americans' health and life perceptions as outgrowths of their views on death. There is considerable literature describing the United States as a death-denying society, a society whose members seem to go to almost any length to postpone death. It is suggested that Americans no longer life, but rather live in fear of death. In this sense, America may indeed be a paranoid society.

Vernon Gunckel offers an analysis of the impact of social change on the role of the funeral director and clergy in the funeral and post-funeral needs of individuals. He also discusses the role of funeral directors and clergy in sponsoring support groups.

Dorothy Ley offers an overview of spirituality and spiritual care in hospice. The role of spirituality and spiritual care is not only a part of the structure of the organization, but it is also a part of the process of managing pain, re-establishing communication, finding oneself, and facing suffering. She also discusses the care of those with AIDS.

In Part VI, Brian Woodrow examines the question of personhood and the biomedical ethical decision of neoeuthanasia. Woodrow suggests the landmark decision of the British Columbia Court of Appeal in July of 1988 was correct in ruling that the human fetus was not a person. Woodrow argues that active euthanasia on newborn infants with severe abnormalities is not killing. He also casts light on using anencephalic neonates for transplantation purposes. He closes with words of caution and challenge.

Gerry Cox and Ronald Fundis discuss the ethical problems of practicing euthanasia. After examining the types of euthanasia, they offer an analysis of the medical, legal, and moral issues facing physicians and families. The administration of certain pain-killing drugs is examined as a possible source of a more subtle form of euthanasia.

Abbyann Lynch addresses four ethical issues regarding organ transplants. After discussing the need for donors, she asks whether donors should choose to be donors or, as in many European countries, be assumed to be donors unless one says no. Is it more ethical to have individuals opt in or opt out? Secondly, how "dead" ought the organ donor be? Thirdly, she addresses the question of growing human fetuses for organ donors. Fourthly, the issue of government funding for organ transplantation is examined. Her analysis should offer a stimulus for further discussion among professionals and the general public.

PART I

Ethical Issues

CHAPTER 1

The Ethics of Death Education

David K. Meagher

In giving thought to this chapter on the "Ethics of Death Education," it reminded me of a poem I read many years ago. This poem, *A Learned Man,* by Stephen Crane, seemed to succinctly describe a major concern about death education and the death educator. Crane wrote [1, p. 119]:

> A learned man came to me once.
> He said, "I know the way—Come."
> And I was overjoyed with this.
> Together we hastened.
> Soon, too soon, were we
> Where my eyes were useless.
> And I knew not the ways of my feet.
> I clung to the hand of my friend,
> But, at last he cried, "I am lost."

Humankind has always concerned itself with death. We have developed rituals, designed institutions, formulated concepts and constructed language to help us cope with our own mortality and ultimate death. In our coping processes, we have created the funeral industry, hospice for the terminally ill, the science of thanatology, and death education.

In the last two years, death education has come under fire by a number of individuals and agencies. A sample of some of the criticisms would include the following statements: "Much of death education is psychological manipulation, it is a form of value modification that is being practiced on subjects (students and participants) by persons who

3

presume that attitudes need to be changed" [2, p. 5]. This critic goes on to ask: "Are we solving anything with this? Or are we only creating new problems?"

Another criticism states that: "Death education is not simply a matter of an educator helping a student/client through a crisis. Programmed repetition of death, despair, and personal evaluation of self-worth in these programs may be turning the participants into suicide victims" [3, p. 34].

A third critic asks: "What are the attitudes the death education advocate wants to change? What are the various death practices for which they seek 'wider acceptance'? The answer to these questions may not be easy to accept. Death education allows or encourages the participant to choose as options various death practices: suicide, euthanasia or abortion. These practices are completely acceptable to the death education practitioner" [4, p. 12].

Are these criticisms completely objective and valid? I think not. Is there justification for these criticisms? I believe there is. Does death education suffer from an almost a priori lack of credibility with respect to efficiency? Upon close scrutiny, this may be so.

Death education—what is it? Death education has been defined as that educational process by which the participant confronts the objective data surrounding the phenomena of death and dying, examines personal attitudes, and develops strategies for dealing with these phenomena as the final stages of life. Death education has also been defined as a process whereby each person is helped to develop from childhood through maturity and to senescence with an acceptance of death as a fact of life. Consistent with these two definitions is the concept that death education is a process to help individuals come to terms with his/her own feelings and attitudes towards death and dying. The death education referred to is not an endeavor limited to schools, but is directed to any and all death education programs. In addition to educational institutions at all levels, death education workshops and seminars are being offered by hospitals, residential care facilities, churches, community organizations, the federal government within its own jurisdiction, and by professional associations, not only for their membership but for the society as a whole. Education programs are offered by hospice through their out-reach programs. Organizations such as the American Red Cross, the Girl Scouts of America, and Cancer Care offer classes on coping with loss and dealing with the dying family member. Death education programs have been presented in newspapers, on television and in a variety of self-awareness, self-development books, such as *Personal Death Awareness* and *The Art of Dying*. In a way, one might define grief counseling as a form of death education. Death education does have, after all, three major components: *prevention, crisis intervention* and *survivor postvention.*

What is death education supposed to do? The literature provides the following answers.

The basic goals of death education have been described as:

1. **information sharing**—including the dissemination of relevant concepts related to thanatology, to the care of the dying and bereaved;
2. **values clarification**—this involves activities which enable individuals to consider a variety of alternatives and then to incorporate these choices into healthful behavior. Included in this outcome is the goal to help the participant consider socioethical issues related to death and to define value judgements that these issues raise;
3. **the development of effective coping behaviors**—including problem-solving skills for self-reliance and helping others to make appropriate adjustments. The goal is to help the participant deal effectively with the idea of his/her personal death and the death of significant others; and
4. **the adoption of a positive attitude toward death and dying.**

However acceptable these might appear to be, these goals contain statements that are grist for the critic's mill and with some justification. Terms such as "appropriate adjustments," "positive attitude," and "effectively dealing with one's death," raise the issue of whose definitions of "appropriateness. "relevancy," "positive," and "effectiveness" will be accepted.

In death education, as in all of education, the concern is with human beings—to do something for them and with them. Is it the intention of death education to change attitudes? Should it be? The response in the literature since the beginnings of death education in the late sixties and early seventies has been an overwhelming **YES**. Simpson wrote in 1979 that the attitudinal objectives in death education are of primary importance [5, pp. 165-174]. In the same year, Hoetler and Epley stated that the prevalent assumption concerning the impact of death education has been the derivation of positive benefits from exposure to death related subject matter [6, pp. 67-76]. There seems to have been a universal agreement that the desired outcome of death education is the influencing or changing of attitudes of the participant. The direction of this change has been defined as toward a more positive or favorable attitude. An assumption underlying the choice of material that is presented in death education is that an adequate and appropriate death education is one that is based upon facing reality and not avoiding it. This is one of the places that lends some credibility to the aforementioned criticisms. What constitutes a positive or favorable attitude toward death and dying? If there is an agreement that a certain attitude is positive and that another attitude is negative, can this agreement be validated by empirical research? But we do not yet fully know which responses to death are healthy and which are pathological.

This brings to mind the question of what constitutes a good death? Is a good death a death that was portrayed in "The Love Story," by Erich Segal, where the wife is dying; her face is made up; the slats of the blinds are angled so the sun shines through from heaven above [7]. In her last moment, she reaches for her husband, touches his hand, and asks him not to worry. Death is shared in a loving, non-fearing way.

When we say "a good death" do we mean "good" for the patient, "good" for the family, "good" for the institution, "good" for the society, or is the term not possible to generically or universally define? Might a "good death" depend on the wishes of the individual? Might not "good" be limited to how the individual wishes to live through his/her own dying?

Increased and heightened personal death awareness is obviously of significance. Whether or not it has fulfilled a role in preventing morbidity or pathological bereavement patterns or produced a better dying process is unclear. Ernest Becker, in *The Denial of Death* wrote that on a conscious level one may accept the eventuality of one's death, but on an emotional level, one may strongly deny it [8]. A positive death attitude may be seen as one in which this conflict is in the process of being resolved. A negative death attitude, conversely, is usually defined as a tendency to accept totally a denial or rejection of one's own death. Too often, though, a positive attitude toward death and dying has been described as accepting one's own death as inevitable. This presents a potential conflict of some interest. Does death education advocate that the dying patient accept death as inevitable in the light of some research that describes the rejection of the inevitability of death as a variable that seems to increase longevity and the quality of life in terminally ill patients? I refer here to the concept of the "survival quotient" which theorizes that terminally ill patients who are able to accept the severity of their disease, but deny the inevitability of their death, tend to live beyond their prognosis. Do we have valid research which clearly describes the negative consequences of a death denial or avoidance? Is there some inherent ethical wrong in an avoidance of death?

Catherine Sanders, in her book *The Mourning After*, describes four types of bereavement emerging from her study of bereavement [9]. One type was identified as the "denial group." Sanders writes that individuals in this group are ". . . needing to employ defence mechanisms in order to deal with crisis" [9, p. 129]. They are what she calls "determined optimists," reluctant to admit common human foibles and keep a "stiff upper lip."

Sanders writes that there has been concern that those individuals undergoing grief who do not ventilate their emotions will be a risk for poor outcome. This was not the case in her study, Sanders reports. The coping mechanism of the "denial group" appeared to be facilitative. They did not deny death itself, but rather they denied their overt emotions surrounding the bereavement. Denial, Sanders concludes, is apparently an adaptive defence that serves them well in crises.

Much of the death education research has been studies which attempt to answer the question: Does death education cause any change in the participant? Much research has focused on the impact of the experience on something called "death anxiety" and/or "fear of death"; not the outcome of avoidance or acceptance or the assimilation and utilization of new knowledge. We tend to hypothesize that lowered anxiety or lessening of fear will bring about a greater acceptance of one's own death and the death of others (more the death of others, I suspect, than one's own death). As Ray and Najman wrote [10, p. 311]: "Since death is in fact inevitable, accepting it might be the least we can do. Not only do we thereby avoid anxiety associated with fear, but we would probably be, in such circumstances, best able to provide and prepare for death." Desired outcomes?

There is a great deal to be desired from this type of research and reading any number of these studies will probably create confusion in the reader.

What do these studies reveal? Why is there confusion? A review of some recent studies might provide an answer. Hare and Cunningham found no difference between experimental and control groups in the fear of death [11]. Of course, these researchers permitted their subjects to choose their own treatment groups.

Lockard, in *Death Studies,* reported that the experimental group in this study had significantly lower death anxiety than did the control group at two weeks, four weeks and one year post treatment [12]. It was reported, though, that neither group deviated from some "defined" middle range of anxiety.

Peace and Vincent compared and correlated two variables: hospice care nurses and non-hospice care nurses experience in death education and their death anxiety [13]. Hospice care nurses had significantly more death education than the non-hospice care nurses, but they were not significantly different from the non-hospice care nurses in the level of death anxiety. Both groups, it was reported, tended to fall within a "defined middle range" of anxiety. Watts reported a "favorable" death attitude change resulting from a relatively brief death education unit [14].

The studies examining the effect of death education tend to employ a death anxiety scale (most often quoted instrument is the Templer Death Anxiety Scale) in a pre/posttest design along with course/ workshop evaluations by participants and self descriptions of attitudes or behaviors by the participants. These instruments are all inadequate means to assess the effectiveness of death education courses. Sanders addresses many issues concerning research in bereavement [9]. She states that stereotypes such as "pathological grief" and "bad grief" are often based on poorly designed research. A major research problem, according to Sanders, is inadequate instrumentation, primarily the lack of reliability and validation testing. The instruments have not been standardized; yet we use them, arrive at conclusions and develop programs of intervention based on these findings. Another major research problem, Sanders believes, is investigator bias. She writes that if one believes that "training will bring about a desired 'better' caregiver or person, one will prove it."

The lack of validity may be the reason why studies employing these instruments tend to produce contradictory results. Fredrich Agatstein, in a 1980 article on attitude change in Death Education, wrote [15, p. 324]:

> Using the criterion of death anxiety reduction or such vaguely defined evaluative terms as **Positive** or **Adaptive** as proofs for our effectiveness leaves a great deal to be desired. We may be implying that the nature of death is known or knowable and that there are objective criteria we ought to be feeling and thinking about death.

It seems to me that it is natural, therefore normal, for one to experience some degree of existential or annihilation anxiety. Some difficulty exists in accepting many of the contained on death anxiety, fear of death, death avoidance scales as indicants of an undesired level of death anxiety, fear or attitude toward death. many items seem to be normal death concerns. An examination of these items on the scales used to determine the presence and intensity of death fear and anxiety (agreement indicates the presence of fear/anxiety) will illustrate the concern. The following items were extracted from a variety of scales in current use.

1. I fear dying a painful death.
2. I am afraid of a long slow death.

3. I am disturbed by the physical degeneration in a slow death.
4. I am disturbed by the thought that my abilities will be limited while I lie dying.
5. Being separated from my loved ones at death makes me anxious.
6. The affect of my death on others troubles me.
7. It worries me to think of the financial situation of my survivors.
8. I dread the helplessness of dying.
9. I have misgivings about the fact that I might die before achieving my goals.

In a survey of over 4,000 students, the above statements are frequently identified as personal concerns, yet subjects do not seem to be extremely afraid of or hesitant in discussions of death, dying, and bereavement; or do they report any extreme difficulty in coping with the death of a loved one. Are these issues, concerns, or attitudes that we really wish to change; or are they changeable only by the elimination of death as a human experience?

Is there a need to change the death attitude of the population? Are anxiety levels in the population so high they impede the individual in his/her quest for a satisfying life? Does death education cause a change in the attitude towards death and dying? Does death education reduce anxiety? If there is any change in the attitude or anxiety, does it translate into modified behavior? If there is a change in the attitude, a reduction of fear and/or anxiety, is the effect long-lasting? Do persons who have completed a course(s) in death cope more effectively with their own death and the death of loved ones? Do care givers who have completed a course on death and dying give more considerate care? Before we begin to develop theories and create programs that reflect that theory, we need to answer these and other questions. In order to arrive at these answers, there is a need for more sophisticated instruments designed to measure behavioral changes induced by death education. Although demonstrably effective, in lessening post bereavement morbidity even specific programs directed toward particular groups of bereaved people that have been aimed at lessening their risk status (i.e., widow to widow, parents of a murdered child, SIDS support groups), still require more study before generalizing. Not to involve ourselves in this process of evaluation and accountability appears unethical. The material of death education must be based on a valid data base: the concepts and theories coming from proven hypotheses.

It may be necessary to define the word **ethics**: ethics is "the study of the general nature of morals and of the specific moral choices to be made by the individual in his relationship with others" (*American Heritage Dictionary*). More importantly, ethics is a system of values that guides behavior in relationships among people. On the other hand, morals are one's personal or private system of values—a conviction about how one "ought" to behave in relation to others. Morals are interpersonal—their force comes from internal feelings that arise when a person has or has not acted in accordance with them (feelings of guilt or pangs of conscience). This definition is very important because a great deal of the content of death education addresses ethics and morals. Some of the ethical issues that are generally included in death education follow:

1. the definition of when life begins and when life ends,
2. the definition of the term "quality of life" and the criteria that constitute acceptable or unacceptable quality,
3. the rights of a person to refuse treatment and if there is a right—who possesses this right; what constitutes an adult and competency,
4. the right of a person to die—living will, including the use of drugs to end life,
5. legislating DNR codes and the withdrawing of life support including declaring nutritional intervention as medical intervention,
6. funeral rituals including a dilemma of personal choice vs. cultural-religious requirements. This is an interesting dilemma, especially for young people who do not see the ritual that their family employed in the past as being satisfactory or relevant at the time of the death of a family member. How do they go about resolving the personal issues or desires and that which their family or religion say must be done,
7. organ donation. My surveys of 4,000 students reveal that a majority of these students would decline the opportunity to be an organ donor. Two major reasons for not being a donor are generally offered. Firstly, there is a complete lack of faith/trust in the American medical care system and its practitioners. Secondly, the students stated that if they were to fill out a donor card or form, their family would be greatly disturbed, and
8. nuclear issues including the politics and economics of nuclear energy and nuclear weaponry stockpiling. Death education confronts emotions: anger, fear, loneliness, and rejection. Death education asks, at times coerces, the participant to confront undesired situations: the death/loss of a loved one, the death/loss of the self, past losses, current losses, and impending/future losses.

In many instances, death education has gone beyond the examination of personal death attitudes for the purpose of self awareness and has become involved in AIDS non-death related issues, the politics of the holocaust, the issues of personal freedom (including the right to suicide, the financial cost of keeping people alive, etc.).

It is imperative that the goal of death education be the process of examining issues and not decisions. Paternalism is not an ethical death education position. The participant has the right to know enough about what is going to occur within the death education experience that he/she is able to make an informed decision about participating. In the case of school death education, the parents of the school child should be involved in the decision making process.

When controversial issues are being presented or discussed, the participant has the right to expect that various views of the issue will be presented and each point of view will be validly presented. Too often participants are made to feel their beliefs, feelings or choices are wrong when they differ from the group.

The creation of ethical principles relevant to the educational process in death and dying must include:

1. *Autonomy and informed consent* — the participant must be permitted autonomous decisions. Before the start of any course, workshop, seminar on death and dying begins, the participants should be required to give consent. This consent requires disclosure of adequate and relevant information that must be comprehended by the participant/registrant. The decision must be completely voluntary and informed. Any plans to use the participants as subjects in a research project must be approved by the participants. The participant has to be respected in **their right to experience/think about** his/her **dying in a personal way.**

2. *Confidentiality* — participants must not be coerced into revealing experiences, feelings, or thoughts about death and dying. The person has the right to control the dissemination of personal or sensitive information about himself/herself. There must not be any use of coercive techniques or material.

3. *Beneficience* — the death educator must try to do good, to further the welfare or well being of the other. The criteria of "good" must be what is beneficial to the participant, not to the educator's own death issues.

In order to act ethically, the death educator must be prepared to provide directly or indirectly necessary psychological/emotional support services to the participant. An ethical death educator must also be available between and after all sessions. The death educator is responsible for the creation of an environment or experience that causes the participant to feel or think about issues that he/she may not have felt outside the death education experience. We must create an environment in which the participant may experience an emotional safety.

4. *Nonmaleficience* — the death educator must take great care not to harm the person with which he/she is working. Harm is the outcome to improper or unethical death education practices. Greater harm results when no one is there to provide support.

Dr. Jonas Salk, a noted physician, was once asked to define the health of a child. He answered the question by saying, "I define the health of a child as being the quality of the adult around the child." Healthy death education might be defined as the quality of the death educator.

In closing, there is a fable that focuses on what we do and with whom we do it. A Chinese angel visited hell. He saw many people seated around a table covered with delicious food of every description. Beside each person there was a pair of yard-long chopsticks. But everyone there was wasting away with starvation, because no one was able to manipulate the clumsy chopsticks adequately to feed himself.

Then the angel went to visit heaven. There he saw another table piled with all kinds of wholesome delicious food. Each person seated around the table was also provided with yard-long chopsticks. These people were happy and contented. They were feeding each other across the table with their yard-long chopsticks. The moral is—the difference between heaven and hell is the people.

REFERENCES

1. S. Crane, A Learned Man, in *The New Pocket Anthology of American Verse*, (O. Williams, ed.), Washington Square Press, New York, 1961.
2. C. Chmelynski, Does "Death Education" Belong in the Classroom, *School Board News*, p. 5, January 1, 1991.
3. F. M. Bordewich, Mortal Fears, *The Atlantic*, February 1988.
4. P. Schlafly, Death Education Comes Into Open, *The Brooklyn Spectator*, April 13, 1988.
5. M. A. Simpson, Death Education—Where Is thy Sting?, *Death Education*, *3*, pp. 165-174, 1979.
6. J. W. Hoelter and R. J. Epley, Death Education and Death Related Attitudes, *Death Education, 3*, pp. 67-76, 1979.
7. E. Segal, *Love Story*, Harper and Row, New York, 1970.
8. E. Becker, *The Denial of Death*, The Free Press, New York, 1973.
9. C. Sanders, *Grief: The Mourning After*, John Wiley and Sons, New York, 1989.
10. J. J. Ray and J. Najman, Death Anxiety and Death Acceptance: A Preliminary Approach, *Omega, 5*, pp. 311-315, 1974.

11. J. Hare and B. Cunningham, Effects of a Child Bereavement Training Program for Teachers, *Death Studies, 4,* pp. 345-354, 1988.
12. B. E. Lockard, Immediate, Residual, and Long-term Effects of a Death Education Instructional Unit on the Death Anxiety Level of Nursing Students, *Death Studies, 13,* pp. 137-160, 1989.
13. H. G. Peace and P. A. Vincent, Death Anxiety: Does Death Education Make a Difference, *Death Studies, 12,* pp. 337-344, 1988.
14. P. R. Watts, Evaluation of Death Attitude Change Resulting from a Death Educational Instructional Unit, *Death Education, 1,* pp. 187-194, 1978.
15. F. Agatstein, Attitude Change and Death Education: A Consideration of Goals, *Death Education, 3,* pp. 323-332, 1980.

CHAPTER 2

Self-Healing for Persons with Cancer: Issues for Health Professionals

Ross E. Gray and Brian D. Doan

Despite the uncertain scientific status of psychospiritual influence on cancer etiology and progression, health professionals working with persons who have cancer cannot afford to dismiss patient beliefs in self-healing. The psychological implications of such beliefs are important in their own right.

This chapter explores the potential positive and negative consequences for patients of popular conceptions of self-healing. Clinical and ethical issues related to health professionals' response to patients are discussed, and a rationale is presented for adopting a flexible, person-centered approach.

The issue of whether psychological factors are relevant to cancer etiology and progression has received increasing attention over the last two decades. Popular bestsellers by Simonton, Mathews-Simonton, and Creighton [1], Hay [2], Siegel [3, 4], and others have brought ideas of psychological and spiritual (hereafter psychospiritual) influence on cancer, including the possibility of self-healing, into the mainstream of North American thinking. According to these writers, the path to self-healing lies in becoming more expressive, loving, positive and courageous people. Specific techniques—such as meditation, mental imagery, and positive thinking—have been advocated as having direct and indirect healing effects.

Individual patients, professionals, and members of the public are almost inevitably aware of these ideas about self-healing. Indeed, in a recent survey of university students and health professionals, the vast majority of respondents indicated a belief that psychological factors contributed to cancer etiology and progression [5]. A majority also indicated that they would use psychospiritual techniques to help battle illness should they ever be diagnosed with cancer.

Despite the popularity of the self-healing notion, numerous studies and reviews from the fields of oncology, psychology, and psychoneuroimmunology have failed to clarify the question of whether, and to what degree, psychospiritual factors may influence cancer [6-10]. A recent randomized controlled study reporting that group psychotherapy prolonged survival for cancer patients is suggestive of benefit for at least some patients under some conditions, but the need for replication and generalization of findings dictates that scientific consensus will be unlikely in the near future [11].

Because this issue of the scientific status of psychospiritual self-healing appears unresolved at present, many health professionals working with cancer patients assume that it need not be taken seriously. We are uncomfortable with such a dismissive stand. Important needs may be met for patients regardless of the question of scientific merit. For example, we think that the aspiration of cancer patients to heal themselves represents, in part, a healthy and natural identification with the age old hero myth [12, 13]. This notion—which we have discussed at length elsewhere—reframes self-healing as the expression of an urge for self-transcendence, i.e., for overcoming our usual human limitations. Without pursuing further this particular example, we wish to stress the point that psychological implications of beliefs in self-healing are important *in their own right*. Such beliefs have important consequences for health-related decisions and behavior.

In the remainder of this chapter we will consider the potential benefits and problems of belief in psychospiritual influence outside of the context of its supposed effect on disease causation and etiology. We will then elaborate a model to guide health professionals on how to be helpful to patients about this issue.

BENEFITS

From our clinical work, we are convinced that many cancer patients experience major benefits from believing that psychospiritual factors influence their illness. In the face of a life situation characterized by loss of control, patients who believe that their health will improve by practicing imagery, by changing their relationships, or by redefining life priorities, typically feel more "in control." This can markedly reduce anxiety and depression. Similarly, many patients find that the meaning in their lives is enhanced when they undertake personal transformation as a means of battling cancer. A psychospiritual approach to illness can assist in directing the person in a reexamination of life issues, and can heighten motivation to act to remedy situations that are problematic or lack positive meaning. We have encountered several homemakers with cancer, for example, who have reported taking charge of their own lives in a new way following their experience with cancer. This was such an important change for some of them that they described being thankful for their illness experience.

PROBLEMS

Belief in self-healing can also give rise to difficulties. We see a substantial number of patients who come to us because their attempts at psychological self-transformation are resulting in increased anxiety. One common source of anxiety involves patients' difficulties in evaluating the success of their psychospiritual efforts, since the literature on psychospiritual control of cancer is replete with sweeping and ambiguous statements. Siegel [3, 4], for example, refers to the need to develop peace of mind, and to give and receive love. Many people have difficulty interpreting how, exactly, these goals are attained and what they would look like if they were attained.

Whereas some patients become anxious about the vagueness of psychospiritual exhortations, others take the approach literally to a degree that involves magical thinking. For example, we have seen patients who believed that specific thoughts or images of cancer or death would trigger a recurrence of their disease. Because it is virtually impossible for the person with cancer to *never* think of illness progression or death, the patient ends up feeling terrified that he/she is actively contributing to a negative outcome.

A related example of how prescriptions for self-healing can make things worse instead of better is of the patient who tries desperately to hold only positive thoughts and images of the future because he/she believes in the power of self-fulfilling prophecy. The constant effort required by this strategy can leave patients tense and exhausted. They may also feel guilt when they experience the natural and healthy urge to take a break from battling cancer and resume some semblance of normal living.

Family members may also exhibit a panicked approach to self-healing, endorsing unrealistic goals of psychological transformation. We have seen many cases where a spouse has taken a rigid "positive thinking" approach, and will not tolerate his or her loved one's expressions of fear, helplessness, or hopelessness, however realistic such expressions might be. Although the intention is most often to support the patient, the effect is usually the opposite—the patient feels misunderstood and rejected.

Sometimes a family emphasis on self-healing can degenerate into frank blaming of the person with cancer—like the man who directed his anger at his terminally ill wife just days before her death, saying, "Why don't you get inside your head and figure out what your problem is? Think of the children!" Such extreme responses are fortunately uncommon, but there are many more cases where family anxiety about self-healing leads to subtle blaming of patients.

Whereas some patients respond to the challenge of self-transformation with high anxiety, others report feelings of failure, with associated guilt, despair, and lowered self-esteem. Some patients feel overwhelmed and intimidated from the time of diagnosis by the prospect of self-healing through transformation. Others experience difficulties later, when disease progresses or recurs. With the increasing emphasis in recent years on patients' personal responsibility for beating cancer, the risk of guilt and despair for terminally ill patients has arguably risen, and mental health professionals can expect to see this more frequently as a presenting problem.

Another potential difficulty may involve the need to ascribe a specific meaning to cancer etiology or progression. Anyone who believes that cancer occurred because of stress or a psychological problem will be able to identify *some* life issue that might possibly account for illness. For example, we occasionally meet patients who are convinced that family members' bad behavior has been the direct cause of their illness. Although some of these patients have legitimate complaints about lack of support from family members prior to or following cancer diagnosis, it seems that sometimes family members have become *scapegoats*. Similarly, we see bereaved families who believe that their loved one failed to make necessary personal changes that would have allowed them to beat cancer. In these instances, ascribing ultimate control to psychospiritual factors typically leads to survivors' complicated grief, with exaggerated anger and feelings of having been rejected by the deceased.

Finally, a few patients reject conventional therapies to pursue only psychospiritual interventions. This is rare in our experience, but certainly distressing where it leads to an avoidable death.

A PERSON-CENTERED APPROACH

Although in this paper we have focused more on potential problems than on benefits, psychospiritual change in the service of self-healing most often has a positive impact on patients' overall sense of well-being [14, 15]. Given this typical benefit for patients, we support the development of community psychosocial programs with a self-healing focus as an important strategy for enhancing patient empowerment [16].

Nevertheless, we consider it important that health professionals not assume *a priori* that a self-healing approach will be either helpful or unhelpful to patients' psychological well-being. A flexible *person-centered* approach focuses on the unique effects of patients' beliefs on their mental (and physical) health. Beliefs that are useful, and foster productive living for some people, may be harmful and hinder adjustment for others [17]. From this perspective, the most important question to ask about a cancer patient's self-healing beliefs is whether or not the beliefs are presently contributing to the patients' quality of life, coping ability and general well-being.

When patients' commitment to self-transformation seems to be enhancing their sense of personal control, hopefulness and emotional well-being, we support and facilitate their efforts. We assist patients who want to learn stress management techniques, and help them address problems that negatively influence their quality of life. We refer those desiring more specialized training in psychospiritual techniques to groups or professionals in the community who offer these services.

Where patients' or their family members' commitment to self-healing is causing unnecessary distress, impairing their coping ability, or resulting in increased alienation, we are less inclined to be supportive of the approach. Where possible, we will intervene and attempt to reframe or resolve specific problematic assumptions without challenging the patients' core beliefs associated with the self-healing approach. By respecting patients' world view, we hope to preserve their sense of personal control, hope, and motivation for living.

By way of example of intervening when self-healing belief is problematic, let us consider the situation where family members are "forcefeeding" an ill person with positive thinking. In these circumstances it could be pointed out that such an approach has the unintended effect of increasing the loved one's distress—an outcome antithetical to the psychospiritual self-healing approach. In most cases, family members can use such feedback to better support the cancer patient, yet without having to radically alter their world view.

Sometimes it may be necessary to challenge a worldview more directly in order to be helpful. For example, when a patient and/or family experience intense guilt about illness progression or death, it can be important to point out that even if psychospiritual factors are relevant (and this is uncertain for any given patient), there are many other factors involved in cancer progression and death. Sometimes, despite heroic struggles, loved ones die—and it is nobody's fault [18].

ETHICAL ARGUMENTS

We have argued that a flexible approach to patients' beliefs about self-healing is clinically optimal. We now wish to show that this approach is ethically necessary.

One of the primary principles of ethical professional behavior is that of providing responsible care to patients [18]. Since it is evident from our discussion above that the self-healing approach poses problems for some cancer patients, a practitioner's dogmatic support of the approach is incompatible with the principle of responsible caring. The worst possible outcome occurs when practitioners who unreservedly advocate the self-healing approach experience a decrease in empathy for patients' distress, and engage in subtle blaming or rejecting of those who are losing the battle against their illness.

Dogmatic rejection of the self-healing approach by professionals could also be considered unethical. Patient well-being may be threatened if the practitioner's skepticism leads the patient to feel more helpless, to give up some degree of hope, or to lose interest in living.

Some health professionals would argue that it is preferable to limit the potential disappointment that patients may later experience by taking a conservative approach to the possibility of psychospiritual influence. It is debatable whether this strategy works for individual patients. Illness progression and impending death are typically distressing regardless of previous expectations. We believe that this strategy serves more to minimize distress for practitioners than for patients.

Another important ethical principle is that professional and scientific integrity be preserved in relationships with patients [19]. This includes the expectation of providing accurate information and avoiding misrepresentation. It is on the basis of this principle that some health professionals feel obliged to disabuse patients of belief in self-healing.

We think that such active skepticism is usually unwarranted with cancer patients pursuing self-healing.

First, our reading of the literature leads us to conclude that the question of psychospiritual influence on cancer is unresolved *in either direction*—but that enough supportive evidence has accumulated to make entertainment of the hypothesis reasonable. Thus, outright debunking of the hypothesis may violate the admonition to provide accurate information. More common, however, are practitioners who do not support it on the basis that efficacy of self-healing has yet to be *proven*. These skeptical scientists claim that they would not hesitate to support self-healing efforts if controlled studies irrefutably showed psychospiritual influence on cancer progression. The problem with this position is that it is unhelpful to patients. Patients cannot afford to wait until all the data are in. In William James' terms [20], their options are *forced*. Health professionals need to recognize that the purely scientific approach has limited utility in dealing with the pressing needs of individual patients.

According to the Canadian Code of Ethics for Psychologists, concern for the well-being of patients, and the obligation to engage in responsible caring, both take precedence over and condition the obligation to maintain a purely objective, scientific stance in communicating with patients. Thus, even if one interprets existing evidence on psychospiritual influence on cancer as insubstantial, then it is clear that the *priority* in communicating with patients about their psychospiritual beliefs is to enhance their coping with cancer—not to modify the status of their scientific understanding. Sometimes, being helpful involves setting aside one's opinions in favor of clients' well-being.

CONCLUSION

In this chapter we have argued that professional interest in psychospiritual influences on cancer etiology and progression should not be limited to issues of empirical verification. Self-healing beliefs are meaningful in their own right, and thus are of major importance to all professionals working with cancer patients.

For many patients, the adoption of a self-healing approach significantly enhances their quality of life. For others, it can be the cause of undue distress, impaired coping, and increased alienation. In the interests of the psychological well-being of the cancer patient, we have suggested that the appropriate professional response to patients' pursuit of psychospiritual techniques is person-centered, and sensitive to their unique impact on the individual patient. The ethical principle to care responsibly for the whole patient must take precedence over health professionals' enthusiasm for, or skepticism about, the validity of the self-healing approach.

REFERENCES

1. O. C. Simonton, S. Mathews-Simonton, and J. Creighton, *Getting Well Again*, J. P. Tarcher, Los Angeles, 1978.
2. L. Hay, *You Can Heal Yourself*, Coleman, New York, 1985.
3. B. S. Siegel, *Love, Medicine and Miracles*, Harper & Row, New York, 1986.
4. B. S. Siegel, *Peace, Love and Healing*, Harper & Row, New York, 1989.
5. B. D. Doan, R. E. Gray, and C. S. Davis, Belief in Psychological Effects on Cancer, *Psycho-Oncology*, in press.
6. A. J. Cunningham, The Influence of Mind on Cancer, *Canadian Psychology, 26*, pp. 13-29, 1985.
7. B. H. Fox, Current Theory on Psychogenic Effects on Cancer Incidence and Prognosis, *Journal of Psychosocial Oncology, 1*:1, pp. 17-31, 1983.
8. J. K. Kiecolt-Glaser and R. Glaser, Psychosocial Mediators of Immune Function, *Annals of Behavioral Medicine, 2*, pp. 16-20, 1987.
9. W. H. Redd and P. B. Jacobsen, Emotions and Cancer, *Cancer, 62*, pp. 1871-1879, 1988.
10. L. S. Sklar and H. Anisman, Stress and Cancer, *Psychological Bulletin, 89*:3, pp. 369-406, 1981.
11. D. Spiegel, J. R. Bloom, H. C. Kraemer, and Gottheil, E. Effect of Psychosocial Treatment on Survival of Patients with Metastatic Breast Cancer, *Lancet*, pp. 888-891, 1989.
12. C. G. Jung, *Man and His Symbols*, Dell, New York, 1968.
13. C. S. Pearson, *The Hero Within*, Harper & Row, San Francisco, 1986.
14. A. J. Cunningham and E. K. Tocco, A Randomized Trial of Group Psychoeducational Therapy for Cancer Patients, *Patient Education and Counseling, 14*, pp. 101-114, 1989.
15. A. J. Cunningham, G. A. Lockwood, and J. A. Cunningham, Relationship between Perceived Self-Efficacy and Quality of Life in Cancer Patients, *Patient Education and Counseling, 17*, pp. 71-79, 1991.
16. R. E. Gray, B. D. Doan, and K. Church, Empowerment and Persons with Cancer. Politics in Cancer Medicine, *Journal of Palliative Care, 6*:2, pp. 33-45, 1990.
17. A. Adler, Individual Psychology, in *Psychologies of 1930*, C. Murchison (ed.), Clark University Press, Worcester, Massachusetts, 1930.
18. R. E. Gray and B. D. Doan, Heroic Self-Healing and Cancer: Clinical Issues for the Health Professions, *Journal of Palliative Care, 6*:1, pp. 32-41, 1990.

19. Canadian Psychological Association, *A Canadian Code of Ethics for Psychologists,* C.P.A., 1986.
20. W. James, *The Will to Believe and Other Essays in Popular Philosophy,* Dover, New York, 1956.

CHAPTER 3

The Silence of God:
The Absence of Healing

Lynne Martins

Perhaps there is no other time in the history of the church where we have been confronted with the kinds of challenges in our pastoral roles that seem to stretch us beyond our resources. There is little debate about the enormous ethical and moral issues that we have had to confront due to the technological advances in medicine. These issues have placed further strain on our overloaded pastoral agendas as we have struggled to minister to the dying and bereaved persons in our congregations and parishes. In the midst of this, whether we have been prepared for it or not, comes the charismatic movement, full of challenges for us theologically.

The intent of this chapter is to examine the charismatic movement and its impact; not to debate the validity of the movement. It is my personal belief that the evolution of the charismatic movement is, in fact, a very positive one. For the purpose of this chapter, the definition of the charismatic movement will be limited to physical healing, or what is also known as supernatural intervention. However, the charismatic movement is by no means defined by this one particular manifestation of God's Spirit and to do so would be an act of theological homicide and a grave misinterpretation of the content. It is this very question of God's supernatural intervention that confronts us to examine the charismatic movement in light of our ministry to the dying and bereaved.

In considering the impact of the charismatic movement, we will reflect on the hindrances as well as the strengths that the movement offers ministries. The following lists of hindrances and strengths as outlined by Michael Green in his book, *I Believe in the Holy Spirit*, are a helpful reference [1].

THE HINDRANCES

A few of the hindrances of the charismatic movement which appear as common roadblocks to ministries are:

1. "Showing off" — by valuing the visible more than the invisible gifts.
2. "To heal without means" (i.e., medical attention) is more spiritual than to heal "with means."
3. "Playing God" by assuring people recovery when they will, in fact, die. Along with this is the pale and inaccurate assurance that Christians are entitled to a pain-free life.
4. Temptation to think it is by one's own virtue that God imparts the gifts of the Holy Spirit.
5. Irresponsible Prayer: which is closely related to playing God.
6. Anti-intellectualism which says, "It's not ours to question the ways of God" or "it must be God's will." This is sometimes present in those whose faith is young or immature.

THE STRENGTHS

The strength of the charismatic movement is without limits. The level at which we can lead the dying and bereaved persons to the healing of God is unequivocal and without reserve.

1. *The charismatic movement is a movement of life,* dynamic spiritual life. In ministering to the dying and bereaved, it is precisely life that gives hope in the darkest despair. It is this affirmation of life that gives breath to hope, and frequently it has been the charismatic movement which has nudged us in this direction.

2. *The charismatic movement is a movement of faith.* Real and deep faith in God. Michael Green suggests that the charismatic movement is a "revolt against the straight jacket of Protestantism, confining the Spirit to an article in the creed of Catholicism, confining the Spirit to predetermined persons and sacraments" [1, p. 204].

3. *The charismatic movement is a movement of holiness.* It is true that some have become more loving, unselfish, dedicated, reliable and prayerful than ever before.

4. *The charismatic movement is a movement of fellowship with diversity.* Every member has a place and a vital contribution. The congregation is no longer an audience; now each member participates.

"The charismatic movement has taught us to believe in God's reality and His ability to break into the tenor of our lives with the invading power of His Spirit" [1, p. 209].

While examining the dangers and the strengths of the charismatic movement is an essential foundation for this discussion, one of the key issues that is undoubtedly left is that of God's omnipotence. This materializes in the question of God's silence in the absence of healing. It appears that this "absence" of healing takes a direct assault on God's omnipotence, especially as we refer to passages such as Romans 8:28 [2] as a defense on God's behalf as we grapple with the mystery of His omnipotence.

The core issue to this argument of omnipotence is that if, indeed, God is a powerful God, He would not need my best attempt to explain, defend or define His power. God doesn't require my allegiance at the expense of another's humanity. Therefore, I do not have to deny or minimize another's pain in order to save God's reputation. Perhaps it is not so much of question of God's power, i.e., omnipotence as it is our understanding of God in His powerfulness.

There is a grave theology that has permeated our thinking and has allowed us to reduce God to be a "cause and effect" God. That is, somehow, there is a cause for everything that happens (because God is in control) and/or our response to God illicits His response to us. In essence, we cause God to respond to us. It seems to have invaded us in a couple of ways: 1) In our attempt to defend God's powerfulness, we have resigned ourselves to believing that God causes or allows these tragedies in our lives for some ultimate good [2, Romans 8:28]. The problem with this is that is creates a deeper chasm for the dying and bereaved as it separates them further from God by forcing them to accept the idea that an irrevocable loss has a revokable meaning. We further compound the pain by insisting that God has "told us" (i.e., pastors, counselors, prayer-partners) the reasoning for the suffering albeit the dying and bereaved are still "unenlightened." This author cannot peddle that kind of theology. Surely, God is more loving than to withhold information while I writhe in pain now racked with two questions: why hasn't God healed me? and why can't I accept His "non-healing?" Dare I say that the dying and bereaved are closer to the compassion of God? I think so. Often they are forced to come to terms with life and shed the shallowness of denial. The rawness of life and pain catapults them into the presence of God. The task is to encourage them to encounter this God who is omnipotent, all-powerful, yet does not always heal.

Secondly, cause and effect thinking leads us to believe that our faith (effect) creates some response in God. The charismatic movement can mistakenly teach us that we are entitled to some response from God because we are exercising the gift(s) He has given us. This is where our idea that God's silence is somehow a type of punishment as a result of our "lack of faith" or misuse/inexperience in expressing spiritual gifts. Rabbi Harold Kushner, in his book *When Bad Things Happen to Good People*, relates [3, p. 10], "The idea that God gives people what they deserve, that our misdeeds cause misfortune, is a neat and attractive solution to the problem of evil on several levels but it has a number of serious limitations. It teaches people to blame themselves. It creates guilt where there is no basis for guilt. It makes people hate God, even as it makes them hate themselves." This is especially damaging for the person who is working through the painful process of making sense of their loss which is a normal part of grief adjustment. In this type of thinking, they are sentenced to an inordinate amount of guilt in addition to their separation from God and alienation from the very Body of people they need.

Faith is a gift from God as much as grace is. Faith is *not* the coin that turns the handle of our gumball machine image of God. Instead, faith is possible because God is faithful. It's His character to be faithful. My part is to believe in God's character (because it never changes [2, Hebrews 13:8]). This is much more freeing than depending on my own ability to believe or to take that leap of faith. If I had to depend on my ability to "believe" in God for faith to happen, we'd had a Monday, Wednesday, Friday and sometimes . . . Sunday type of God.

Faith is a result of God's grace toward us. He imparts faith as a gift of grace and asks us to participate in that gift. Faith does not become passive, but is pursuant of this faithful God. God's faithfulness is something I can rest on, put my weight down on. The Reverend Earl Palmer, a Presbyterian minister in Berkley, California, puts it this way [4]:

> Faith means deciding to trust in Christ's character throughout our life-building journey. In the good weather and the bad. That's what faith is. Faith is not a heroic act that we do. Faith is a response to the evidence of God's faithfulness. Faith is a response to *His* character. Faith is also an ongoing relationship to God.

Because the issue of faith so often comes into our ministry with the dying and bereaved, it is essential that we do not conclude that another's life is lacking faith due to the action or lack of action by God we perceive in their lives. Life is simply not this neat and tidy. We are not at liberty to alleviate our own uncomfortableness and sense of helplessness by suggesting such simplistic theological explanations to those who are staring pain, suffering and death in the face daily.

Our understanding of God must make a radical shift from the question of **why** (which can only be answered with a be-**cause**) and be replaced with the question of **who**. To continue to ask why only leads to other unanswerable questions: why me? (which suggests that I am to blame or deserve this tragedy or that the tragedy should befall someone else). **Why** is a question that seeks to find blame and ultimately alienates the suffering person from God. To shift the question to **who** opens up the possibility of a relationship with God. Let us ask, **who** is God in the midst of my tragedy?

We can expect many things from this God when we ask the question of "who." We are infinitely comforted by a God who "never leaves or forsakes us" [2, (Joshua 1:5)]; a God who is on our side [2, (Romans 8:31)]; Who "never changes" [2, (Hebrews 13:8)]; Who "gathers our tears and records them" [2, (Psalms 56:8)]; and who is the same God who stands alongside the "unhealed" as well as the "healed."

In this type of reconciling with God, we acknowledge the ambiguity of God—the God who is powerful yet does not always heal. Ambiguity is not a new concept for the dying and bereaved. Consider the person with cancer—looks fine on the outside but is dying on the inside. It is the mystery of God which lays the foundation of ambiguity and ultimately the bridge of doubt for people to believe again. It is within this mystery, that the paradox of faith is ignited. If we forbid people to enter this arena of ambiguity, we deprive them from the knowledge of God on a very intimate level. What a tragedy it would have been if King David had not doubted God. The Psalms are filled with chapters of questions and doubts in the midst of pain and silence. Mostly, we are uncomfortable with ambiguity because it leaves us feeling helpless and vulnerable. But it is this vulnerability with God that opens us to a deeper level of intimacy with Him.

We must allow for doubt. Doubt is not the same as faithlessness, but is a creative step back into the presence of God. Faithless doubt is a downward spiral that asks questions but never intends to listen for answers. Faithless doubt breeds in the bitterness conceived when some one or something must be blamed for the loss. Creative doubt is that which begs the question—God who ARE you? This is far from destructive and faithless. Questioning God is often seen as doubt. But it is in the questioning that communication is re-established with our Creator. It may be the first time in weeks or months that the dying or bereaved person has had an honest conversation with God. Mostly their questions are mere expressions of the enormity and terror of their pain. It is only one of the many necessary responses as a person struggles to integrate the tragedy into their lives. Nonetheless, their questions make us squirm.

As Rowland Croucher, author of GRID, has brilliantly stated [5, p. 3], ". . . faith is not about certainty. Certainty makes faith invalid and unnecessary." Its core is the mystery. When we "figure" God out, we are in trouble. God is not a puzzle to be solved but a person to be experienced. The ambiguity of God is our bridge of hope through our sea of doubt and despair. [5, p. 4]

> The essential difference between orthodox Christianity and the various heretical systems is that orthodoxy is rooted in paradox. Heretics, as Irenaeus saw, reject paradox in favor of clarity and precision. But true faith can only grow and mature if it includes the elements of paradox and creative doubt. Hence the insistence of orthodoxy that God cannot be known by the mind, but is known in the obscurity of faith, in the way of ignorance, and in the darkness. Such doubt is NOT the enemy of faith but an essential element within in. For faith in God does not bring the false peace of unanswered questions and unresolved paradoxes. Rather, it can be seen as a process of unceasing interrogation.

It is this allowance of doubt that rebuilds the bridge of hope. Hope that brings assurance of God's presence is a hope that does not disappoint. Hope is grossly misrepresented when it has conditions attached to it. "I hope God will heal me" makes hope contingent on healing. It also suggests two additional flaws: 1) hope becomes a graduation process where hope is consecrated when physical healing is imparted, and 2) to have abundant hope without physical healing is somehow a second-class, dimestore version of hope. We seem to be critical and skeptical if a person has genuine hope when physical healing has not occurred. People need hope that reconciles and rebuilds. A hope that recognizes God's hourly intervention with us is, indeed, a direct affirmation of His omnipotence. This also helps to refocus our emphasis on what is "supernatural." Is it *more* supernatural for God to physically heal than it is for Him to invade our lives on a daily basis?

Understanding what is "supernatural" intervention helps us to pray responsibly. We are free to ask for God's healing but understand that God stands with us in either state we continue in.

In closing, it has not been my intention to give easy, text book answers to this question of the charismatic movement, the question of healing, the silence of God and the bridge of doubt. Instead, perhaps it has created new pathways that we can meet our parishioners on and travel together.

REFERENCES

1. M. Green, *I Believe in the Holy Spirit,* William B. Eerdmans Publishing Co., Grand Rapids, Michigan, 1975.
2. Amplified Bible, Zondervon Publishing Co., Grand Rapids, Michigan, 1965.
3. H. Kushner, *When Bad Things Happen to Good People,* Schocken Books, New York, 1981.
4. E. Palmer, *Is Your House Built on Rock or Sand?,* Lecture, San Marino, California, 1985.
5. R. C. Croucher, *GRID-Christian Leadership Newsletter,* World Vision of Australia, Issue entitled: Living With Ambiguity, Melbourne, Victoria, Summer 1988.

PART II

Pastoral Issues

CHAPTER 4

Pastoral Care with the Dying and Bereaved

Delton J. Glebe

This chapter proposes to look at Pastoral Care with the Dying and Bereaved from these three perspectives: *motivation, model,* and *method.* In motivation we discover the source of the uniqueness of Pastoral Care especially in crises dealing with the dying and bereaved. A look at models reveals three predominant theories of grief which influence the kind of care given. In method we acknowledge its great significance in so far as "the medium becomes the message," and we discuss levels of communication, defense mechanisms and approaches to care and counselling especially in the Pastoral Carer's relations with the dying.

First of all, *motivation* will be examined as a source in contributing to the uniqueness of Pastoral Care. In a presentation given at Ancaster, January 1989, Henri Nouwen shared the influence of two voices during his life-journey [1]. One voice said: "Show me you can do it, walk on your own feet, be a man I can be proud of." This latter phrase, he says, was unmistakably the voice of his father!

For this voice success, degrees, diplomas, professional status are important. Henri followed this voice with zest. He became a priest-psychologist. He said, if being a priest was not important enough he could always point to being a psychologist. He achieved teaching appointments at Notre Dame, Yale, and Harvard. About his Harvard appointment he said, "Surely my father will be proud of me now." He wrote and published one book after another.

But he discovered that one's identity may be based too much on the applause of others. He said, "You can preach a sermon on humility then wonder what others thought of it." He confided, "The more successful I was the more desperate I became"—lonely, restless, anxious. He realized, "You can preach the gospel to the whole world and lose your own soul." He said, "I was missing something." He finally realized, "I had to find that first love again."

This first love refers to the other voice in his life's journey. He identifies this other voice in the words of the First Letter to John. "Let us love because God first loved us." "Because God first loved us." He admits it is a struggle to keep in touch with that first love, to truly believe in that first love. It is a struggle always to keep our second and third loves connected with that first love!

That first love which says, "You are my beloved son on you my favor rests." "That love of Jesus that allows us to be in the world without being of it." "That love that holds us safe and gives us a sense of who we are long before we start seeking an identity." "That love which knew me before I could think, which knitted me together in my mother's womb, which moulded me in the depths of the earth." Nouwen's description of "that first love" grabbed me. It has a lot to say about motivation in ministry.

Pastoral care means living our second and third loves always connected with that first love. The writer of I Corinthians 13 sounds a similar note: "If I speak in the tongues of persons and of angels but have not love, I am a noisy gong or a clanging cymbal." Imagine a noisy gong or a clanging cymbal at the bedside of the dying, in the house of the bereaved or in the pulpit at a funeral! To paraphrase another part of Corinthians 13, "If I have preaching power and understand all mysteries of care and all knowledge of counseling but have not a love always connected with that first love, I am hollow and empty."

Some years ago in a divinity school in Chicago the young Turks on the faculty chided the Dean for not having his Ph.D. The Dean replied, "You have a Ph.D. but I have agape." A Ph.D. may facilitate the imagination and expression of agape. But a Ph.D. and all the clinical certification in the world without agape does not add up to Pastoral Care. Pastoral Care is living our second and third loves always connected with that first love. Facing the bereaved and dying with honesty and integrity is the acid test for authenticity in Pastoral Care. This is the source and motivation for the authenticity which makes Pastoral Care unique. "We love, because God first loved us."

Circulated among you is a sheet showing a list of "Dynamics of the Grief Process." This list of grief dynamics is the result of many meetings with various groups which I conducted over a period of ten years. The participants were asked to identify dynamics of the grief process which they themselves had experienced or which they had perceived in others. You will notice that out of twenty dynamics identified, fourteen involve considerable pain. As one young widow in one of my university courses on grief and dying said, "When my husband died last June I was grateful for having learned previously the dynamics of grief. I knew that the craziness in my grief was normal and healthy. But I had no idea how much it hurts." The process is called grief work because it is hard work and painful. But pain is not grief's last word. Look again at the list of dynamics of the grief process. The telos, the purpose, of grief is reaffirmation, resurrection! Jean Vanier, in his recent volume, *The Broken Body,* advises us not to "shrink from suffering, but enter into it and discover there the mystery of the presence of the risen Jesus. He is hidden there . . ." [2, p. 62].

Resurrection hidden in the pain of grief, this is a uniqueness of that first love. And that first love is the uniqueness and motivation in Pastoral Care of the bereaved and dying.

It is helpful to have not only an awareness of motivation in Pastoral Care but also an awareness of various models of grief.

Secondly, *Models of Grief.* Models of grief are various theories about grief and their implications for Pastoral Care. A precise definition of grief is impossible because it is a powerful and complex process. Because grief is a process, it is always in flux. Grief varies with the nature of the loss. Grief over the loss of a child is not precisely the same as grief over the loss of a ninety-year-old grandparent. Grief varies with the uniqueness of the person in terms of experience with previous losses, age, religion and personal characteristics [3]. Grief varies with the person's previous experience in interpersonal relationships. If the person has had warm and trusting relationships, then the support of family and others is readily received. If the person has had negative interpersonal experiences, then also care givers may be mistrusted and avoided. Grief varies also with the attitudes and practices of the culture and subcultures. The variance may range from open wailing and weeping in one culture to stony stoicism in another.

MODELS FOR UNDERSTANDING GRIEF

R. Scott Sullender, in *The Journal of Pastoral Care,* has identified three models useful in the effort to understand grief which is of primary importance in Pastoral Care for the bereaved and dying [4].

Grief as a Reaction to Loss

Grief is seen here as an emotional reaction to the loss of a significant person or thing. The loss of things may include body parts and material possessions or changes in one's life. Grief as a reaction to loss is seen as a searching for what has been lost. This searching includes anxiety, restlessness, preoccupation with the lost person, certain forms of spiritualism and focusing on places associated with the lost person. The search is given up when the loss is accepted [4, p. 244]. Negotiating with the loss or accommodating oneself to the loss also serves as realistic grief processes.

This model of grief helps us to see that any change in life can be a loss event and therefore a grief experience. In pastoral care Granger Westberg uses this approach to grief. He discusses the loss of a loved one in the context of the countless "little griefs" of everyday life. A person's response to a traumatic loss can be assessed by the Pastoral Care giver by looking at how the person has responded to previous little griefs. Such a quick assessment can help the Pastor in choosing the appropriate way of helping the bereaved [4]. Sullender says [4, p. 245]:

> Professional pastoral carers need to be especially sensitive to this large diversity of loss experiences. . . . Pastors may encounter subtle and baffling behaviors in parishioners that they do not recognize as a form of grief. Sometimes these subtle 'little griefs' are more difficult to minister to for the Pastor precisely because they are more subtle. People do not consider their loss to be serious enough for grief and, therefore, do not take measures to appropriately nurture themselves.

These little griefs can become stock-piled like time bombs and explode unexpectedly in terms of psychosomatic ailments or delinquent behavior. For these little griefs, we fail to express that pain too deep for words which can be expressed better non-verbally in rituals, ceremonies and funerals.

The model of "grief as reaction to loss" does not explain all the symptoms of grief; therefore, another model is needed, Grief as Separation Anxiety. This view, says Sullender, is best expressed by Pastoral Counsellor David Switzer. Switzer sees acute grief as amazingly similar to an anxiety attack. Hence Switzer sees grief as a form of separation anxiety. Sullender quotes Colin Parkes saying: "I think it is fair to say that the pining or yearning that constitutes separation anxiety is the characteristic feature of the pangs of grief" [4, p. 247]. Sullender agrees with John Bowlby who sees separation anxiety in the human infant as the prototype of all adult grief. Says Sullender, "The grief of the adult finds its origins in the anxiety of the infant" [4, p. 247].

There are implications in this model of grief for the Pastoral Carer. If grief is essentially separation anxiety then support, community, and empathy will help in the terrible pain of separation. This model also shows why "talking it out" is such good grief therapy. Talking is a symbolic way of staying in close touch with the lost loved object [4, p. 247].

Grief as Separation Anxiety

Model Two is *Grief as Separation Anxiety* and has been particularly meaningful to me personally. My wife and I babysat, played with and held our one-year-old granddaughter Pamela on a Saturday night. Twenty-four hours later on Sunday night we held her lifeless body in our arms. One year and two years later I was afflicted by anxiety attacks related to the trauma of her death. The devastating thing about anxiety is that while rooted in the past it is future oriented. Sullender points out that anxiety alarms and arms the human psyche not at the something that has happened but toward a something that it fears is yet to happen. This is precisely what happened to me. The anxiety appeared to be about some loss that was going to happen when actually it came from a loss which had already happened, the loss of Pamela.

As important as this model is, its future orientation does not adequately deal with that aspect of grief which needs to make peace with the past.

Grief as a Function of Attachment

In this model the task of grief is to help the person face reality, withdraw attachment from the lost, and thus find freedom for new attachments. But since this process is piecemeal, it is extraordinarily painful. Sullender (1979) says [4, p. 248]: "Sorrow is in proportion to the power of the attachment." This will help the Pastoral Carer understand "why persons with unhappy relationships to a lost person will often grieve just as intensely as those with happy relationships" [4, p. 248]. Here grief is connected not with love but with attachment.

Sullender quotes Edgar N. Jackson, a renowned member of the Pastoral Care Community, saying that through grief [4, p. 248]:

> . . . a person seeks to disengage oneself from the demanding relationship that existed and to reinvest one's emotional capital in new and productive directions for the health and welfare of one's future and society.

Here grief is necessary. Otherwise a person's emotional life remains trapped by the past and one is unable to re-enter, reorganize, reaffirm and reinvest oneself in the present and future.

Sullender refers also to Pastoral Care writer William Rogers who also sees grief as a function of attachment. He says that grief is not caused by the loss of a loved one but by the value the griever has put on that relationship. Says Sullender, "Grief exists because the griever valued and gave meaning to that which is now lost" [4, p. 249].

This explains also why a grief crisis is an identity crisis. In grief, one's identity is thrown into confusion. Here, too, it is not the loss in itself which determines the intensity of the grief but the importance of the lost loved one for the survivor's identity. The Pastoral Carer can assess the intensity of a person's loss by ascertaining how central the lost loved one was to the griever's own sense of identity [4, p. 250].

Available to the Pastoral Carer are at least these models of Grief: Grief as Reaction to Loss, Grief as Separation Anxiety, and Grief as a Function of Attachment. Sullender concludes [4, pp. 250-251]:

> Grief's purpose . . . is always the restoration of the person's capacity for love. Grief is therefore health oriented. Theologically, grief is God's answer to the existence of loss and death. Grief is God's intended way of healing the human psyche and restoring the bereaved to human attachment. Grief is therefore essentially good by nature. By implication then, our task as pastoral carers is to encourage the free and full expression of grief. It is the best path of healing.

Even for the dying, grief is life oriented. Grief can enrich dying into "living your dying." This is effectively and humorously illustrated in a cartoon-styled five minute film by our National Film Board called "Why Me?" The film focuses upon a patient and his physician who tells him that he has only five minutes left to live. In response to the bad news the patient goes through various grief reactions. The film comes to a climax as the patient prepares to leave and the doctor says: "But Mr. Spoon you have only 30 seconds left." The patient replies, "Right Doc, and I'm going out there to live every last second to the fullest" ("Why Me?").

From models of grief we turn now to *Methods* in Pastoral care with the Bereaved and Dying. We will look first at levels of communication in relating with the dying.

Each person will die his/her own death in his/her own unique way. However, there are guiding principles for the Pastoral Carer's communication with the dying.

In an unpublished paper entitled "The Dying Patient" [5, p. 4], Dr. Claude Guldner says it is most common for such communication to begin on the impersonal level. The person will talk about the illness or surgery or treatment. The person will describe hurts, pains, symptoms and bodily changes. The person will differentiate between how she/he feels now from how he/she felt when physically fit. The person becomes highly sensitive to bodily feelings and will notice new sensations like never before. These new sensations are not always painful. Says Guldner, ". . . in fact many persons talk about these new sensations much like a pregnant woman will speak of her baby's movements. It is a totally new awareness of the physical self" [5, p. 4].

The next level to which communication moves is the interpersonal. Says Dr. Guldner, "The person may have talked of this aspect before, but did not do it at the emotional level he/she will now" [5, p. 4]. The primary concern will be for family, how they will get along, the burden of finances and employment. The total effect of the illness on family and friends becomes a primary concern now. One way in which the Pastoral Carer can help preserve the dying person's dignity is to encourage him/her to take some practical steps which can be communicated and set into motion even from a hospital bed. Rather than take over for the dying person and thereby create further dependency and loss of dignity, the Pastoral Carer instead helps him/her to clarify what can still be done by the person even in these limiting circumstances.

Eventually the dying person may move to the third level of communication namely, the intrapersonal level. Here the person's very subjective responses to what is happening will begin to emerge.

The person may move through the three levels during each visit. But as the dying person feels safer in sharing with you and sees that you can "hang in there" even in the face of morbid details, the person will delve more deeply into his/her personal reactions. As your relationship deepens the impersonal level will diminish and disappear and communication will carry on at the interpersonal and intrapersonal levels. This may indicate also that the dying person has accepted the fatal facts and can now move directly to the personal meaning it has for her/him [5, p. 4].

The Pastoral Carer will try to support the dying person to preserve his/her identity, dignity and sense of worth. I received a telephone call from the village where I grew up. Charlie's son told me that Charlie was very ill but what worried him most of all, "Charlie was depressed, could I visit Charlie next time I came up to the village." Charlie had been the farmer across from the farm where I grew up through childhood and adolescence. During my next visit to the village, I stopped in to see Charlie. Among other things I shared with him was how important he had been to me during those formative years of my childhood and adolescence. Some few weeks later I again received a telephone call from Charlie's son. This time he said: "What did you do to Charlie!" And I thought, "Oh, oh, did Charlie get worse or commit suicide!" But I had enough courage to ask, "Why?" His son explained, "Charlie's depression is gone." With a little honest appreciative response, Charlie's sense of worth and integrity had been restored. Charlie also requested that I preach his funeral sermon. That was an unusual request because in those days, forty years ago, the pulpit in Charlie's church was not easily opened to outsiders like me. I believe Charlie wanted me to speak the final words about him because somehow he trusted his personal identity and integrity would be safe with me. If the dying person is immobilized, then letting the person talk over past accomplishments and share acquired knowledge will help the person retain a sense of identity and self-worth.

The dying person may also have a strong need to correct old wrongs. This can include confession to the Pastor. Or the person may want direct action and reconciliation. Where possible this may be supported and facilitated by the Pastor. Or the person, says Dr. Guldner, "may only be able to talk about how things should have been different." This, too, is confession.

The dying person's desire to maintain relationships with others and to share whatever the person can with survivors is a significant help in preserving the person's identity. The dying person may also talk about important people in his/her life who have already died. Encouragement for the person to talk about these also seems to be important because it develops an important connection between the living, the dying and those who have already died. Dr. Guldner concludes, "The Pastor may offer his care through sustaining relationship with dying persons who need help with the burden of dying" [5, p. 5].

Guldner helps me in becoming aware of at least three levels of communication: the impersonal, the interpersonal, and the intrapersonal in relating to the dying person. The third level of preserving the identity, dignity and sense of worth may well be the most significant. At the same time this level may also be the most threatening because the Pastoral Carer must face honestly his/her attitude toward his/her own mortality as well as the imminent mortality of the dying person.

Dr. Guldner emphasizes that it is the impending death of another in which the Pastoral Carer senses some foreshadowing of his/her own finitude. Whether we like it or not, our ego will try to protect itself from facing its own vulnerability to death. Guldner points out that no matter how great is our concern for the dying person, a conflict starts in us even before the person's death. On the one hand we want to be with the dying person. On the other hand we want to pull away in order to avoid recognizing our own finiteness and mortality. Says Guldner, "Out of this conflict there is a terrible isolation and loneliness which the living force upon the dying" [5, p. 3]. This is true of all who are close to the dying person including the Pastoral Carer. "It is very interesting," says Guldner, "that the majority of intense fears of death are found not in the sickly but in the relatively healthy" [5, p. 2]. Confronted by a dying person the Pastoral Carer's denial system provides protection. We may be unaware of our denials and defensiveness. But they will reveal themselves in the ways in which we relate to the dying.

There are, of course, neurotic ways of relating to people. In neurotic behavior one is tied up within oneself. Dr. Peter VanKatwyk relates this to work with the dying [6]. As a worker with the dying, a part of one's responses can get hooked into an anxiety deep within oneself. It is like the "wounded healer" where one gets connected with one's own inner wounds and where one relates to one's own inner anxiety about dying. The Pastoral Caregiver may assume an aura of calm and control. But somewhere deep below that calm and control may lurk unhealed wounds and unrecognized anxieties. These underground forces, while remaining incognito, may surface in the ways the Caregiver relates to the dying.

Karen Horney, in a book called *Our Inner Conflicts,* identifies three kinds of neurotic ways of relating to people [7]. They are "Moving Toward People," "Moving Against People" and "Moving Away from People."

The first such way is in Moving Away. Here the Carer is caught in an avoidance pattern. There will be a tendency to surround oneself with images of health and vigor. This will result in avoiding certain people who do not fit the image. Here the Pastor will tend to avoid visiting the dying with the well documented excuse of "being too busy." Or the Pastor will assign the task to the Associate or Assistant or Student with the rationalization that it is a good learning experience for them.

The second neurotic way of relating to people is the opposite to the first, namely, Moving Toward. Here is the tendency to surround oneself with the sick and dying. Here one spends most of one's time with the elderly and dying. Sermonizing will put repeated emphasis upon concern about the sick. Here one tends to become a people collector possibly as a reaction to one's perceived sense of loneliness and unacceptance. Here one is caught up in one's own wounds and will populate one's life with people which reflect one's own wounds. In the "wounded healer," we are drawn by our own wounds. In that encounter we can find our healing. But this becomes neurotic when it is one's major all consuming project. And when this project becomes autobiographical it can become self-justification or narcissism, covered with a veneer of self-righteousness and holiness! It is an almost obsessive compulsive pre-occupation with the sick and dying. It is incapable of "detached concern." It can be a highly productive neurosis. This caregiver finds more life with the dying than with the living. But the healthy have little or nothing to offer.

The third neurotic way of relating to people is Moving Against. This is the heroic way of denying death. It is a triumphalistic approach to death. There is an intolerance for people who feel depressed. One always has to be "up"! All forms of death like sadness and sorrow are taboo. One has to be happy, on a high, all of the time. This heroic approach has an intolerance of death reality in any shape. It can violate the dying in the name of holiness. The hospital room of a colleague of mine, terminally ill flat on his back was invaded by such heroic enthusiasts. With a religious high they harassed him. They insisted, "If you believe in Jesus, there won't be a cloud in the sky anymore. All your troubles will vanish like a bubble." But my colleague was a realist. He knew his Lord but also the sting of death. What an episode of violation! Their approach is a rejection of their own death, a rejection of the dying person's death and a rejection of the dying person. If one does not buy their "heroicism" one is not saved. Here is no possibility of "living your dying" or "death as a part of life." Here one splits off absolutely the experience of dying. Moving Against, Moving Toward, and Moving Away are Karen Horney's three neurotic ways of relating. They apply not only to everyday relationships but also to Pastoral Care relationships with the dying!

In 1954-55 I was in a graduate program in Psychology of Religion and Pastoral Care at Boston University. The issue those days was Directive versus Non-directive counselling. It was C. F. Thorne versus Carl Rogers. For almost a decade I tried to be Rogerian. It has been said that the Rogerian method is best suited for the church because the church is a volunteer organization. Nevertheless, I eventually discovered I could never be a pure Rogerian. However, I also saw the fallacy behind the answers given by candidates being examined for certification in CAPE. When asked about their counseling method at least eight out of ten replied, "I'm eclectic." How can you not "pass" an eclectic?

What an array of methods and approaches have emerged in the past forty years from Jay Adams to Fritz Perls. Robert W. McClellan, in *Claiming a Frontier: Ministry and Older People,* [8] expresses counseling methods in a succinct way appropriate to ministry related also to the bereaved and dying. These approaches to ministry are differentiated by means of a preposition: Ministry to, Ministry for, Ministry with, and Ministry of.

Ministry to the bereaved and dying will remain an important method for persons who need services offered to them from pastoral care to community services. My predecessor dean of our divinity school was in the hospital terminally ill with a brain tumor which left him speechless and handicapped. There I was at his hospital bed reading the scripture to a person who had been an expert in teaching them!

Ministry for the bereaved and dying will also continue because they will have special needs which they cannot meet themselves. The same terminally ill dean had also been a professional musician with a Ph.D. in music from the University of Berlin. One of my colleagues gathered together the equipment, tapes and records to provide appropriate music for our dying colleague during his final three months. His physician marvelled how he sat in silence in the face of death surrounded by his favorite music. This would not have happened had not someone been aware for him and provided for him. It was the single most important thing done for him to live his dying days.

Care must be taken, however, that ministries not be done to and for the bereaved or dying which they can handle themselves and which are done to meet the needs of the Caregiver. Public Broadcasting System (PBS) has a tape on Donahue and Kids, in which children with cancer are interviewed. One teen-age girl emphasizes that not only should they not have everything done for them but also they, the afflicted, should be called upon to do things for others. Ministries to and for are valid and useful under appropriate circumstances. But the two ministries which intrigue me are Ministry with and Ministry of.

Ministry with the dying is meaningfully articulated by Richard L. Schaper in the *Journal of Religion and Health*, under the title of "Pastoral Accompaniment of the Cancer Patient." Schaper says [9, p. 138]:

> Cancer confronts a person with her or his mortality. On the inner journey of coming to terms with this, the pastor accompanies the patient in a way analogous in which a music accompanist supports a soloist, providing attentive relationship and supportive context.

In speaking of the pastor-patient relationship Schaper says, "Accompanist and soloist listen to each other on a level beneath that of the music that flows between them and relates them. Almost always it is the soloist who leads" [9, p. 140]. The accompanist's attention is focused upon the soloist whom the accompanist is supporting. But there may be times when the soloist takes cues from the accompanist.

Schaper explains, "The pastor seeks to offer the cancer patient both attentiveness and free space" [9, p. 140]. The patient is allowed to lead in order to allow respect for personal integrity and for the uniqueness of that person's life situation. Both the uniqueness of the person and the uncertainty of the course of events are unpredictable. Therefore, both Pastor and patient have no score for guidance.

The Pastor could stick to a score like that of Elisabeth Kubler-Ross' stages of denial, anger, bargaining, depression and acceptance. These stages do enlighten our understanding of grief's emotional processes. But this score can just as often misguide the accompanist-Pastor from concentrating full attention upon the dying person whose grief and dying are as individual and complex as his/her fingerprints. There is the temptation for the Pastor-accompanist to be misguided by "how he thinks it should be." Says Schaper, "when this occurs it is as if the Pastor has become musical conductor instead of accompanist and insists upon following the conductor's score" [9, p. 141]. Schaper tells of a co-pastor who insisted on taking a young man "through the death and dying stages" so that in the next crisis he would not be afraid. Schaper admits, "I have recognized elements of this same attitude in my own relating to patients" [9, p. 141].

The Pastor-as-accompanist implies also that he/she represents a community of faith which gives validity to the patient's inner struggle of the spirit. The pastor's presence and relating as an accompanist affirms the patient's much needed sense of unique worth as she/he faces the issues of meaning in her/his death and life.

For me, the Pastor-as-accompanist is an exciting attempt to image ministry with the grieving and dying. Dr. Peter VanKatwyk describes the Helping Mode of "being with" as "facilitative" [6]. The concern here is "what must I be" to be of help to the patient. For a ministry with the patient, Schaper suggests be an accompanist!

There is also the *ministry of*. Ministry of implies that the aging, grieving and dying have a contribution to make to the living and healthy. Dr. Elisabeth Kubler-Ross sub-titled her volume *On Death and Dying* "What the dying have to teach nurses, doctors, clergy" [10]. In ministry of the patient is seen as a source of learning and love, faith and life.

Dr. Henri Nouwen in his Ancaster presentation gives a dramatic example of this. He was asked to be the priest of one of Jean Vanier's communities in Toronto. Soon after he arrived he says [1],

> . . . they thought it would be good for me to take care of Adam. Adam is twenty-five years old. Adam does not speak. Adam cannot dress or undress himself. Adam cannot walk alone. Adam has a severe contortion in his back. Adam does not recognize you or at least can't let you know. Adam suffers from seizures. Adam can

never be alone. [Henri cared for Adam. He says,] I was afraid. In the morning I had to take him to the bath tub, take off his diaper, dry him, brush his teeth, shave him, put on his clothes, give him breakfast. Here I was with Adam. Why did God send me to Adam?

Nouwen continues, "Something happened to me. Gradually I fell in love with Adam. It wasn't a romantic love. But something was happening to me. Something I had never experienced before." Adam's father said: "We call him peacemaker. He brings us peace, love, which nobody else can bring us." Says Henri [1],

> . . . this broken young man is chosen by God to tell me something I so badly needed to know. I had read so many books about God and theology. But Adam is telling me something no one else can tell me, not even the best professors or the best students. Adam is telling me: 'being is more important than doing,' 'the heart is more important than the mind,' 'together is more important than alone.'

Adam has told me something about that first love." Says Henri, "I would never be able to offer people consolation and comfort if I was not somewhere deeply sure in my heart that God held me safe wherever I would go, whatever I would do or whatever would happen." Through Adam, God taught Henri to trust that first love.

We have come full circle now. We started with motivation for Pastoral Care of the bereaved and dying coming from that first love. We end now with a ministry of, wherein that first love reveals new awareness to the Pastoral Caregiver through most unexpected sources, through the broken, the bereaved and the dying.

Dynamics of the Grief Process

Shock	Impatience
Guilt	Self-pity
Ambivalence	Joy
Anger	Communal strength
Pain	Hope
Depression	Relief
Panic	Growth
Loneliness	Memories
Somatic distress	Identity Crisis
Emotional expression	Reaffirmation

REFERENCES

1. H. Nouwen, Christian Discipleship in the Modern World, audio tape, Ancaster, Ontario, January 12, 1989. Quotations are not necessarily verbatim.
2. J. Vanier, *The Broken Body,* Anglican Book Centre, Toronto, 1988.
3. R. S. Sullender, *Grief and Growth,* Paulist Press, New York, 1985.
4. R. S. Sullender, Three Theoretical Approaches to Grief, *The Journal of Pastoral Care,* pp. 243-251, December 1979.
5. C. Guldner, *The Dying Patient,* unpublished paper.
6. P. L. VanKatwyk, The Helping Style Inventory: A Tool in Supervised Pastoral Education, *The Journal of Pastoral Care,* pp. 319-327, Winter 1988.
7. K. Horney, *Our Inner Conflicts: A Constructive Theory of Neurosis,* Norton, New York, 1945.
8. R. W. McClellan, *Claiming a Frontier: Ministry and Older People,* University of Southern California Press, 1977.
9. R. L. Schaper, Pastoral Accompaniment of the Cancer Patient, *Journal of Religion and Health,* pp. 138-148, Summer 1984.
10. E. Kubler-Ross, *On Death and Dying,* MacMillan Co., New York, 1974.

CHAPTER 5

Ministry to People with AIDS

Jean Crabtree

The bottom line with AIDS is that it is a universal killer, a multi-million dollar business, and the greatest challenge ever to our health care system.

From 1984-88 in Ontario alone, the total number of AIDS diagnoses increased twenty-fold. Seventy percent of these cases are reported in the Metropolitan Toronto area. Toronto has a large gay community and, according to some reports, gay men from other areas of the province and country who believe they may be infected with the AIDS virus move to the city because it is a place where gays find more social acceptance and where there is access to highly specialized, confidential medical care.

From our experience to date, it is projected that the numbers of people diagnosed with AIDS will continue to increase. By 1991 in Metro Toronto we had 1,258 cases, 2,460 in the province of Ontario, and 7,000 cases across Canada.

AIDS has, to date, for Canadians been a disease of the gay community in the bigger cities of our country. However, it is only a matter of time before the heterosexual population and smaller centres and even rural areas will be grappling with the reality of AIDS in their midst. When AIDS is no longer a disease of strangers but one of our neighbors, new issues and problems arise for us.

Women's College Hospital is an acute care teaching Hospital in downtown Toronto. The Hospital has a reputation for being a place that lives up to its motto "to teach, to heal, with special care." Because of the Hospital's proximity to the gay community and its reputation for excellence of care, it has attracted a significant number of AIDS patients.

The number of AIDS admissions has grown faster than the Hospital anticipated.

Year	First Time Admitted	Annual Admissions
1985	1	1
1986	12	12
1987	65	94
1988	51	123
1989 (January-May)	14	

On the average, the Hospital has ten AIDS patients who stay about 15.9 days per admission.

Women's College Hospital uses the Medicus Tool to classify patients according to the level of care required. AIDS patients require levels 3 and 4 which is close to the level 5 required by patients in the Intensive Care Unit. Pastoral Care statistics reveal the same intensity of involvement—up to three times greater per admission than that given to non-AIDS patients.

A diagnosis of AIDS raises many complex issues for the health care provider. These are only part of the picture. For patient, lover, family, and caregiver, there are a whole range of ethical, moral, religious and spiritual concerns.

The admissions to Women's College Hospital reflect what is still true for most of North America: AIDS is a disease of gay men. "Straight" society can tend to see these people as deviants or perverts to be shunned or feared. The religious community may see them as outcasts, or sinners who have brought upon themselves the just rewards of their sinful lifestyle. It is difficult, if not impossible, for us to think about AIDS without dealing with the reality of homosexuality. If, because of our religious convictions we believe homosexuality to be a profoundly evil or immoral condition, then it will be very difficult for us to give supportive pastoral care to those in great need.

The United Church of Canada, in facing the issues of Sexuality, Lifestyle and Ministry has been torn apart by bitter controversy as congregations, ministers and the national church take opposing and what seems to be irreconcilable positions. The divisions are deep on how to understand what the Scripture teaches about homosexuality. I wonder what will happen if we learn that one of our ministers has AIDS.

In one week, news reports told of members of an Anglican Parish in Halifax, Nova Scotia, being very upset because their priest was giving too much time to people with AIDS. In the same city, a Church group wanted to purchase a house where people with AIDS could live faced the anger of neighbors because this house was across the street from a school. The neighbors feared the children would be in danger from AIDS patients.

How can responsible pastors and church members respond to homosexuals with AIDS, especially when their religious tradition takes a position that all homosexual acts are in themselves evil, unnatural, and contrary to God's intended purpose of procreation within the context of heterosexual marriage? No doubt, at times, some clergy will do so at a great personal cost and pain. Even if a particular denomination takes a liberal stance, there will be a price to pay for there will be some members of the congregations who will find our involvement with people with AIDS unacceptable.

Professor William Zion of Queen's University, Kingston, in an essay "AIDS and Homosexuality: Some Christian and Jewish Responses" reminds us that Jesus, along with the rabbis, taught us not to judge our neighbor [1]. We are, like those who would have condemned the women caught in adultery, challenged by the words of Jesus: "If any of you is without sin, let him be the first to throw a stone at her" (John 8:7). Zion goes on to say [1, p. 40]:

> The hardness of our hearts, our lack of compassion, our indifference to the suffering—are all overwhelmingly sinful compared to those dying from a disease contracted in their attempts to reach out to the other.

Theories and statistics are important to understanding AIDS and the problems which confront us, but for pastoral care-givers, the primary concern must be with people. They are called to support those in their care and to stand in the gaps of their lives with and for them.

Women's College Hospital has chosen to support AIDS patients emotionally and spiritually through the services of a multidisciplinary Team. The resources are limited in finances, people and time and team members have many other calls upon their time. Nonetheless, this is a model that works and one that can be readily adapted to other health care institutions. The Team consists of a psychologist, social worker and chaplain. Sometimes each team member will see a patient, lover or family member, at other times only one member will be involved; at yet other times, the Team will be caring for the caregivers.

From a chaplain's perspective this is what has been accomplished and what has been learned since the first AIDS patient was admitted in 1985. A call to the Intensive Care Unit brought me into contact with a tearful, frightened looking young woman whose husband was dying of AIDS. She apologized for her lack of fluency in English. The doctor had just told her that her husband would soon die. How could this be, she asked, when he was only thirty-two, and a recent arrival in Canada who wanted so much to live? The doctor had also told her that she and their two-year-old daughter might also test positive for the HIV antibody. "What am I going to do?", she asked. Their story unfolded. As a young man, her husband had been an intravenous drug abuser but had put that behind him when they fell in love. Coming to Canada was to be a new start in life and now. . . . He did not die that day. Nor did he ever regain consciousness. As the week went on, we planned a funeral. She was unfamiliar with Canadian funeral practices. Her husband had been baptized in the Catholic Church but had long since given up attending Church. Yet she would like him to have a Christian burial. We discussed how and what to tell her daughter and sources of emotional, spiritual, and social support were explored.

Since that meeting I've met with many young people, mostly men, who have been diagnosed with AIDS or ARC (AIDS Related Complex). These men, their partners and their families have freely shared their stories with me and other staff members on the AIDS Psychosocial Support Team. Together, staff, patients, lovers and families have learned much from each other and supported one another. As staff, we learned to confront our own fears about AIDS. We learned that it is a hard disease to catch. The virus is transmitted only through the exchange of blood of body fluids—not by touching, not by being in the same room, not by sitting close to the patient or eating offered food or sharing the Communion Cup. We learned that it was not always necessary to wear gowns, gloves and masks—although specific precautions are called for in handling blood and body fluids and when a particular infection is identified.

Harder than dealing with the medical protocol was the emotional response to the patient with AIDS, his lover and family. So far the majority of people with AIDS are gay men under forty. They are generally strangers to many of us, and we have long been conditioned to fear strangers. As parents we teach our children to avoid strangers. The strangers who have AIDS confront us with all that we are most uncomfortable of publicly dealing with: death—sex—strangers. As health care providers we held the same stereotyped views as society at large and had the same fears of catching AIDS. Some believed that patients with AIDS had brought this disease upon themselves and should not be expecting the health care system to waste valuable resources in caring for them when they were going to die anyway. As we got to know the people with AIDS, we learned of their emotional and physical suffering we were able to lay aside most of our fears, prejudices and judgements.

Some patients with AIDS are very demanding. The nature of the disease often calls for a lot of nursing and medical intervention. The physical status of the patient can change dramatically from day to day. Because of these changes the patient often rides an emotional roller coaster. Some patients feel discriminated against as they interpret the delays that are so often an inevitable part of hospitalization as hostile reactions to them because they are gay and have AIDS.

Most of the patients admitted to Women's College Hospital with AIDS or ARC are homosexual or bisexual men. They have particular problems that differ from a child who has contracted AIDS from a needed blood transfusion. A significant number of the men we see are self-employed. So when they become ill there may be no one else to run the business. They may not be eligible for sick benefits. As their health declines they may see their financial resources dwindle and may become unable to afford their own accommodation any longer. They may be forced to move in with family or friends or apply for welfare. Moving in with family or friends may have strings attached. The family may not welcome their sons's lover or gay friends—thus cutting him off from important supportive relationships.

Simon was admitted very ill and frightened of dying. On the admission form he listed George, his lover, as next-of-kin. His mother did not know he was gay. He was convinced that if he declared his sexual orientation, his family (who were devout Catholics) would disown him. So very careful visiting arrangements were made to ensure George never met Simon's family in his hospital room.

Simon had long ago given up on the institutional church. He had listened to one too many sermons condemning homosexuality. But as death neared, he was rethinking many things, and was surprised at this yearning to be reconciled to the Church, to receive the Sacrament of the Sick, to be assured of Christian burial. We often discussed faith issues. Simon could not believe that the God who created him would send this awful disease to punish him for going against the teaching of the Church. Together we looked at Jesus' dealing with the questions of sin and sickness. Simon came to a real sense of peace as he understood that God's grace and love is unconditional.

I was not at the Hospital the day Simon died. His lover, George, telephoned me to help him find some words to pray. George couldn't go to the funeral. He knew Simon's family would not want him there.

When Simon's family finally learned that their son was gay and dying of AIDS they focused their anger on George, blaming him for leading their son astray and giving him AIDS. They told their parish priest that Simon died of cancer. Their grief was lonely. Their anger remains. George attended the Memorial Service held by the AIDS Committee of Toronto and joined a survivors grief group.

Other families whose sons die of AIDS tell of being isolated by friends and neighbors. Because of the stigma attached to AIDS many families often do not get the emotional support they need from each other, let alone the community.

Lovers and gay friends are often excluded from the funeral rites. These folks' grief is just as intense as the biological family's and it may be even more lonely. They may not be able to reveal their grief without revealing their sexual orientation. Then, too, they have added fears and guilts to complicate their grief. Did they infect their lover? Will they be diagnosed with AIDS?

People with AIDS, their partners and gay friends are also faced with on-going chronic grief as they learn of the diagnosis of AIDS or the death of yet another person they know and care for. Maurice counted ten friends in two months who had died of AIDS. "I'm always going to funerals," he said. He went on to describe the emotional impact of coming to the Hospital to visit his lover and meeting, unexpectedly, on the same floor a business contact who had recently been admitted with AIDS. "And who can I talk to about it?" he said. Dr. Rosemary Barnes, Chief Psychologist at Women's College Hospital, points out that people with AIDS deal with all the concerns other patients have about fatal illness—plus more. She defines some issues common to life threatening illness:

- fear of death, disfigurement and pain
- loss of control and autonomy
- upset of established relationships
- loss of future
- adjustment to patient role
- difficulty in maintaining emotional equilibrium, and

specific to AIDS:

- stigma of association with homosexual contacts and/or drug use
- concerns about contagion and isolation

For gay men there may also be these additional stresses:

- conflict over sexual orientation

- guilt related to past sexual behavior
- uncertainty about future sexual attractiveness
- fear of disclosing sexual orientation to family, friends, employers.

Unlike cancer patients, people with AIDS have no real hope of remission. People with other fatal illnesses may have the opportunity to go through a denial period as they come to terms with their diagnosis. With AIDS this may not be possible for there is often a short time span between diagnosis and debilitating illness. Patients speak of how awful it is to pick up a newspaper or magazine, to turn on the radio or TV and read or hear yet another story about the finality of their diagnosis. They know of no one who has been cured. Symptoms may be relieved but for how long. Some patients with disfiguring infections may withdraw from social contacts or may be asked to leave their jobs. Some find living with AIDS so difficult that they choose suicide. On a recent edition of 60 Minutes a young man described his involvement in the suicides of many AIDS patients.

Patients with AID Related Complex (ARC) live under the added stress of not knowing whether they will develop full blown AIDS or remain antibody positive. They wonder how to plan for the future, or if they have a future. Those with ARC who go on to develop full blown AIDS often say that bad as this, it is better in some way to finally know where they stand. At first it was believed only a small percentage of those who tested antibody positive would develop AIDS. Experience indicates that this was too optimistic a view.

Asked if he believed AIDS to be God's judgement on homosexuals, Stephen Manning, Director of the AIDS Committee of Toronto, stated that he saw it as more of a judgement on the rest of us. It challenges us as a society to a response of love, compassion and action that we may not be able or willing to make.

Ministry to people with AIDS, their lovers and families, does not mean we set out either to cure homosexuality or to condemn it. We are called to support and enable patients, lovers and families to verbalize their fears, their concerns, their hopes. AIDS is a fear-filled disease for those whose lives it touches. We minister effectively when we show by our presence and actions that we care.

As pastoral caregivers, some of us may never see a patient with AIDS. We may be brought face to face with parents who disclose to us that they have just learned their son who moved to the city is gay and dying of AIDS, or we may learn that a woman has just discovered that her husband of twenty years is bisexual and has AIDS. Faced with what may be a double grief as well as the perceived need to keep their news secret, they may have no one else but their pastor to turn to for support.

Whether we minister to patients, their lovers or families, we will help best when we reflect God's unconditional love for all people. James Wharton is quoted in *AIDS: A Manual for Pastoral Care* [2, p. 40] as noting that it is inappropriate to "preach at" one who is in crisis. The appropriate pastoral response is to the stated needs of the patient or family member. It will usually be a listening ministry with the agenda set by the one to whom we minister. In the same volume, we are brought the suggestion by Alan Keith-Lucas from a social work perspective that effective help and support is offered when three caring elements are present: reality, empathy and support [2, p. 35].

> Reality: This is it.
> Empathy: I know that it must hurt.
> Support: I am here to help you if you want me and can use me
> (or . . .). You don't have to face this alone.

As a Christian minister, I believe the stand I must take in ministry to people whose lives are torn apart by the diagnosis of AIDS cannot be dictated either by my denomination or by individual members of the Church. I must be able to believe that Jesus' words in Mt 25:34-46 mean also people with AIDS. I must act upon that belief—Jesus said these words we have heard so often [Matthew 25:34-36]:

> Come, you who are blessed by my father: take your inheritance, the Kingdom prepared for you since the creation of the world. For I was hungry and you gave me something to eat, I was thirsty and you gave me something to drink, I was a stranger and you invited me in, I needed clothes and you clothed me, I was sick and you looked after me, I was in prison and you came to visit me.

May God give us grace and strength to be his presence through the signs of love and affection we show to those who live with AIDS.

REFERENCES

1. W. Zion, Aids and Homosexuality: Some Jewish and Christian Responses, *AIDS in Religious Perspective*, Queen's Theological College, Kingston, Ontario, 1987.
2. R. H. Sunderland and E. E. Shelp, *AIDS: A Manual for Pastoral Care*, The Westminster Press, Philadelphia, 1987.

BIBLIOGRAPHY

Flynn, Eileen P., *AIDS: A Catholic All for Compassion,* Sheed and Ward, Kansas City, 1985 (ISBN 0-934134-731).

James, William Closson (ed.), *AIDS in Religious Perspective,* Queen's Theological College, Kingston, Ontario, 1987 (ISBN 0-88911-509-5).

Kubler-Ross, Elisabeth and Mal Warshaw, *AIDS The Ultimate Challenge,* McMillan, 1987.

McNeill, John J. S. J., *The Church and the Homosexual Person,* Sheed, Andrews and McMeel, Inc., Kansas City, 1976.

Reed, James (ed.), *Human Sexuality, Approaches to Sexuality and Christian Theology,* Anglican Book Centre, Toronto, 1986 (ISBN 0-919891-49-7).

Sunderland, Ronald H. and Earl E. Shelp, *AIDS: A Manual for Pastoral Care,* The Westminster Press, Philadelphia, 1987 (ISBN 0-664-24088-7).

Shelp, Earl E., Ronald H. Sunderland, and Peter W. A. Mansell, *AIDS: Personal Stories in Pastoral Perspective,* The Pilgrim Press, New York, 1986 (ISBN 0-8298-0739X).

CHAPTER 6

Clergy and Lay Persons Working Together

Dorothy Southall

As a national trainer for Widowed Person's Service, a program under the umbrella of A.A.R.P., I have had the privilege of meeting with laity and clergy across the nation. Because my stay at each place is brief and our training intense, the people involved feel free to openly express themselves concerning everything involved in their grief process. Over and over I have heard the concerns of both laity and clergy and feel strongly that there is a great need for better understanding between the laity and clergy.

A positive approach is needed for this working together. Fault-finding and blaming the others will only delay the understanding. As I have listened to these people's stories, I have realized that some were real and some were exaggerated. Real or not they were real to them and are problems for both laity and clergy.

There are a number of questions which I feel all should think about as we begin to look at the situation as it occurs today. These questions are:

1. How do you rate your religious group in their Clergy-Laity co-working in grief experiences?
2. Do you know the number/percentage of widowed persons in your religious group?
3. Do you know the average number of deaths annually in your religious group?
4. Is death, grief, bereavement a "No, No" subject in your religious group?
5. Do you take part in ongoing grief and bereavement work?

6. For laity, a) have you talked with your clergy concerning knowledge of death, grief, bereavement?; b) have you asked for help in groups concerning (6a)?
7. For clergy, have you talked with your congregation and asked their desire for more information on said subjects?
8. Do the people in your group feel that their religion helps them with what they are going through or does it get in the way? No doubt you have seen it happen both ways.

The clergy was very cooperative with me, and we were able to arrive at specifics concerning what they want laity to do in grief and bereavement situations. I have compiled these and consolidated them into the following:

1. Courtesy concerning letting the clergy know when people are ill or have died rather than assuming that the clergy knows.
2. Understanding that the clergy is not a puppet to be manipulated, that the clergy has personal beliefs and practices of the church that are sacred and they will not compromise.
3. Forgiveness if the clergy fails to live up to expectations. Clergy are not infallible. Having feet of clay is felt by many. Some have their own problems with death/dying and grief/bereavement. A Catholic priest told of his struggle in the making of his will. It was over a year before he could put it on paper.

If the clergy is very close to the person who died, he or she may be having personal grief and may back off from the immediate family. They won't really forsake them but will delay their help.

If the clergy continually does things wrong that is one thing, but if the mistake is seldom, they ask forgiveness.

4. Let the clergy help in planning the services, share suggestions and help the family. The clergy wants to know what the laity desires. They are not mind readers. They ask that the laity be specific and open. If they don't know what they want, they can say that. This gives the clergy the opening for giving options.
5. Know that the clergy has many tasks. Although they are often willing, they cannot give all their time to each beloved one.
6. Support the study and the discussion of death, funeral practices and the grief process as a part of the ongoing work of the congregation.
7. Be willing to support a grief support system to be used as the need arises. This includes ongoing work with better understanding of the bereaved.

8. Take the initiative to see that such an ongoing program could be started, continued and supported. They desire the laity to give their willingness to explore work and study.
9. The laity needs to support those concerned persons who get the program started and working.
10. Support the clergy in getting the program coordinated and working.
11. Work in small groups, getting the groups ready to discuss the establishment of a grief-bereavement ministry to then work with the minister in drawing up a proposal to be presented to the decision-making body. This body of persons, with the minister, can open the way for appropriate study and planning implementations.
12. Trust that the clergy is a man/woman of God and will counsel and serve from that perspective.

Today we have a more philosophical laity; however, the clergy need not fear and think they have to pull the ranks. Management skills can be put into use. The things the laity would like for the clergy to do follows:

1. Be there. Rabbi Earl Grollman, upon hearing of two boys drowning off the coast of Massachusetts, immediately went to the scene. Later he was asked to counsel both sets of parents. When he asked them why they, who were not Jewish persons, wanted him to counsel, they replied, "You were there." The laity realizes this immediate attention cannot always be given but expect it as soon as possible.
2. Listen-nonjudgementally-allow openness. The laity wants permission to express feelings, doubts, wishes and to ask questions (even when there are no answers). They may not really want to hear answers.

I read that clergy had a hard time allowing grieving persons to scream at God. Some people need to express rage without being judged.

3. Limit length of scripture reading and/or prayer as needed or asked for on the initial visit.
4. Although it is likely unnecessary to mention, avoid cliches. They are still used by some well meaning clergy and may help some laity; however, they are hurtful to others. Examples: "It is God's will," "I know how you feel," "Now you have an angel in heaven," "You'll get over it," "God only gives you as much as you can bear," "Time heals all wounds," "They are better off," "They would want you to be strong."

5. Encourage input in funeral and burial arrangements. They want to know what options they have.
6. Remember them later. A survey showed that only three percent of widowed persons expected or received help from the clergy following the death of their spouse. This being remembered could be a phone call, short note or short visit. They desire that you use the name of the one who died—not drop it or avoid using it.
7. Be a facilitator—not the person who does all the work. They hope that you can refer persons who have had similar grief experiences and who have worked through their grief to be of help.
8. Show strength and acknowledge feelings. They know that Jesus wept and would not be offended to see a tear in your eye. They understand that there is a time for all things.
9. Be accepting of the new person who emerges. People are never the same. Some are much better.

Clergy and laity can work together in research. This would include finding out the number of families in the local group, the number of deaths annually (also for the past five years), number of persons in each family and their experiences of death, and who in the church group (outside their immediate family) each feels closest to and would want near them when a death occurs.

There is a need for clergy and laity to work together in education both within the immediate group and the community. There are many people who desire to help, but feel inadequate.

Clergy and laity need to open lines of communication and keep them clear.

An openness to the idea of suffering God and remembrance of Israel as a suffering nation should not be neglected. Along with this idea of a servant people will be helpful in people being aware of their need to help others in grief experiences.

Study courses relating to dying, death, grief and bereavement can be started. Workshops can be held. Training sessions for working with newly bereaved persons can be helpful. Ongoing training will also be needed. Continued updating information, acquiring helpful resources and always being on the lookout for persons who do specific work is needed. Key persons can include the grief ministry coordinator (the clergy or appointed by clergy), one-to-one outreach volunteers who are willing to take training and do ongoing work (called "shepherding persons" by some), hospice workers, funeral directors, minister of music, kitchen chairperson, worship service planner (for special remembrances such as candlelighting, lilies, etc.).

There is a need for a willingness to work together. If communications are clear and open much will be accomplished. The work will not be accomplished overnight, but each step taken forward will be a great help for all. It can be very rewarding for everyone in the congregation and the community.

CHAPTER 7

The Church:
A Model for Adjustment for
the Dying and Bereaved

Lynne Martins

Paradoxically, the church has the power to console or condemn, incorporate or isolate individuals and families who are in various stages of grief or mourning. Unlike any other institution, the church can also offer the greatest sense of adjustment, hope and integration of the dying and bereaved person(s) into the life of the church.

This chapter looks at the church as a model for grief adjustment and integration. The healing aspect of the church lies in the person of Jesus Christ. The clergy are "mini-churches" carrying the task of ministry and healing hope of Jesus Christ to the dying and bereaved. My beliefs about the role of the church evolved through the losses I experienced between the ages of 17 and 25. During those eight years, three members of my immediate family died. During each death, I was deeply involved in the church. However, the response from each church was very different. Some responses were powerful, others were painful. I am ultimately convinced that the church wants to help, but does not always know how to help. It is my conviction that the church is the one place where I can be reinstated in the flow of life following a tragedy.

THE STRENGTH OF THE CHURCH AS A MODEL

Psychologically

The church provides several elements needed in the grief process. "Jesus Christ is the same: yesterday, today and forever" (Hebrews 13:8).

Stability — The church lends stability because of the structure it provides. Both physically and spiritually, the church provides a sense of ritual and routine which contributes to the bereaved persons' need for order during the chaos of death and bereavement. (Example: The bereaved person can count on the location of the church day after day, week after week. As daily tasks become overwhelming, a sense of disorientation and confusion set in. It is extremely difficult to concentrate. Anything that can diffuse the sense of powerlessness, even something as incidental as remembering the actual location of the church, can be beneficial.)

Familiarity — This is closely related to stability, but the point of familiarity is in terms of the structure of the church found in such things as the order of worship, Sunday school classes, other groups of people that are familiar to the bereaved. If the bereaved has been in a smaller group within the church, the element of familiarity is greatly enhanced. Familiarity is found in the fact that the person does not have to go through additional changes and adjustments of meeting new people and rituals of the service, but are stabilized by familiar faces.

Continuity — The church has become part of the dying and bereaved person's history. They have known the past, experienced the present, and covenant with them for the future. The continuity the church also provides: 1) the affirmation of the tragedy that the person has been through (they have witnessed it—and are horrified by the loss which affirms the shock, horror and disbelief experienced by the bereaved); and 2) the absence of change (which is a critical point to healthy adjustment, especially within the first year). These two points are of great benefit to strengthening the bereaved person psychologically.

Spiritually–Faith Found in Others

Because of the psychological elements the church provides, another strength is found in the faith of others. While I am unable to express myself to God in the midst of my darkest hours, my fellow partners in Christ "stand in the gap" for me. I sit silently in church, unable to utter a single word, prayer or praise to God but am absorbed by the history and continuity of faith around me. No words are needed. There is healing and encouragement in being able to participate in my catatonic state. I will not be able to tell you what the sermon was about or who sang special music, but I was brought into the presence of God, which will be the only One who can heal my brokenness.

The faith and life of those around me provide me with the necessary buffer I feel I need to question God, to express my rage and dislike toward my Creator. I am not sure at this particular moment whether or not I'll be annihilated for my questions, because I am not sure which side of the fence God is on. The best possible ministry that could come to me is the freedom to doubt without being accused that my faith is faltering. My questions are not really a lack of faith, they are merely an expression of the enormity of my pain and helplessness that beset me. To ask a grieving person not to doubt God robs them from an authentic meeting with their Creator. Grief has a way of stripping us of the games we sometimes play with God and others. The faith of others will eventually point me back to God and provide the necessary arena to question and doubt which will ultimately help me make sense of my loss.

Physically–Accessibility and Variety of Gifts

Another strength of the church lies in the physical accessibility and variety of people available to minister to the bereaved. The church provides a built-in network of people who can aid the bereaved in the adjustment process. The physical numbers represented in a church gives testimony to the fact that other people have faced losses and survived them. The numbers also attest to the fact that I am not alone. No where will there be access to as many diverse gifts guided by the person of Christ and the Holy Spirit. (Example: A group of retired people organized and managed the estate sale for me when my mother died. By that point I was able to enjoy the memories that the sale provided and was quite relieved to have their expertise with a project that overwhelmed me. I often wonder if I really would have felt the freedom to enjoy the sale without the loving, tender support of Ivan and Lucy Wilharm and friends. I even remember that Lucy made her special creamed cheese chocolate cupcakes. There is a lot of sound theology in cupcakes shared in an estate sale, especially when it rains. Faithfulness of God is demonstrated in the faithfulness of His people.)

CORPORATE MOURNING:
INTEGRATION OF THE BEREAVED

The greatest threat to adjustment and healing is isolation. It is extremely important for the bereaved person to be integrated into the life of the church. All ages affirm life and can be instrumental in lending healing to the bereaved.

"A little girl lost a playmate in death and one day reported to her family that she had gone to comfort the sorrowing mother. 'What did

you say?' asked her father. 'Nothing,' she replied. I just climbed up on
her lap and cried with her."

Acknowledgement of Death

After gaining permission from the family, a public acknowledgement
of the death can minister in several ways:

1. Whether the death is impending or actual, the acknowledgement
   will be the foundation for the grieving process to begin. The
   acknowledgement of a tragedy gives permission to the bereaved
   person to grieve. This also gives the congregation the green light
   to respond.
2. The acknowledgement of death is the beginning of the affirmation
   of the decreased person's life. Their life counted, it will be missed,
   we are all grieved that this catastrophe has happened.
3. A corporate acknowledgement of the death also relieves the
   family from having to relive the horror of sharing the "bad news"
   over and over again.
4. The bulletin or church newsletter is the most practical means of a
   public acknowledgment. A short note to remind people that a
   death has occurred will be very meaningful to the grieving family.

Holidays, anniversaries — Flowers can be given in remembrance of
the deceased. One Presbyterian church sets aside a section in the
bulletin both at Christmas and Easter just for this purpose. Poinsettias
and Easter lilies are given in remembrance of a loved one who has died
and their names are printed in the bulletin.

All Saints Day — This is a special day set aside for remembering
the dead. In the Jewish tradition, two days are set aside. Traditionally,
the deceased person's name is read aloud during a special service. For a
person to hear the name of the deceased reminds the world that
their life was important: they are missed and are still remembered.
It validates my sadness and grief. In our focus to be resurrection Christians, we must be careful not to overlook some of the rituals
and traditions that could be instrumental to the healing of bereaved
persons.

The Strength of Community: Small Groups

Integration withers if it is left on the corporate level. Anywhere the
deceased has been involved will serve as a catalyst of healing for the
bereaved.

Sunday school class — Healing would be expedited if time were given to remembering the deceased, and acknowledging the pain and despair of the bereaved. (A young child named Billy died suddenly in a car accident. The volunteer teacher had the wisdom to invite a discussion about death. She encouraged the children to write a short story about what they remembered about their young classmate.) What a healing legacy was given to Billy's parents and a healthy response to children's questions about death.

Choir, committees, Sunday school teacher, etc. — Look for the places where the deceased "lived" in the church. This will provide the necessary network for the grieving person to draw upon. This also relieves the clergy from the unrealistic expectation that he/she is the only one who can help.

Para-church support groups — While these groups (bereavement support groups, etc.) are very beneficial, I would caution the church to be aware that without the ongoing life of the church, these groups can make a person feel even more isolated and desolate in their bereavement experience. It is ideal for a person to experience the specialized support groups simultaneously with the ongoing network of the church. We need to remember that identity with a bereavement support group is a temporary identity and not one that we want to sentence the grieving person to. We are a "fix-it" society and must be aware of this pitfall. I have also come across some churches where the attitude is such that to send a person "off" to a group fulfills their sense of duty without then having to be touched by the individual's pain.

INDIVIDUAL MOURNING:
THE FIRST YEAR ALONE

I hesitate to break down the bereavement process so systematically because of the individuality of the bereaved. Each person and situation is very unique and should not be held to any type of rigid time table or progression of stages. The year following a death is a year of "firsts." The first month, the first holiday, the first birthday, not to mention the numerous social functions and daily routines which also induce a "first" encounter of some type. The community of the church provides a buffer to face the first holidays and anniversary dates alone.

0-3 Months: Sitting and Listening Phase

Ministry is most difficult because we are keenly aware of our helplessness during this phase. However, helplessness can become the greatest asset and can become the common ground between the minister and the bereaved. Admit your helplessness. That will be an automatic bridge to the bereaved person. They are well acquainted with the feeling of helplessness. You no longer need to be an "expert" with an answer, but a person with ears. I have given extra attention to the first phase because it establishes the rapport with the person and sets the stage for a healthy progression of the grieving process. An excerpt from *Life Together,* by Dietrich Bonhoeffer, emphasizes our need to listen [1, pp. 98-99]:

> The first service that one owes to others in the fellowship consists of listening to them. Just as love to God begins with listening to His Word, so the beginning of love for the brethren is learning to listen to them. It is God's love for us that He not only gives us His word but also lends us His ear. So it is His work that we do for our brother when we learn to listen to him. Christians especially ministers, so often think they must always contribute something when they are in the company of others, that this is the one service they have to render. They forget that listening can be a greater service than speaking.

> Many people are looking for an ear that will listen. They do not find among it Christians because these Christians are talking when they should be listening. But he who can no longer listen to his brother will soon be no longer listening to God either; he will be doing nothing but prattle in the presence of God too. This is the beginning of the death of the spiritual life, and in the end there is nothing left but spiritual chatter and clergical condescension arrayed in pious words. One who cannot listen long and patiently will presently be talking beside the point and be never really speaking to others; albeit he be not conscious of it. Anyone who thinks that his time is too valuable to spend keeping quiet will eventually not have time for God and his brother, but only for himself and for his own follies.

> . . . Christians have forgotten that the ministry of listening has been committed to them by Him who is Himself the great listener and whose work they should share. We should listen with the ears of God that we may speak the Word of God.

Charles Swindoll, Pastor of the Evangelical Free Church in Orange County, California, summarizes the importance of listening in an excerpt from his book, *Killing Giants and Pulling Thorns,* where he quotes Joseph Bayly [2, p. 38].

I was sitting, torn by grief. Someone came and talked to me of God's dealings, of why it happened, of hope beyond the grave. He talked constantly. He said things I knew were true.

I was unmoved, except to wish he'd go away. He finally did.

Another came and sat beside me. He didn't talk. He didn't ask me leading questions. He just sat beside me for an hour or more, listened when I said something, answered briefly, prayed simply, left.

I was moved. I was comforted. I hated to see him go.

In our haste to fill the uncomfortable silence we often quote a familiar verse—"For we know all things work together for good for those who love God and are called according to His purpose" (Romans 8:28). Be aware that vision for the future is NOT possible during this phase. Reassurance that "all things work together for good" is of little value since the task of looking ahead is impossible. We must also be careful not to suggest that an irrevocable loss has some revokable meaning. Romans 8:31-32, 37-38 are much more comforting as they reinforce the idea that God is present and cannot be separated from them—no matter what. Real ministry comes in the form of availability to reassure the bereaved that: 1) they are not alone, and 2) they are not expected to face the loss alone. The more concretely you can show that, the more healing it will be.

3-5 Months: The Forgotten Phase

Because the bereaved are moving out of the numb stage, their emotions are met with a great deal of intensity. Unfortunately, this is the time most people expect the bereaved to be getting "back to normal" and become exasperated and frustrated with them. In general, the bereaved feels very alone and abandoned.

Ministry means a personal phone call, visit or note to remind them they are not forgotten. Establishing routine contacts will be very meaningful to the bereaved. Now is a good time to suggest other resources such as support groups or individual counseling. Books and other literature may be given at this time. Encourage the bereaved to attend some of the outings and social functions they attended previously.

A recently widowed woman was attending a birthday party for a co-worker which happened to be near Christmas. In a room surrounded by familiar faces, she sat quietly off to the side, silently weeping. I noticed, and went to stand behind her. What I observed was powerful. One of her closest friends sitting beside her, who appeared to be completely absorbed in the activities of the party, had her hand tightly clinched around this woman's. It was a powerful demonstration of sensitivity and ongoing care for this woman's grief.

6-8 Months: Tell It To Me Again Phase

The intensity of loss seems to peak somewhere within the first six months of the loss depending upon the type of loss that has been experienced. The bereaved emotions are similar to a child's yo-yo. These months will be sprinkled by some "good" days. This is also the time when the bereaved need to rehearse their loss over and over to make sense of what has happened. This is essential to be able to incorporate the loss into their life. Rehearsing the loss again and again is the only way a person can reduce their grief into bite-size pieces to digest the loss into their lives. Ministry that asks the history of the deceased person will be most beneficial. Photo albums, movies, cards, notes and any other memorabilia of the deceased will be an instrument of healing for the bereaved. An afternoon compiling a photo album will provide healing for years to come. This stage of remembering provides the necessary bridge to continuing life. Until the death is adequately remembered, it cannot be laid to rest. A common fear is that the deceased person will be forgotten. A simple ritual of reviewing the life of the deceased somehow ensures that they are not and will not be forgotten. A lot of listening and sitting is needed in this stage as well. More than likely, if you are close to the person, you will see the most raw emotions expressed. You will begin to notice that the person is able to envision small glimpses of life. They may be able to participate in life of the church in the completion of mindless tasks (i.e., bulletin stuffing or other bulk mailing projects, etc.)—no emotional energy expended, yet their place in the community is validated and maintained.

9-12 Months: Onward We Go Together

Ministry comes in the form of helping the person to envision the possibilities of the future. This includes helping them monitor their involvement in church. Too often, "busyness" is mistaken for adjustment. Encourage the bereaved to slowly get back into the activities of the church, but never use involvement as a substitute for the grieving process.

During the first year, one practical aspect is helping the bereaved handle the personal belongings of the decreased. The rule of thumb is SLOW. Personal belongings are important memories and should not be given away until ready to do so. Often people rush to rid themselves of the memories so they do not have to face the pain. Encourage people to hang onto the belongings, store them away until they are really ready to let go of them. (Give alternatives instead of solutions: boxing up clothes for storage instead of having to make every decision about every article of clothing, until they are able to do so.)

NETWORKING AND SUPPORT SYSTEMS

Support for the Bereaved

Several community organizations offer help for the bereaved. Unfortunately, support groups are created on the basis of need and are usually not ongoing. However, one call can often provide many resources. It is important to help the bereaved help themselves. Healing and adjustment come from regaining some of the strength that has been taken away by the upset of the loss. A few good networking ideas for the bereaved are:

> Chaplains who can bridge the gap for the clergy/counselor with the family at the point of crisis.
> Church groups offering bereavement support groups.
> Hospices offering bereavement support groups.
> Senior Citizen Centers with ongoing resources for loss issues.

Help for the Helping Professional

There are four things that are essential for the preservation of the helping professional.

1. You must come to terms with your own mortality, defenses and fear regarding death and bereavement. Otherwise, you will pass your uncomfortableness onto the bereaved.

2. It is vitally important for you to realize your role with the bereaved. Unless you are a full time counselor, your role needs to be one of a switchboard operator. The greatest ministry and service you can offer the bereaved is to connect them with a network of people and resources. It is unrealistic to think that you alone will have the time to spend with the bereaved. One bereaved family is a full-time job for a pastor. If you try to be self-sufficient you commit a grave disservice to the bereaved, the congregation and yourself. It is intense, demanding and extremely draining work.

3. Educate your staff and congregation about how to care for the bereaved. If they see caring modeled, it will not be difficult to maintain the role of the switchboard operator.

4. It will be of utmost importance to have a support network of your own to help you process your own loss issues due to the nature of your job. It is ideal to have both a professional support network and a social network. Bereavement is hard work and we all need a break from time to time.

REFERENCES

1. D. Bonhoeffer, *Life Together,* Hoffman, Verlag, West Germany, 1954.
2. C. Swindoll, *Killing Giants and Pulling Thorns,* Multnomah, Portland, Oregon, 1978.

RESOURCE LIST

The following resources are an accumulation of reading and experience. I have highlighted some of the books that are especially appropriate for the four phases of healing and adjustment that I have mentioned.

The resource list is divided up into five groups: adults, children, parents, spouses and various situations. Some of the resources are appropriate to give to comfort the bereaved and some are listed as resources for the helping professional. Several resources are given a code to indicate which stage that particular resource is appropriate for. The code is indicated by: *1 = Phase 1; *2 = Phase 2; *3 = Phase 3; *4 = Phase 4.

Adults

Bayly, Joseph, *The Last Thing We Talk About* (formerly entitled *The View From a Hearse*), David C. Cook Publishing Co., Elgin, Illinois, 1969. — This book is easy to read and understand. It is an overview concerning death, how our society views it, and his own personal account of the loss of his three sons.

*3 Berkus, Rusty, *To Heal Again,* Red Rose Press, Encino, California, 1985. — A fantastic booklet with soothing illustrations and short phrases about grief and adjustment. Very powerful and moving.

*3 Colgrove, Bloomfield and McWilliams, *How To Survive the Loss of a Love,* Leo Press/Bantam Books, Allen Park, Michigan, 1976. — This is a book of short poems, thoughts and concrete suggestions drawn from life experience, in a variety of loss situations. Humorous in parts, highly recommended.

Jackson, Edgar, *The Many Faces of Grief,* Abingdon Press, Nashville, Tennessee, 1977. — Deals with several aspects of grief such as anger, guilt, loneliness, humor and several other normal responses. Leans toward a professional audience, but gives an insightful understanding of the grief process.

Kubler-Ross, Dr. Elisabeth, *On Death & Dying*, MacMillian Co., New York, New York, 1970. — A fairly technical look at death and dying. Audience is geared toward those in the helping profession. Dr. Kubler-Ross pioneered the understanding of the five stages of grief and it is explained in detail in this book. She offers some of the best information on the subject.

Kubler-Ross, Dr. Elisabeth, *Questions & Answers on Death & Dying*, MacMillian Co., New York, New York, 1974. — In this book Dr. Kubler-Ross answers questions directed toward her years of experience as a general physician and her work with the terminally ill. Very interesting, many case histories.

*2-3 Landorf, Joyce, *The Mourning Song*, Flemming Revell Co., Old Tappan, New Jersey, 1974. — This is a biography of Ms. Landorf's experiences through the death of a child, a birth, and the journey of the terminal illness of her mother. Very well written, extremely comforting.

*1 Manning, Doug, *Don't Take My Grief Away. (What To Do When You Lose a Loved One)*, Harper & Row Publishing Co., New York, 1984. — Excellent!! This is a great book to give anyone who is newly bereaved. Can be given immediately to the person. One of the finest, most concise, honest books on the subject. Written by a pastor. Highly recommended.

*2 Mumford, Amy, *It Hurts to Lose a Special Person*, Accent Expressions Publishing Co., Denver, Colorado, 1982. — This booklet comes with an envelope for mailing. A book of comfort with scripture passages and thoughts about grief. **See end note.

Simos, Dr. Bertha, *A Time To Grieve*, Family Service Association of America, New York, New York, 1979. — A theoretical, in-depth explanation of the stages and processing of grief and loss. Also indicates aspects of complicated grief. (Ch. 3). Directed toward the helping professional rather than the bereaved person.

*2 Swindoll, Charles, *For Those Who Hurt*, Multnomah Press, Portland, Oregon, 1977. — A good booklet to offer.

Swindoll, Charles, *Who Can I Turn To?*, Multnomah Press, Portland, Oregon, 1980. — This booklet is written for those who are suffering from a terminal illness. It is very good. Written from a dying husband's perspective.

Group Series for Adults

Bayly, Joseph, *If I Should Die Before I Wake*, David C. Cook Publishing Co., Elgin, Illinois. — This is an excellent six week study on the subject of death and dying. Candid, honest, intense. Includes teacher's manual, cassette tapes and student's manual. Audience: college age and beyond.

Children

Furman, Edna, *A Child's Parent Dies*, Yale University Press, New Haven, Connecticut, 1974. — Excellent book to help understand the effects of death upon a child. Leans toward a professional audience.

Jewett, Claudia, *Helping Children Cope with Separation and Loss*, The Harvard Common Press, Boston, Massachusetts, 1982. — A marvelous resource book. Offers excellent suggestions in aiding children through losses such as death, divorce, separation, etc. Offers many therapeutic techniques, games, etc. One of my favorites.

*1 Mumford, Amy, *Love My Hurt Away*, Accent Expressions Publications Co., Denver, Colorado, 1983. — Fantastic! Great booklet to sit and read with children. Discusses meaning of words like: soul, mortuary, casket, grave, etc. Booklet also comes with an envelope for mailing. (**See end note)

Stickney, Doris, *Water Bugs and Dragon Flies*, The Pilgrim Press, New York, New York, 1982. — A short fable for children. Would be a good resource to introduce the subject of afterlife/heaven.

Wolfe, Anna, *Helping Your Child to Understand Death*, Child Study Press, New York, New York, 1973. — Another resource for helping adults aid children in their understanding of death.

Parents

Grollman, Rabbi Earl, *Explaining Death to Children*, Beacon Press, Boston, Massachusetts. — Excellent resource for a clear understanding of how children interpret death. A very complete work.

Kubler-Ross, Dr. Elisabeth, *On Children & Death*, MacMillian & Co., New York, New York, 1983. — Written from her personal experience working with terminally ill children and their families. Covers a broad spectrum of difficult circumstances. Psychological and philosophical in nature, technical but informative.

Rando, Therese, *Parental Loss of a Child*, Research Press Co., Champaign, Illinois, 1986. — Address numerous instances of parental loss. While somewhat theoretical, many practical aspects and helps are given. A handbook for any professional.

Spouses

*4 Nye, Miriam Baker, *But I Never Thought He'd Die. (Practical Help for Widows)*, Westminster Press, Philadelphia, Pennsylvania, 1978. — Practical book for spouses from a woman's perspective. Written from personal experience, tackles a variety of issues and offers practical solutions. Sensitive and on-target.

Various Situations

Briggs, Lauren, *What You Can Say When You Don't Know What To Say*, Harvest House Publishers, Eugene, Oregon, 1985. — Written from personal experience, Ms. Briggs gives much insight into what is needed and what should be avoided in our contact with grieving people.

Grollman, Rabbi Earl, *Explaining Death to Children,* Beacon Press, Boston, Massachusetts, 1967. — A very complete work. Includes interviews, case histories, development stages of a child's understanding of death. Technical. Excellent.

Pamphlet: *Mom's Really Sick: Here's How to Help.* — Gives several practical suggestions that aid and help a mom who is struggling to "maintain" normal routines in her family in the midst of a terminal illness. (**See end note)

**These materials may be ordered through:
    Focus On The Family
    Colorado Springs, Colorado
    USA

Focus On The Family also offers a series of tapes on death and dying. Write for a pamphlet.

PART III

Selected Canadian Experiences

CHAPTER 8

Understanding the Spiritual and Cultural Influences on the Attitudes of the Bereaved

Paul Sakalauskas

> Show me the manner in which a nation
> or community cares for its dead and
> I will measure with mathematical
> exactness the tender sympathies of
> its people, their respect for the
> laws of the land and their loyalty
> of high ideals.
>
> *Gladstone*

Every society has developed belief systems that help them cope with difficult tasks that they encounter throughout life. This chapter explores ideas on how these systems affect the bereaved.

It is important to examine Western values as they relate to others from around the world. These values also have specific influences in the way societies deal with rituals. Many factors are involved in the way an individual reacts to death. This chapter illustrates some ideas on how these influences work, for the purpose of making graphic the many variables affecting how one grieves. Finally, it looks at the subtle differences between two countries, Canada and the United States. They are very closely related, but view life and death differently.

There is no stronger thought or idea than the one that is conceived in one's own mind. During our lifetime we are exposed to a great deal of information, but are very selective in the data retained. We reject all information contrary to our beliefs tending to shy away from ideas that do not match our own. This process is built on two factors, the *spiritual*, and *cultural* influences of an individual.

The spiritual beliefs shape the way individuals view the world around them. They are intensely personal and they help cope with many of life's "up's and downs." They govern the way we act and react during our life and have a profound influence on us during crisis. In the October 1985 issue of *Ladies Home Journal*, an article about Jane Fonda quoted her as saying [1, p. 206], "I've believed in God, though I have no formal religion. One of my regrets is that I wish that I would have given my children what I didn't have because I think being brought up with formal religion gives structure and ritual to our beliefs—a way to think about the great issues of life."

Culture, as defined by the *Living Webster Encyclopedic Dictionary*, is the total of human behavior patterns and technology communicated from generation to generation. Another definition is that culture is the sum total of everything that is learned and shared by members of a society [2]. These two definitions emphasize the forceful impact on an individual's behavior by his surroundings, experience, and relationships.

From the combination of both the spiritual and cultural beliefs, societies have developed rites and rituals that evolve by trial and error over time and guide people through the different experiences of life. They help people adapt to major change, reinforce the basic principles of a society, and bring order to the disorder of life's transitions. They are particularly helpful during times of great upheaval because they escort an individual or group through those threatening periods.

To comprehend the spiritual and cultural influences on bereavement, it is important to examine and understand what particular values and beliefs are held by our own culture and how they compare to others. Many problems between different people can be viewed as a conflict in the fundamental values held by each [3].

In North America, our values have been shaped by the idea that man is master. Nature is something that we control and it must be shaped to our particular needs. Achievement and progress are the result of one's efforts to practice this control. Success is also gauged by the level of one's social and economic status. To increase one's level is a definite sign of success and being competitive is one of the major paths to that end.

When we are performing a task, a definite result must be obtained. There has to be a reason for every action and an outcome for every activity. In most situations, those results have to be concrete and measurable. If this does not happen, then the activity is viewed as something that is not worthwhile.

Freedom and the ability to express oneself is important. The ability to make one's own decisions when they affect the individual is thought of as a very important and basic right. The North American way of life is greatly influenced by pioneer mentality. The individual alone is responsible for what happens. If something happens or goes wrong, the individual must correct it for no one else will. The individual must be rugged and strong; to be otherwise is a sign of weakness and failure.

When we compare North American values to other societies, the one point that stands out is the emphasis on the individual. In many parts of the world, the main focal point is the importance of the group. This is largely due to the fact of history and development of the society. In areas such as Europe, the communities have been long established with very little migration. Because these communities have been in existence for a long period of time, an allegiance has developed to them and the individual has a responsibility to the community.

In places where survival depends on migration and cooperation, it is most important to understand that to work for the benefit of all also benefits oneself. Respect is shown to members of one's family because the family represents the past, present and future. The past is represented by the elders—they would be the teachers and historians. They are the link with one's heritage. The present is represented by the individuals who work and maintain their community. The future is represented by the child. He is the sign of hope and reaffirmation of the continuation and value of life. The family unit is central to one's existence, each part of the family deserving respect for what they represent. Without the family unit, a community could not survive.

In North America, the elderly are thought to be of no use. Their productivity ended when they retired. The ever increasing problem of teenage suicide may be indicative of the fact that western culture is now ignoring the youth. As the baby boomers grow to middle age, they are the dominant force. People do not seem to want as many children as they used to have. The family is not as important to the way of life as it was several years ago. The focus now is on more material gains. The importance of a group is, therefore, defined by who has the greatest purchasing power as consumers.

Western culture has a missionary complex. It is our belief that what we do and the way we do it is the only way. Because of this attitude, there stems a lack of understanding of the other's beliefs. When someone considers theirs to be the correct belief or action it is very difficult to even consider other possibilities.

Death is a universal experience and probably the most severe crisis anyone will ever experience. Man has always struggled with the idea of why it happens. Today, according to Dame Cecily Saunders, "death is a mysterious, awe inspiring and scary event. We live in a society where death is not an immediate reality it used to be" [4, p. 15]. In North American and other advanced cultures, death is removed from everyday existence, people die in hospitals or nursing homes. Very few die at home. In fact, in these institutions people do not die they expire or as in one hospital in Hamilton, an individual is classed W.V.S. (Without Vital Signs). Death is looked on as an embarrassment to life-affirming, success-oriented societies.

Based on the values held by North American society, mainly that the individual is responsible for his own success, it follows naturally that death is looked on as a particular failure by those who give care. A failure to prevent it from happening and also to understand why it happened. We become failures in our work because we lose productivity for the time needed to grieve. Therefore, the period of grief is perceived to be as short and very private. People are unsure of what they are supposed to do and how they are supposed to feel, leaving them uncertain about how long and how much to grieve [5, pp. 29-30].

In other parts of the world, death is regarded as a part of life. It is a time that the community must come together to give support to one another. In Japan, for instance, we see the giant automaker, Toyota, consider bereavement an illness that has befallen the worker. The length of the leave is left up to the work group with tasks being covered by the survivor's co-workers. It is also understood that the bereaved person will take as much time as needed [6, p. 202]. It is ironic that even many funeral homes, where need for the time required to heal is continuously seen, the leave that is designated for a spouse is usually listed as a maximum of three days.

Jean Stairs, who is the bereavement councilor at the Markey Dermody and Cresmount Funeral Home in Hamilton, has observed in her experiences with the bereaved that the emotions of an individual are greatly affected by their personal spiritual and cultural beliefs. This creates many different patterns in an individual's grief work.

Guilt and anger are emotions that play a very important role in bereavement. Guilt can stall the grieving process when one's spiritual and cultural background states that we are responsible for all actions and events that take place. Individuals may punish themselves for specific events that they feel they could have changed. There is a great deal of unfinished business about which people may feel guilty. Missed opportunities and a great many "I should have's" only create barriers to the task of coming to terms with death. As someone has stated before, "God can forgive you, but can you forgive yourself" [7]. On the other hand guilt can be a factor which leads to forgiveness or absolution. This takes place when an individual's faith points out that loss will occur, that it is a part of life and that there is forgiveness even for the most serious offenses [8].

Anger can compensate for an individual's feeling of powerlessness. It becomes a spiritual question when one's background teaches that a Deity controls everything. The emotion of anger gives the individual the feeling that he has control. That an individual is angry at God, the doctor, the clergy, the funeral director or whoever should be there at a particular moment, is probably an attempt to gain control of what may seem to them a never ending emotional tailspin.

Sorrow is an emotion that hurts. When someone very close dies every waking hour hurts. It is not uncommon to hear people say "it hurts so bad." Sorrow is intensified when the belief system is weak. Feelings of anxiety and hurt are sometimes increased. In special situations where the death is sudden or from causes such as suicide, sorrow is sometimes even greater. Self pity is common in grief reactions. The degree though, has a marked difference depending on the cause of death, the type of relationship with the deceased, and also the belief systems one has.

Hope is what man needs to continue, and Kubler-Ross places Hope in a special category. It is something that weaves through the grieving process holding everything together [9, pp. 139-156]. Those without hope have a great fear of the finality of death. A death close to us makes one more aware of our own mortality, and in most situations, that is a terrifying thought.

This fear of death and one's own mortality is well illustrated by the following incident. It took place when I was dealing with a thirty-year-old teacher whose father had just died from cancer. His father's death was very painful and he had suffered a long time. The son, during the arrangements, was very preoccupied and lost. In talking with him about his father's death, he finally was able to admit that the thing that bothered him most at that time was not the actual death of his father but the cause of his death. He was extremely terrified that the cancer was hereditary and that he himself would contract the disease and die in a similar manner. He felt that when he reached his father's age the disease would strike him. His father's death heightened the awareness that he, too, could die in a similar manner, to the point that he was totally preoccupied with the thought.

Man is the only animal that creates rituals to deal with the death of another human being. Even in prehistoric times, man had developed some sort of ceremony when death took place. The purpose of those ceremonies may have been to appease the gods, to assure oneself that they would not be bothered by the spirit of the individual who has died or it may have developed as a show of respect because of the status of the individual in that particular society. What all these reasons have in common was that they, in some way, delivered a degree of comfort to those who were left behind.

Several years ago, there was concern within the Funeral Service profession on the decline of traditional type funeral services. It seems that many individuals were changing their ideas on what a funeral service should be for themselves and for someone close to them. In a very complete study done by Amy Seidel Marks and Bobby J. Clader in 1982 on Attitudes Toward Death and Funerals, it identified what those changes are and to what degree the public had changed. Most people would want a funeral service to be held for themselves or for their families [10, p. 49]. They identified that more young people (under the age of 45) would want to have a typical funeral service. The definition of typical is one that would be reflective of a person's economic bracket and one that is inexpensive or "no frills" is one that is simple but decent and not the cheapest possible [10, p. 56].

During the year of 1988 Cresmount Funeral Home in Hamilton served 413 families. Of those funerals, thirty-one or 8 percent were classed as Immediate Disposition Services. By looking at the figures, one might think the percentage is high and those families received no service whatsoever, but on looking deeper, it is interesting to note that seventeen of those families asked for assistance in arranging a memorial service either in the funeral home or the church. To these families, this type of service was very meaningful and at the time fulfilled the necessary requirements (as they saw them) regarding the funeral. Overwhelmingly the families who asked for assistance to arrange the memorial service also asked to have a minister supplied because they did not have a church affiliation.

In looking at the type of services Cresmount offered to the public, it was important to ascertain if the clergy in the area would consent to a nonreligious, Humanist Service if a family requested. Since 1984, the overwhelming majority of people would still prefer clergy to conduct the service in a more traditional manner. Some feel that they must do this because of what others may think or they may feel that it is still the right way of conducting a funeral. There is a strong sense that the time surrounding the funeral is still a very spiritual time.

The bereaved family today is looking for some sort of relief from the pain they are experiencing. Today, with all that is written or spoken about the bereavement process, there seems to be an attempt by the present generation to recapture the things that our grandparents knew or did naturally [11, p. 4].

Thus far, we have looked at the special values and patterns of grief in a two dimensional manner. Because man is a social creature, our ideas are influenced by dealings with other people. The extra dimension that could be added is that of social interaction.

Over the last one hundred years, there has been a great migration from troubled areas around the world to what many believe to be the "promised land"—North America. For whatever reason they chose to come, they have all had some sort of influence on the way we view life. North American society has become diverse in cultures and rituals. This diversity has also created the need for a greater understanding of the different ways in dealing with death and bereavement.

The immigrant or refugee brings with him his own ways of viewing life. His behavior when a death occurs is therefore strongly influenced by the spiritual and cultural background of his upbringing. But the longer he lives in his new land, he is also very much influenced by new surroundings. The way he may view death and bereavement could be a mixture of old and new. This type of mixture can sometimes be very deceiving to the caregiver.

Several years ago, at Christmas time, Cresmount received a call from a family whose mother had just died. It is the policy to close the funeral home on Christmas if possible, so as to give the staff the opportunity to be with their families. This is explained to families and they are quite understanding. It is rare to have visitation on Christmas day. Unfortunately, for the funeral director on call, this family was Ukrainian. They were not pleased to find that they could not have visiting when they wanted. They stated it is not their Christmas and that the Ukrainian community would not be observing it until January.

During Christmas Day, there were very few people in to pay their respects. What bewildered the funeral director, who had to work, was that the whole family sat in the coffee lounge during the afternoon and exchanged a multitude of Christmas gifts. In most instances, these new North Americans married and raised families in their adopted lands. Their children would be exposed a great deal to the heritage of their parents but are more influenced by the existing society. The Ukrainian family did not mislead us about the fact that it is not their Christmas when they made arrangements. In the funeral home, it was for their children's sake that they had gifts and presents.

The difficulty in care giving stems from the misunderstandings that develop when there is interfacing between customs. There may seem to be a double standard perceived because the family's actions are not consistent with the care givers' perceptions of the situation.

At present, we are witnessing a large migration from Third World countries. Because of the lack of knowledge about these areas in general, the rites and rituals surrounding the time of death may seem very unusual and not conforming to our beliefs. Several of these cultures express their grief very strongly. and in manners very foreign to us. The intensity at which they grieve is very high and to many this is extremely uncomfortable. Some of the rituals and customs tend to be exotic and somehow appear not to fit in with our own views on how things should be looked after, i.e., it is very difficult for staff of a funeral home to allow people to come in and dress a body, or prepare it for special services. It is something that the majority of the population would not do. To others it may be a religious requirement.

In dealing with other cultures, it is astounding to witness the extent people will travel to attend a funeral. I have directed services where the funeral home was asked to supply statements for airline discount purposes. The need to be present at the funeral because the individual who has died may have been from the same village or area is one of the major reasons for attendance. An overwhelming majority of those who have travelled a great distance could only be listed as friends.

In comparison, the study by Marks and Calder identified that although attendance at wakes or visitation is very high, there was an indication that attendance at funeral services is lower [9, p. 21]. This could be indicative of the fact that North Americans tend to be more private in their grief. In other cultures, it is important to be able to share in one's bereavement. The community is their extended family and the death of one of their members is a loss to all. Therefore, to them, travelling a great distance for the funeral service is not given second thought, it is just done.

There are a great many differences that are encountered between cultures when it comes to mourning practices. They could sometimes be very subtle, or they are extremely radical in their differences.

Canada and the United States, being so close, tend to be viewed by many as having similar patterns of behavior and values. Both countries share the same language, watch the same television programs, and read the same newspapers. There is no question that they have a lot in common.

Even though we share many similar beliefs, there is a distinct difference in the way we view life and death. There is a great tendency to consider that the American way is the North American way. But there is a subtle difference in the way that Canadians deal with death. This is, in part, due to the historical background of each nation and also the different experiences felt by the people in the two countries.

Canadians in general tend to be more reserved than their American counterparts. Alex Trebbick, the host of the popular game show Jeopardy, states that Canadians make poor game show contestants. They are too subdued for the networks liking; they are not spontaneous and exuberant; and they are conservative. The same can be said about Canadians' reactions to death.

Three separate incidents that illustrate the point concerning the differences between the two countries follow. Each incident had a profound affect on me because it reinforced the idea that we have been very fortunate to live in Canada, a country that values peace as a way of life.

The first incident took place several years ago. I was fortunate enough to have an English teacher who saw the opportunity to use that particular moment to emphasize a very important time in history.

At the time, the Vietnam war was coming to a close and he had arranged for our class to spend a day at a high school in Buffalo. It was a very interesting experience for my class mates and myself; we were exposed to issues with which we did not have to deal. The draft loomed over the American student's heads and the fear of being killed in war was something with which they had to live with. As for us from Canada, our daily concerns were paled by the enormity of what the young Americans had to deal with. It was difficult to truly understand the great pressure that was placed on those students at that time.

The second incident occurred several years ago when I attended a wedding in the United States. During the ceremony the clergy related to those present, the first time he had met the groom. It was at the church cemetery, years before. He noticed a young boy praying very intently at a grave. When he approached the young lad he asked him what he was doing. He was told that he was asking his brother to watch over him in his life and guide him. He was hoping that he could experience the things that his brother would never have the opportunity to experience. His brother was killed in Vietnam.

The third incident occurred when I was involved with the funeral of a Canadian citizen who served with the U.S. Marine Corp during World War II. The family had informed us that several active Marines were to be present on the day of the funeral as an honor guard. Their participation meant a great deal to the family. The seriousness that they conducted their duties was most impressive. In comparison to veteran's services that I have conducted in the past, they exemplified the true military honor that should be bestowed on someone who put their life on the line for others.

These three instances all emphasize the point that there are different experiences that shape the way we view life. Canadians, within the last thirty years have not had to worry about going to war or having a friend or relative die in combat. The ceremonies for veterans reflect the closeness of loss that Canadians do not experience. For Americans, the realization that death can occur does not come from film clips on television alone but from the personal experience of many people across the U.S. This type of experience can only alter one's beliefs and behaviors at the time of death.

There are so many different factors that affect the way people grieve and react to death. It really does not matter whether you belong to a society that prides itself on being a "melting pot" or one that boasts "a multi-cultural heritage," there will always be specific influences on the way a person reacts. Bereavement is a very personal matter. Misunderstandings develop between individuals when there is a lack of knowledge as to the background and culture of those involved. It is most distressing to those who are in need during "crisis moments" to find the caregiver passing judgement on reactions that to them are only natural.

It is also difficult for the caregiver to deal with a situation when the reactions of the individuals they are caring for do not parallel their own specific beliefs of the situation.

It is only through understanding people, their background, and their beliefs that care giving professionals can begin to be helpful. There are many problems that individuals must deal with when a death occurs. The caregiver should not be one of them.

REFERENCES

1. Jane Fonda Article Title, *Ladies Home Journal*, October 1985.
2. E. B. Taylor, *Primitive Culture*, (7th Edition), Bretano, New York, 1924.
3. Handout published by the Canadian International Development Agency, Ottawa.
4. R. Bell and Dame C. Saunders, *Presbyterian Record*, Don Mills, Ontario, February 1989.
5. M. Osterweis and J. Townsend, *The Mental Health Professional and The Bereaved*, U.S. Department of Health and Human Resources, Rockville, Maryland, 1988.
6. M. Osterweis, F. Solomon, and M. Green, (eds.), *Bereavement, Reactions, Consequences, and Care*, National Academy Press, Washington, D.C., 1984.
7. Batesville Management Services, *Earl Grollman, Living When a Loved One Has Died*, Film Strip, Batesville Indiana.
8. P. Krauss, *Why Me? Coping with Grief, Loss, and Change*, Bantam Books, New York, 1988.
9. E. Kubler-Ross, *On Death and Dying*, MacMillan Company, New York, 1969.

10. A. S. Marks and B. J. Calder, *Attitudes towards Death and Funerals*, The Center for Marketing Sciences, Northwestern University, Illinois, 1982.
11. J. Congram, *A Time to Mourn*, Presbyterian Record, Don Mills, Ontario, February 1989.

CHAPTER 9

Through the Valley of the Shadow: Developing a Visualization Process for Healing Grief

Ted Creen

Each year there is more information available regarding death, grief and bereavement. We do seem to be opening up this once almost "taboo" area. Books, speakers, and tapes now are all available. Much has been written about the stages of grief, the process of bereavement. Yet for many people much or most of this information remains inaccessible. At a time when they need good information about what they may be going through, the impact of grief often makes reading difficult. Add to that the fact that some information is cast in a technical language, means that books just do not get read. In attempting to work with people in grief, I have searched for a good "vehicle" to carry to them information important for their healing in a way that they will accept such information. Such a search led me to the concept of metaphor.

Metaphor has always been a strong part of our language and literature. Certainly in the Christian tradition we continually go back to the parables of Jesus, the gripping stories of the Old Testament and its heros, and the poetic descriptions of the Psalms. Metaphor is visual language. I find that our culture is returning to visual forms (e.g., the impact of television). People may tune out a sermon or lecture. They will still listen to a story.

Along with this, has developed the increasing awareness of the importance of validation, the affirmation of our present reality. It is often a fact of the grieving process that may put pressure upon us to go "too far, too fast" for us. We develop a sense that it is not OK to be where we are.

Even in preaching, the temptation not to validate where my hearers are, but to proclaim high standards that may be beyond the present ability of the hearers to achieve. Pastorally then, in validating the life experiences of my hearers, I have come to look at grief as a journey—a process. I need to confirm a sense that I comprehend where a person is in her or his personal journey. While I warn against "getting stuck," I affirm that I will try to walk beside them where they are.

Putting together these considerations, the need for metaphor and the validation of one's own personal grief journey, I turned to Psalm 23. That psalm with its powerful visual descriptions has always had a strong hold on people. Even those unfamiliar with much else in the Bible often request Psalm 23 for a reading at family funerals. Part of the pull can be found in the phrase "through the valley of the death," a phrase that has a strong resonance in the grief of people. The picture of grief as a journey through a deep and dark valley immediately begins to complete the process of validating people in their grief. They can see, feel, and experience their own valley of shadows.

From that point, I began to put together a visualization process for dealing with grief from the Psalms. I discovered some immediate and very helpful visual constructs, such as:

- a valley suggests an unusual place, different from the overall landscape, as in grief people often describe the feeling of being "lost"—"in unfamiliar territory even in the same place" and "in a dark shadow," with the accompanying feeling of deep fear. Visualization of one's personal valley legitimizes it and assists in coming to terms with its reality.

- through the valley suggests a journey, a metaphor I feel is of utmost importance. Rather than being either "in grief" or not, or being in some stage, a journey is much more suggestive of the reality being encountered. A journey allows for expressions of fear, anger, etc., which often are dealt with negatively (particularly in religious circles).

- the very powerful "of shadows," an apt description of the helplessness, fear, hopelessness encountered in grief. Assisting a person to describe (in words, poetry, drawing) the extent of their dark shadow begins the healing process.

From the visual constructs of valley, journey and shadow, I began to try to help create for bereaved a "map" of their personal journey and their valley of shadows. I encourage people to keep a "logbook" of their journey (i.e., a journal that they can go back to, to understand the changes they will go through). I urge them to "be gentle with themselves" and to resist pressure to go too far too fast. In journaling, I emphasize openness to feelings, however conflicting those feelings may be. I outline that feelings are, and should not be judged.

The first stage of grief, normally considered the time of shock, I picture as the entering of the valley, the steps into darkness. From my visualization process:

> You are walking along a quiet pathway.
> It is afternoon and the son is warm on your back.
> You have been enjoying the day, good things have come to you.
> It is not until the sun is blotted out by the surrounding
> hills that you realize you are in a valley. Then suddenly
> it is dark, very dark.
> With the darkness comes a sweeping at you a confusing array of
> feelings:
> a sense of unreality: Where did the pathway go . . . why does it feel
> like it is dropping out from underneath my feet . . . maybe this is
> just a bad dream, the sun will be out again and all will be pleasant
> again.
> It hurts to keep on going feeling lost like this . . . stop, can't turn
> back. . . . But now I can't even see where the valley began, is there
> someone to hold my hand and support me in this darkness . . . what
> is happening to me? Will the darkness ever end, am I trapped here,
> abandoned by the shepherd? I have lost my dearest travelling companion—Is there any point to going on?

From here I involve the person in describing the darkness in their valley: how dark? what feelings? what reactions? etc. Then I input information about this stage of the grief: initially to validate the shock with all its manifestations, that, particularly in acute grief, one needs to know they are in the deep dark shadow of grief, not going crazy, as they might feel.

I extend the metaphor of the valley as I explore the next aspects of grief: anger, guilt and despair. Here is the heavy travelling, the real work of grief. In keeping with the metaphorical picture I describe these aspects in the forms of piles of rock that may completely block the pathway through valley. From this visualization:

> I had you visualize that on this stretch in the valley there are
> large piles of rock that may block your journey. I would like to
> explore three common such blockages, give them names and help
> you to deal with each one in turn. They are anger, guilt and despair.
> The biggest danger is getting to such a blockage and allowing it to
> stop you dead, and hinder your progress for a long, long time. So we

will need to take the piles of rock apart, set them to one side and continue onwards.

There is a second danger that is taking part of the pile of rock apart, enough so it seems like you can go on . . . but then putting a lot of the rock not to the side of the pathway, but into your backpack . . . carrying it with you until it wears you down so much you have to stop. This is what can happen to unresolved anger, guilt or despair. No, we must get the rocks out of our way. Again, though, remember, you are encountering obstacles that are very, very common on any journey through the valley of the shadow of death . . . if you do have to take some time to deal with these obstacles you are still OK. It is only when you refuse to move them, or pile it all in your backpack that you will get into trouble.

From here I work through the three piles in turn—guilt, anger and despair. Following that I picture a "turning point" where the valley levels out and begins to lead upwards. At this point I deal with fear— the fear of change. On the upward journey, I picture a roadway with many "detours," the detours being the times in grief we get back into deeper grief, particularly anniversaries, birthdays, Christmas. Then at the end, the pathway breaks into many possible paths—the reality of the choices necessary following a loss and what Worden would call the "reinvestment of emotional energy into new relationships."

Some further aspects of developing this visualization process follow. I include, when appropriate, a definite spiritual component. Quite naturally extending from the visual picture of Psalm 23 is the portrait of God as shepherd. For those struggling with faith during their journey of grief have them quite intentionally visualize the shepherd and have that visualization travel with them. From the visualization:

I would like you at this point to again visualize the valley of shadows you have entered . . . the darkness . . . the many, many feelings and emotions . . . the unreality.

You may have felt very alone; but I would like you to realize that going with you through the valley is a shepherd . . . he has not abandoned you; he promised never to leave his sheep.

In your inner mind, your imagination, begin to picture how this shepherd looks to you; perhaps from an old picture you remember, maybe as a healing light, or simply as a source of warmth, perhaps a reassuring hand on your shoulder or back, or even a mixture of all of these.

Take some time to create for yourself an inner picture of this shepherd that is very real for you.

Then picture the valley and yourself within it. Now bring your inner picture of the shepherd very close to you . . . allow him to walk up from behind until he is in step with you. He wants to travel with you. In his hands is protection. He carries a rod and a staff to ward off any enemy.

At times in your journey, you may feel that the shepherd has left your side. He hasn't, you simply, for a time, have lost touch, lost contact with him. You can make contact again by bringing your inner picture of the shepherd back to your side again.

You may have many things you would like to share with the shepherd. Go ahead and tell him everything. Or you may just want to receive his loving, healing touch. Remember, he is there for you . . . there is nothing he would not do for you now.

With their own personal shepherd, I can have a person bring that picture into their minds at particular points (e.g., when dealing with guilt).

Finally, in Christian tradition, the metaphor of shepherd is applied not only to God but also to those who in the name of God seek to serve those who are hurting. Those undergoing grief need a friend, a personal shepherd to walk them through their valley. In training people to seek to be helpers to those in grief, I have found the visual metaphor of valley helpful—that they be able to comprehend the valley of the one they are walking with and not make presumptions about the person in grief as well as understanding the "terrain" that will be travelled.

In conclusion, I have found this metaphor to be quite useful in helping people deal with grief. I have used it in various ways in presentations to groups. I have put a ninety minute presentation of the visualization on cassette tape which people can listen to all or in parts. I encourage you to discover other metaphors that may have power to enable people to understand the complexities of grief.

CHAPTER 10

Irreplaceable Objects:
An Imaginal Approach to the
Mourning of Inconsolable Losses

Greg Mogenson

> . . . the interesting part of love is usually its decay, that is, the impossibility. When it falls apart, when it doesn't work, when all the pathologies appear (and aren't disguised in bliss). You see this decay in dreams when the old lovers don't want each other anymore, when an old attraction, an old pattern doesn't work. And then you are haunted by them, the old figures, for years afterward. They return like ghosts. The eros is getting psychized. Then you have something very painful but very interesting to work with. What are those ghosts returning for? [1, p. 180].

IMAGINAL OBJECTS

The inner experiences which constitute the content of the mourning process bear witness to the irreplaceability of our lost objects. The dead friend who no longer visits, the dead parent who no longer calls, and the dead spouse who no longer warms the bed beside us persist in the imagination with an unprecedented vividness. Viewed from the "inside," mourning is as much the beginning of an imaginal relationship as it is to the ending of the material one. The unconscious, as Freud said, cannot represent negation [2, p. 353]. The same voice that announces the death of a dear one calls into being a personified

This chapter appears in Greg Mogenson's book, *Greeting the Angels: An Imaginal View of the Mourning Process,* Baywood Publishing Company, Inc., 1992.

category of the imagination as well. Although our loved ones are "gone" they are also "not gone."

The specific *pathos* which characterizes mourning is a function of the paradoxical relationship between absence and presence. Although the inner images which continue the existence of the lost object in the mind may be as sweet as the acceptance of the absence of the outer object is bitter, the two do not belie one another. Indeed, we reconcile ourselves to the one reality only to the extent that we have reconciled ourselves to the other. Like two locked boxes each containing the other's key, death (object loss) and the imagination unlock each others mysteries.

Of course, if it were simply that the dead appear in the mind as they had appeared to our senses while still alive, we could discount their importance. Indeed, if they were nothing more than memory images, reaching out to them in imagination would be a category error similar to the category error the bereaved make when they reach across the bed to embrace a spouse who is no longer there. But the figures which animate bereavement, though similar to the persons who once animated our lives, manifest themselves in a fashion distinct from their previous existence. We are surprised by what they say and do. We see them as we never saw them before. Being dead they are now no longer attenuated by what we had required them to be and may now appear as they actually are.

It is not just that "we don't know what we've got till it's gone." The corollary is also true. Losing an object is the psyche's way of finding it. By becoming absent the object becomes wholly psychological. By losing its life it gains the eternal life of the imaginal psyche. It becomes a subtle body, an imaginal object, an image, an angel.

In bereavement, the ontological assumptions which tell us that a loved one no longer exists are shaken by the ontological assumptions through which the absent object, now an imaginal object, persists. Suddenly we realize that we have buried them alive in our materialistic assumptions about what constitutes reality. Suddenly we realize that we have always buried them in our materialistic assumptions about what is ontologically real. But now, perhaps for the first time, we begin to appreciate their value. They are the necessary persons of the permanent mind. Where once we saw them imperfectly through the dark glass of our own projections, we now see the faces they wore before they were born.

FREUD'S BIAS

In answer to the question—"in what consists the work which mourning performs?"—Freud writes [9, p. 154]:

The testing of reality, having shown that the loved object no longer exists, requires forthwith that all the libido shall be withdrawn from its attachments to this object. Against this demand a struggle of course arises—it may be universally observed that man never willingly abandons a libido-position, not even when a substitute is already beckoning to him. This struggle can be so intense that a turning away from reality ensues, the object being clung to through the medium of a hallucinatory wish-psychosis. The normal outcome is that difference for reality gains the day. Nevertheless its behest cannot at once be obeyed. The task is now carried through bit by bit, under great expense of time and cathectic energy, while all the time the existence of the lost object is continued in the mind. Each single one of the memories and hopes which bound the libido to the object is brought up and hyper-cathected, and the detachment of the libido from it is accomplished. Why this process of carrying out the behest of reality bit by bit, which is in the nature of a compromise, should be so extraordinarily painful is not at all easy to explain in terms of mental economics. It is worth noting that the pain seems natural to us. The fact is, however, that when the work of mourning is completed the ego becomes free and uninhibited again.

This account of the work of mourning, an account which underpins much of the subsequent research on the mourning process, is based on a materialistic bias. For Freud, mourning is a fixation of libido to objects which no longer exist, a fixation which painfully resists, but sooner or later succumbs, to the reality principle. Although he does not view mourning as a pathological syndrome, he speaks of it, nevertheless, as if it were. Mourning implies a "turning away from reality." The lost object is being "clung to through the medium of a hallucinatory wish-psychosis." The process is said to make great demands on "time and cathectic energy."

There is something soulless about Freud's account of this most soulful of processes. Although he sensitively portrays something of the pain of mourning, he is wholly insensitive to the lasting value of the lost object. Mourning, in Freud's account, consists of little more than the breaking of the habits associated with the object, habits which continue to bind us to the object despite the fact that the object is gone.

Freud's blind-spot here is a consequence of viewing the lost object exclusively from the standpoint of drive-theory. Since the object no longer affords an avenue to the reduction of the drives, it must be replaced by a more suitable one. From this perspective, the pain of mourning is merely the pain of withdrawal. Though "man never willingly abandons a libido-position, not even when a substitute is already beckoning him," "deference for reality gains the day" when repeated attempts to gain satisfaction from the absent object, as its existence is "continued in the mind," fail. Like an addict recovering from an addiction, the ego recovers from its lost object.

But does the drive-theory account of the mourning process do justice to the experience of the widow ruminating in her chair? Is her dead husband nothing more than a lost object? Was there nothing unique in her loss? Is he really as replaceable as drive-theory maintains? Should she go out on another blind date when she is only now beginning to see what her husband means to her?

Perhaps Freud's difficulty in "explain[ing] [mourning] from the point of view of mental economics" resides in the fact that instinctual drives are not the only currency in which the process trades. The fact that a portion of libido remains committed to an object long after that object has ceased to exist in the world of "really, real reality" may mean that something else is going on. Perhaps the energy is changing its form and being utilized in another way. Perhaps the bereaved widow brooding over the image of her dead husband is making him into a part of her inner life, a part of her soul. Present now precisely through his absence, the dead man initiates her into the ontology of loss. She sees him in dreams, standing beside her dead father, smiling. From the point of view of "reality," of course, her husband has become extinct. From the point of view of the imagination, however, he is now eternal. "Bit by bit," the eros, as Hillman has said, "is getting psychized" [1, p. 180]. The very man with whom she once explored life, or rather, his imago, is now initiating her into the imaginal.

Of course, the inner world of mourning need not be seen as conflicting with the establishment of new outer relationships. In fact, when relationships to the dead are maintained it makes it less likely that their images will be reincarnated in the form of projections which distort our relationships with other people. A particularized awareness of the dead is necessary if there is to be a particularized awareness of the individual uniqueness of the living. A heart that grieves, a heart that communes with the dead in reverie, is immune to falling in love on the rebound. By welcoming the ghosts, the bereaved may find themselves to be no longer haunted by them.

Despite the materialistic bias which characterizes Freud's analysis of mourning, in letters to bereaved friends and colleagues he displayed a more compassionate understanding of the process. Indeed, in a letter of condolence written to Ludwig Binswanger, Freud supplemented his ideas about mourning in a fashion that shows that he was not unaware of the value of the nostalgic tie to the dead which the bereaved may wish to cultivate [4, p. 386]:

Although we know that after such a loss the acute state of mourning will subside, we also know we shall remain inconsolable and will never find a substitute. No matter what may fill the gap, even if it be filled completely, it nevertheless remains something else. And actually this is how it should be. It is the only way of perpetuating that love which we do not want to relinquish.

MOURNING AS SOUL-MAKING

Peace, peace! he is not dead, he doth not sleep—
He hath awakened from the dream of life—
'Tis we, who lost in stormy visions, keep
With phantoms an unprofitable strife,
And in mad trance, strike with our spirit's knife
Invulnerable nothings.—We decay
Like corpses in a charnel; fear and grief
Convulse us and consume us day by day,
And cold hopes swarm like worms within our living clay [5, p. 425-440 lines 343-351].

This stanza from Shelley's poem, Adonais, is not a denial of the death of Keats. Shelley, in writing this verse, is not enacting the mourning process as Freud described it in "Mourning and Melancholia." His assertion, "Peace, peace! he is not dead . . .", cannot be read as clinical evidence that Shelley is clinging to Keats through the medium of a "hallucinatory wish-psychosis." On the contrary, the elegy is Shelley's attempt to bury Keats in the cultural imagination. The mourning process enacted in the poem is closer to the account of the process Freud gives in his letter to Binswanger: "Although we know that after such a loss the acute state of mourning will subside, we also know we shall remain inconsolable and will never find a substitute." The images of the poem resolve the "acute stage of mourning" not by denying the loss or be replacing it, but by precisely imagining Keats' irreplaceable uniqueness. To the extent that Shelley is able to absorb the emotion stirred by Keats' death into images he need not "vex, with inharmonious signs/The silence of that heart's accepted sacrifice" [5, pp. 425-440, lines 314-315].

In Adonais Shelley is not detaching our "memories and expectations . . . from the dead" [6, p. 858].[1] Nor is he auditioning others to take the place of Keats in the world's affections. Such moves as these

---

[1] The sentence reads: "Mourning has a very distinct psychic task to perform, namely, to detach the memories and expectations of the survivors from the dead."

would constitute the soul's *un*-making. Rather, Shelley is gathering the young poet to his own images, locating him amongst the fellowship of the dead, making him into soul. Keats, we are told, is now "a portion of the loveliness/ Which once he made more lovely . . . " [5, lines 379-380]. In verse 14 a wake is imagined in which "All he had loved, and moulded into thought/From shape, and hue, and odour and sweet sound,/ Lament[s]" him [15, lines 118-120]. And in verses 45 and 46 Shelley imagines Keats entering the company of other young poets who died before achieving the fame that was their due. "Robed in dazzling immortality" these "inheritors of unfulfilled renown," cry out to Keats, "Assume they winged throne, thou Vesper of our throng!" [5, lines 397, 409, 414].

Though this may not be as science would have it, it is, as Freud comments in his letter to Binswanger, "as it should be." With the writing of Adonais, Shelley created a vehicle capable of perpetuating that love for Keats which we do "not want to relinquish" [5, lines 352-360].

> He has outsoared the shadow of our night;
> Envy and calumny and hate and pain,
> And that unrest which men miscall delight,
> Can touch him not and torture not again;
> From the contagion of the world's slow stain;
> He is secure, and now can never mourn
> A heart grown cold, a head grown grey in vain;
> Nor, when the spirit's self has ceased to burn,
> With sparkless ashes load an unlamented urn.

While it is entirely fitting that Keats, the poet who coined the term "soul-making," should be perpetuated beyond his death in the subtle body which Shelley's elegy provides him, it would be a mistake to think that the bereaved widow ruminating in her chair may not be mourning in the same poetic genre. True, she may not be a strong poet, and her dead husband may not have been "the morning star among the living," [5, line 1][2] but if his loss was as irreplaceable for her as the cultural loss of Keats was for Shelley, she, too, will have to perpetuate in images the lover whom her heart cannot relinquish.

INTERNALIZING THE IRREPLACEABLE

When "death does us part," the "for better or for worse" which constituted our life with the deceased may at first seem dead as well. The

___

[2] Line 1 of the epigram, attributed to Plato, which Shelley prefixed to the poem.

period of depression that follows the loss of a significant relationship devastates the identity of the survivor. Indeed, to the extent that we are disconnected from the deceased we are also disconnected from ourselves.

> Patient: I feel like a zombie. I was at a party last evening, but I was not really myself. Without Elizabeth to laugh at my jokes, I no longer seem to have a sense of humor. I could always see life's ironies with her.
>
> Therapist: You miss the laughter. You find that your *sense* of humor is cancelled out by *her* death. Is that your brand of irony?
>
> Patient: Who is it who died—Elizabeth or me? It's like without her I have no soul.
>
> Therapist: You cannot get in touch of that particular part of yourself which she touched?
>
> Patient: Yeah, you know, I had always thought of myself as being my own person. I hadn't realized how much I was me through her.
>
> Therapist: Is that bad?
>
> Patient: No, just surprising. I suppose that all my friends bring out different sides of me. It's just that the side of me and the side of life which Elizabeth connected me to is gone.
>
> Therapist: Strange, that now, in her apparent absence, you are learning so much about her and about yourself.
>
> Patient: How's that?
>
> Therapist: Well it's like that meditation of John Donne's. It is precisely because "no man is an island" that the bell that tolls for anybody also tolls for you.
>
> Patient: Elizabeth would like that.
>
> Therapist: Do *you* like that?
>
> Patient: Yes.
>
> Therapist: So there you are yourself again, enjoying the ironies. Hello, Elizabeth.

As the outer persons die, the inner world becomes more densely populated and a discipline for connecting to them becomes imperative. With each loss the imagination becomes the place we live from precisely as we once had lived through others. They are there, backing our reflections, informing our perceptions, guaranteeing us continuity of self in a world convulsed with change. And although we may now be more consciously aware of how these others are us, they are also not us. We can still have it out with them just as we did before.

Like the photographs in the family album, the images of the dead populate the soul. The mourning process is the laboratory in which the images life has imposed upon the film of death are developed. Everything that has died and that we encounter as no longer there is the negative from which our inner life emerges. There is Elizabeth all in white, and me at twelve, and me again at twenty. Whole boxes of negatives that have never been printed, never been grieved. But now this immense loss, this loss in which I'm lost, holds me in the darkroom of the mourning process until all the lost souls come back to life in the emulsion of the mind.

REFERENCES

1. J. Hillman, *Inter Views*, Harper & Row, New York, 1983.
2. S. Freud, *The Interpretation of Dreams*, James Strachey (trans.), Avon Books, New York, 1965.
3. S. Freud, Mourning and Melancholia (1917), in *Collected Papers*, Vol IV, J. Riviere (trans.), Hograth Press and The Institute of Psycho-Analysis, London, 1925.
4. E. Freud (ed.), *Letters of Sigmund Freud*, Basic Books, New York, 1960.
5. Shelley, *Adonais* in *The Complete Poetical Works of Percy Bysshe Shelley*, T. Hutchinson (ed.), Oxford University Press, London, 1914.
6. S. Freud, *Totem and Taboo*, in *The Basic Writings of Sigmund Freud*, A. A. Brill (ed. and trans.), Random House, New York, 1938.

CHAPTER 11

Lifetime Losses:
Seeking a Balance

Michael Bull

I would like to begin this chapter with a story. Recently, I travelled with my family from London to Wellington, Ontario, a small, quaint, friendly town which is very close to Camp Trillium—a camp for children with cancer and their brothers and sisters. One of the reasons for the trip was to attend a board meeting of Camp Trillium. The second reason, however, was to take my oldest son, Jeff, who is thirteen years old, to the camp where he was to begin his first summer job as a helper in the kitchen. After we arrived at the camp on Saturday, Jeff went off to begin his orientation and his duties, as my other son, my wife and I wandered through the new campsite and explored its progress. Throughout Saturday and Sunday, I could see Jeff busy doing this and that, barbecuing chicken, setting tables, rinsing dishes, and doing many other kitchenly tasks. I wondered how he was managing and how he would handle this major life event, that of being on his own and having to take care of himself. However, being a father of a thirteen-year-old, I also was careful to keep these questions to myself, knowing that newly adolescent boys basically know everything that needs to be known and do not feel the need for parental guidance or advice. So I kept occupied with my meeting and Jeff kept busy with his work.

As Sunday afternoon wore on, though, I was conscious of a growing feeling, an anxiety, a tension, as the time for our departure and Jeff's remaining approached. Finally, my meeting was over. I sought out Jeff to begin the process of separation. I found him tucked away in the staff lounge, sitting quietly with his brother, from whom he seemed to be , seeking some solace. When Jeff saw me, tears came to his eyes as he approached me and inquired forlornly as to whether one of the family could stay at the camp. The time had come, the time we all had known would come but had not wanted to face. It was also time for me to "handle" this situation. I felt it incumbent upon me to "handle" it, seeing as I am the father, the parent, and even worse, a social worker who should be able to "handle" such things. So I put my arm around Jeff's shoulder and we went for a walk into the woods. We talked about why our plans did not allow someone to stay, but that mom and Chris would be back in a week when camp started. We talked about how Jeff was needed to help in the kitchen and the importance of hanging in there. We talked about how Jeff could call us anytime and keep in touch that way. We also had tears in our eyes, both of us, and I gave Jeff a hug and told him how proud I was of him.We finished our walk and later the three of us said goodbye to Jeff and decided to leave the camp sooner, not later, so as not to prolong the situation. The five-hour drive home was different. I bought Wendy's burgers for three, not four. Chris had no one with whom to share the back seat of the car. There was no brotherly arguing which usually accompanies our trips. Although we didn't talk about it much, and instead used the technique of "I wonder what Jeff is doing now?", we all were missing Jeff.

I share this story because it illustrates for me the idea of lifetime losses. In that experience of watching my son move ahead in his life, of seeing him make the transition from child to young man, from dependence to independence, I was losing something. For the summer, I was losing the daily presence and company of my son. I also was losing something less tangible, more symbolic—I was in the process of losing my son as a boy, a child, and seeing him more as an adult. I was losing my role as the parent of a child, someone who feels the need to be all-knowing and all-protecting. I am now the parent of a teenager, and the times we spent with Jeff as a baby, a toddler and a young boy are gone and, in a sense, lost.

Lifetime losses—what do we mean? Lifetime losses are those events which occur throughout our lives, events which mark a change, a transition from something that was to something that is now or will be. Arthur Carr writes [1, p. 3], "To a surprising degree, we are confronted with and tested by loss and separation throughout life." As you read this chapter, I would like you to get in touch with some of the losses you have experienced throughout your life.

From the day of birth, we begin to experience losses. Perhaps our first loss is that of the umbilical cord. Carr notes that because our body plays such an important role in mediating between the outer world and our inner self, changes in our body are seen as significant losses [1].

Later, as infants, we are weaned and experience a loss of comfort and gratification. Baby teeth fall out and a first hair cut occurs. Appendix and tonsils are often lost through surgery. As we grow older, we lose our youthful physiques of adolescence. Women talk of "losing their figures" after childbirth. Menopause brings the loss of childbearing. With aging comes the loss of sight, hearing, skin and muscle tone, hair, energy and other functions and capabilities.

Another significant area of losses occurs among the relationships we have with those important to us. It is our humanness, our ability and need to have close, satisfying relationships, which makes us vulnerable to these relationship losses. Ned Cassem defines loss as the rupture of an attachment [2]. Such rupturing again begins in early childhood; weaning has already been noted. Most of us can picture the "rupturing" which occurs when mother and father first leave their child with a sitter—the strain and loss are felt acutely by both parent and child. The first day of school marks another change/loss in the parent-child relationship. Other losses occur as friendships change, moves are made, job changes take place. We "lose our heart" when we fall in love; in adolescence, this can happen almost daily! With marriage comes the loss of our old relationship in our family of origin, and with children comes a change in the relationship with our partner. We may feel the loss of that special romantic aspect of a relationship; as the song says, we can lose that "lovin' feeling." My wife will tell you that she loses me at about 10 o'clock at night as I nod off in the easy chair! Major losses are experienced as loved ones die throughout our lives, or as marital relationships break down, resulting in separation, divorce and family disruption.

Some of the losses we experience are more subtle, more symbolic in nature. These may be the loss of a goal, a hope, a fantasy. Couples who cannot have children lose the dream of being parents. The goal of achieving a particular level of financial or business success may never be attained. Birthdays, for some, represent the slow but certain loss of youth. A colleague of mine, when he reached his fiftieth birthday, stated that he had lost his dream of writing a book by that particular age. We can "lose face" and experience a diminishing of ourself esteem.

Many of the losses I have described thus far could be called developmental or *transitional losses*—those which occur as a result of normal changes and developments in the lives of most of us. There are other losses that are not part of normal development and thus cannot be anticipated; these are situational losses. *Situational losses* come out of specific, unexpected events which do not occur to all people. Car accidents, wars, hurricanes, droughts—these are events which lead to situational losses. And in this group of events is the diagnosis of illness, particularly a major, life-threatening illness such as childhood cancer.

Let us reflect a moment on the losses associated with the diagnosis of childhood cancer. Theresa Rando has written extensively about families with a seriously-ill child [3]. She accurately describes the dilemmas faced by these families as survival rates improve and diseases like childhood cancer become more chronic in nature:

- numerous remissions/relapses
- increased financial, social, physical and emotional pressures
- long-term family disruption
- longer periods of uncertainty
- intensive treatment regimens and their side effects
- dilemmas about decision making and treatment choices, and if a child is not doing well
- progressive decline of the patient and the responses of others
- lengthened periods of anticipatory grief

What Rando describes, and many of you have experienced, is a lifestyle which conjures up two images—one of a roller coaster ride, and the other of a walk on a tightrope (two activities which one would not relish having to do at the same time, but which many parents seem to accomplish very well)!

The process of anticipatory grief, which Rando refers to and has studied extensively, is generally defined as grieving which occurs prior to an actual loss [3, 4]. Much of the work in this area has focused on families whose child or other member died, and the process these families went through before the death. This is unfortunate because I believe that all families whose child is diagnosed with a serious illness go through the anticipatory grief process, and that this process is determined not by whether the child eventually dies, but by the many other actual or anticipated losses associated with having a sick child. These illness-related losses become, then, a part of our total lifetime losses and this is why the theme of lifetime losses seems important to explore.

One curious and unique behavior of people, something which no other animals do, is worry not only about things which do happen, but also about things which might happen. This could be called our "what if" thinking. Sometimes, this ability is not very useful, particularly if it is not kept in perspective and we worry about things which are highly unlikely to happen. This is what can occur when a child or spouse does not arrive home at the expected time, and we begin creating "what if" scenarios. "Where is she? She should have been home by now. What if she got tied up at work? Well, she would have called. But what if she couldn't call? What if she was in an accident? Yes, but the police or hospital would have called. Then, what if that mass murderer has escaped again and she's been kidnapped by him and he's speeding off with her to some Godforsaken place. . . ." In reality, she had a flat tire and decided to use her last quarter to call the motor league rather than her husband because she figured he would have enough common sense to realize that there was a good reason she was late. Actually, in terms of lifetime losses, I can remember going through this type of thinking in one of my earliest anticipated loss situations, when I was babysitting my sister at night and my parents did not come home on time. So we learn this kind of "what if" thinking early.

When the diagnosis of childhood cancer is made, "what if" thinking begins and can be very helpful. It allows families to deal not only with the present realities but begins to prepare them for what might be a reality in the future. In order to "be prepared," one needs to anticipate what lies ahead. "What if" thinking also assists in decision-making and problem-solving and in this sense is useful. To make appropriate choices, families need to anticipate the options, get needed information about each, and make the best decision they can.

Rando identifies some of the losses which childhood cancer families experience both in the present and through anticipatory "what if" thinking [3, p. 12]:

- the loss of previous functioning, health, abilities
- the loss of the future that had been planned
- the loss of hopes, dreams and expectations invested in the relationship
- the loss of security, predictability, control
- the loss of the notion of personal invulnerability

Rando notes that these losses incorporate aspects of the family's past, present and future. Let us explore a bit further, then, the link between previous lifetime losses and current illness-related losses.

There are two major connections between previous losses and the losses associated with the diagnosis of childhood cancer. The first is the link between how one coped with previous losses and how one deals with current illness-related losses. Two authors suggest models for looking at how we cope with loss. In her chapter, "Learning to live through loss," Marilyn Rawnsley identifies four universal situations or behavioral patterns in response to loss [5, p. 13]:

1. Activity vs. passivity—the degree of active control one takes in responding to loss as opposed to just letting it happen.

2. Adequate vs. diminished self esteem—how positively or negatively one feels about oneself in the face of loss.
3. Unresolved or delayed grief—the grief that is carried over from previous losses (discussed further below).
4. Independence vs. dependence—the level of one's ability to act independently, or with appropriate support, rather than to regress to earlier dependency.

Arthur Carr writes about three loss response patterns [1, p. 4]:

1. Optimism vs. despair—the degree of hopefulness and determination one can maintain in the face of loss.
2. Passive resignation vs. angry unwillingness to "let go."
3. An assumption that "fate" is benevolent vs. malevolent.

I would invite you to take a moment to think about some of your losses, either previous or more currently illness-related, and try to determine which response patterns you may tend to use. Are your responses in relation to illness similar to responses to other lifetime losses? Do you see any progression from less useful to more useful behaviors and responses? What behaviors would you like to change in responding to loss?

The second major link between previous lifetime losses and current illness-related losses relates to the carry-over grief that one brings from the past into the present. This grief has been called unresolved, delayed, postponed or suppressed grief, and it can be described as the grief feelings which did not get fully expressed or worked through at the time of an earlier loss. These feelings are experienced or renewed at the time of a current loss. The person or those around him/her generally have a sense that the response is disproportionate or exaggerated in relation to the current situation [4].

Another indicator of left-over grief is the stimulation of grief feelings by watching someone else experience a loss, or by watching a movie or hearing a song which triggers intense feelings. Given the difficulty some people have in expressing their grief, and the reduced support in society for grieving and grieving persons, unresolved grief is a major factor in determining how many people react to current losses. A TV movie or a feature on a telethon that readily brings a tear to my eye, seemingly out of proportion to the situation, is due in part to the doses of grief accumulated through my work with the seriously ill, dying and bereaved. If you are aware of this in yourself, you might consider the root of these delayed feelings and at least be aware of how this emotional "baggage" affects your current loss responses.

I would like, finally, to explore how we can more constructively deal with the many losses we have or will experience in our lifetime. I think, to begin with, we need to consider our general attitudes about loss. Philippe Aries, a social historian, writes about society's attitudes toward death through the past several hundred years [6]. He describes the attitude in the 20th century as Forbidden Death, an attitude that "life is always happy or should always seem to be so" [6, p. 87]. Death and loss are to be seen to the least possible degree and sorrow is not to be in evidence, as it is repugnant, bad manners, morbid, and perhaps a sign of mental instability (I am reminded by this of how many grieving people wonder if they are going crazy). We aggressively resist loss—we try to regrow hair, we get rid of wrinkles, we put in new parts as our body wears out. Loss, then, is something to be resisted, defied, or denied, rather than accepted as part of life and dealt with accordingly.

There are, however, two viewpoints on how useful such an attitude of denial is. Some argue that denial and an unwillingness to accept loss are risk factors in coping [7, 8] while others state that denial is a natural response to a threat and allows positive thinking to assist [9]. I recently encountered a colleague whose niece had Non-Hodgkin's lymphoma. She told me, "My sister said she knows you from when her daughter was treated at Children's Hospital. She could never bring herself to talk to you about her daughter's illness because, if she did, it would mean accepting the seriousness of the cancer. She didn't want to do that."

I don't know for sure where the truth lies on the issue of denial, although I suspect there is a point at which denial is more harmful than helpful. A concept that I like is one called "aikido." Aikido is a martial art based on the principle of respecting the integrity of the enemy while still maintaining your own integrity. It includes the notion of "going with the flow" rather than resisting the flow, on the one hand, or being totally swept away by the flow, on the other. An illustration of aikido is the story of the substitute teacher. On the day of the teacher's assignment to one class, the students, seeing an opportunity to have some fun (in the true tradition of getting substitute teachers), decided to all drop a book on the floor at a predetermined time. Finally, the moment arrived and thirty books hit the floor noisily. The teacher, momentarily distracted, looked up from her work and gradually went to the side of her desk. The class awaited her next move. Finally, slowly, the teacher picked up one of her books, dropped it on the floor, and said, "Sorry I'm late." Rather than losing face or losing control, the teacher respected the flow of the situation while maintaining her integrity. Another aikido story tells of an old man who was approaching death. His son came to visit him one day and, realizing that his father's days were limited and that some preparation might be in order, he asked his father, "Dad, where do you want to be buried, in Brooklyn or Forest Lawn?" The old man, wise from his years and respectful of the enemy, Death, propped himself up on his elbow and after some deep thought, said with a sparkle in his eye, "Surprise me!"

Along a similar line, the Chinese have an ideogram for crisis with two figures. The first symbol describes crises as danger; the second describes crises as opportunity. We cannot always control the events which affect us but we can control the way in which we perceive these events. If you can see loss as an opportunity for change or growth, you will probably achieve these. We also know from crisis theory that when you effectively deal with one situation, you develop skills for dealing with future crises. A type of inoculation occurs, strengthening you for future challenges. I remember one mother whose daughter had been diagnosed with leukemia. This daughter also had Down's Syndrome. The mother presented as noticeably less upset than many other parents I had seen at the time of diagnosis. When we discussed this, the mother was able to state that having had to deal with her daughter's Down Syndrome and the loss of the "normal" child she had hoped for, she could now deal with just about anything. Coping with an earlier loss had helped her with the losses associated with childhood cancer.

There are two potential risks in not dealing effectively with the losses in our lives. One is that of unresolved or delayed grief discussed earlier. If we can avoid viewing loss as a forbidden topic and go with the flow of our losses, we are likely to express much more of our feelings around the loss and leave less unresolved. Building a support system which helps you express your losses is a vital part of this. People with good support have consistently been shown to cope more effectively. This might mean developing a network of friends with whom you can talk comfortably about loss issues. And of course, many self-help groups grow out of the need for mutual sharing about losses. Widow groups, mastectomy groups, Sudden Infant Death groups, retirement groups, and of course, cancer parent groups, of which Candlelighters is perhaps the best known. Using the support of a professional counsellor may also assist if difficult and more intense feelings continue.

One thing that I have done to unplug some of the unresolved grief I mentioned earlier is to expose myself intentionally to a situation which will trigger a grief response. I recall specifically watching the original version of "It's a Wonderful Life," the story of a man who, on the brink of suicide, is helped to see how meaningful his life has really been. A friend of mine had recently died and I had not been able to grieve as fully as I wanted. Knowing that the movie might trigger some feelings, I stayed up late one night and watched the movie on my own while the rest of the family slept. Gradually, my tears began to flow and I had the good cry I had hoped for. I heard of a father who did a similar thing to deal with the anger associated with loss. He would go to garage sales and buy inexpensive china cups and saucers. When he felt the need to express his anger, he would go to his garage and hurl the dishes against the concrete wall. No one was being hurt and he unloaded his anger very effectively.[1]

The second risk in not expressing loss feelings effectively is that of "unfinished business." Unfinished business refers to the words that do not get said, the deeds that are left undone, and the regrets and guilt feelings which are left when opportunities are not taken. One way in which losses and changes have been recognized historically is through rituals. A ritual is a way of formally acknowledging an event, often in a way that is repeated so that business is not left unfinished. Funerals are obvious loss-related rituals, but many such rituals are changing and seem less effective in structuring expressions of loss and the finishing of business. Graduations and marriages, for example, seem to be taking on less symbolic meaning in terms of the life changes involved. We may need to work at creating or sustaining our own rituals. I was talking recently with an eighty-five-year-old lady who spoke of the annual reunions held by her family. This was a ritual that sustained the interaction among generations and allowed words to be said and deeds to be done before the oldest generation was gone. Support group meetings are like a ritual that can help people focus on their illness-related losses. It is gratifying to see in the newspaper announcements of retirement parties and anniversary open houses to mark endings in relationships and activities. Recently, a London bus driver retired and, to commemorate his last shift, his family spread themselves out over the route and at each stop a different relative or friend would board with best wishes and a gift. That driver would never drive that route again and his family had not let it go unnoticed and uncelebrated, nor had they let their feelings go unexpressed.

Similarly, the psychoanalytic literature talks about transitional objects, things which help us let go of one thing and move on to another. In childhood, dolls, stuffed toys and blankets can serve as transitional objects as the child moves tentatively from the parent toward increased freedom. After childhood, it seems that the things we collect, things that are mementos, serve as transitional objects to mark certain endings and losses. High school pins and school sweaters help us deal

---

[1] Editor's note: this temporary feeling of relief, may or may not result in having worked through the anger.

with the loss of youth and the "good ol' days." Yearbooks, photo albums, ribbons and medals, a pressed flower—things which sometimes seem like junk destined for the next garage sale—are reminders of what is finished and help us remember and, in a way, re-grieve these losses each time we pull them out.

What can you do to acknowledge endings and remembrances in the future? This is my little balancing skier. Much of what has been presented so far and much of what you do as families of children with cancer is about balance. Balancing the present with the past and the future. Balancing life with loss. Balancing illness with health. Balancing normal with the unusual. Maintaining the balance required to ride the roller coaster and walk the tightrope. I would encourage you at some point to get one of these balancing figures to remind you of the balance you need to strive for and of the fascinating way in which you achieve this balance.

I wrote earlier about anticipatory grief and "what if" thinking. Anticipatory grief is, I believe, a gift. It alerts us to possible losses in the future and allows us to plan for how we might take care of business before it is too late. I know there are some who argue this point, saying, "If I'm going to have a loss or a problem, let it come fast and unannounced." I can not dispute that position and I am sure it works for many. However, many others regret not having known what lies ahead and then not having a chance to finish things up. I would suggest that the diagnosis of cancer is an opportunity, albeit an unwelcomed one. The opportunity is to assess what is now and what will be lost, but the sad part is that many of us go through life assuming we have all the time in the world.

George Carlin does a routine about the two-minute warning, a signal that goes off two minutes before we die so we can prepare and go out in style. He suggests we begin to pass the hat for our own memorial fund, or that we get to the front of the line at a faith healer's just as the two minutes are up. Maybe a diagnosis of cancer is like a two-minute warning that awakens us from the sleepy pace of life and reminds us how time is passing. I am experiencing this now as my own parents grow older and I become aware that all the time in the world is not there. I am realizing this more, too, with my own son who is gone for the summer. So when he called during his first week away from us, I found myself telling him that we loved him. I could not remember when I had last said that to Jeff. But I am aware that I still have some work to do because, while telling him we loved him, I did not tell him that I loved him.

There is an Indian saying which goes, "Live each day with death over your left shoulder." Last summer, I heard a suggestion about how we might do this. The speaker suggested that when we are doing the mundane things of daily life, we stop and ask ourselves a "what if" question—"What if this were the last time I ever did this?" What if this were the last time I drive to work, or washed the dishes, or kissed my wife in the morning, or tucked the kids into bed? It was noted how this though increases one's awareness of the precious nature of time, and helps one live in the present, not leaving business unfinished. He also noted how it increases one's humanness.

I would like to go back to the word BALANCE and use it as a guide to summarize some of my key points:

B: business—finish it to live with fewer regrets;
A: anticipate losses, do not ignore them;
L: laughter helps us to keep life in perspective;
A: aikido—go with the flow while keeping your integity;
N: now—live in the now, it is all we have for certain;
C:
    celebrate endings — rituals, memories, symbols
E:

Let me finish with a quote from a young woman whose husband had lymphosarcoma [2, p. 16]:

> To all of you, I would say . . . —live out your love for one another now. Don't assume the future; don't assume all kinds of healing time for the bruised places in your relationships with others. Don't be afraid to touch and share deeply and openly all the tragic and joyful dimensions of life.

If we can live our lives a bit more like this, then we will experience our losses a little differently—with fewer regrets, with less emotional baggage and with a greater sense of accomplishment and meaning. My wish is that the diagnosis of childhood cancer will not be perceived as only a danger, but rather as an opportunity to deal better with lifetime losses.

REFERENCES

1. A. C. Carr, Bereavement as a Relative Experience, in *Bereavement: Its Psychosocial Aspects*, B. Schoenberg, I. Gerber, A. Weiner, A. H. Kutsher, D. Peretz, and A. C. Carr (eds.), Columbia University Press, New York, 1975.

2. N. H. Cassem, Bereavement as Indispensable for Growth, in *Bereavement: Its Psychosocial Aspects*, B. Schoenberg et al. (eds.), Columbia University Press, New York, 1975.
3. T. A. Rando, A Comprehensive Analysis of Anticipatory Grief: Perspectives, Processes, Promises and Problems, in *Loss and Anticipatory Grief*, T. A. Rando (ed.), Lexington Books, Lexington, Massachusetts, 1986.
4. J. W. Worden, *Grief Counselling and Grief Therapy: A Handbook for the Mental Health Practitioner*, Springer, New York, 1982.
5. M. M. Rawnsley, Learning to Grow through Loss: A Focus for Preventive Mental Health Services, in *Preventive Psychiatry: Early Intervention and Situational Crisis Management*, R. DeBellis and C. A. Lambert (eds.), The Charles Press, Philadelphia, 1989.
6. P. Aries, *Western Attitudes toward Death from the Middle Ages to the Present*, The Johns Hopkins University Press, Baltimore, 1974.
7. V. R. Pine, Dying, Death, and Social Behavior, in *Anticipatory Grief*, B. Schoenberg et al. (eds.), Columbia University Press, New York, 1974.
8. A. D. Weissman, Coping with Untimely Death, *Psychiatry, 36*, pp. 366-377, 1973.
9. W. Weiner, A Positive View of the Defense of Denial: Implications for Treatment Services, in *Preventive Psychiatry: Early Intervention and Situational Crisis Management*, S. C. Klagsbrun et al. (eds.), The Charles Press, Philadelphia, 1989.

PART IV

Children and
the Death Experience

CHAPTER 12

Attitudes About Childhood Death: An African Perspective

Connie Guist

As a graduate student in nursing at the University of Wisconsin-Milwaukee, I participated in a six-week course of Community Health Nursing at Maua Methodist Hospital in rural Kenya in June and July, 1987. I was one of six nurses who traveled to Maua Kenya, in East Africa, with an instructor who is also a licensed nurse in Kenya and had been employed at the Maua Methodist Hospital school of nursing in 1985 and 1986. Therefore, she knew the community well and was instrumental in laying the foundation for this research. The research project itself was not part of the course requirements, but was conducted because of my interest in bereavement in childhood death and a desire to take advantage of an opportunity to learn more about attitudes toward childhood death in relation to this population.

HEALTH PROBLEMS IN KENYA

As in many developing countries, Kenya's health problems reflect poverty, malnutrition, and competing priorities in the economic and political arena. A sensitive indicator of the level of general health of a population, especially the well being of mothers and infants, is infant mortality.

In 1985, Kenya's infant mortality rate was reported at 76 per 1000 live births and ranked 79th in the world. According to UNICEF in 1985, one of every three Kenyans who dies is below the age of five [1]. However, with the overwhelming problems experienced by a developing country such as Kenya, it is easy to overlook the impact that the rate of infant death has on the population and how health care providers deal with the families experiencing the death of an infant or young child.

Although several studies by Boylan [2], Kaufman [3], Kune [4], Mwangi and Mwaba [5], and van Ginneken and Muller [6] have defined and statistically described childhood mortality, no definitive work was found in the literature that addresses the impact of the death of a child on Kenyans or how health care providers in this culture feel about childhood death. Personal communications with two nurse experts in the area of transcultural care and childhood bereavement, Madeleine Leininger [7] and Ida Martinson [8], also failed to identify any research done in the area of grief and bereavement in the Kenyan population.

Culture and Health Care

The importance of looking at the culture of people in relationship to health care and attitudes toward death is identified in the nursing and Thanatology literature. O'Brian [9], Leininger [7], and Clinton [10] stress that health care providers must consider cultural heritage in order to effectively provide holistic health care. Rando [11, 12], Kalish and Reynolds [13], specifically identify the interrelatedness of ethnicity, culture and religious and philosophical background as important psychological factors which influence attitudes, feelings, beliefs and the grief reaction to death. Many studies indicate that various cultures generate and develop strategies to deal with death which are related to and depend on culturally determined conditions unique to that culture. With this in mind, the purpose of this study was to describe the attitudes of some of the student nurses at Maua Methodist Hospital (MMH) to increase awareness of these attitudes in this cultural context. In order to set the stage for this study, I would like to describe the area where Maua Methodist Hospital is located.

Kenya is an independent republic in East Africa approximately twice the size of Texas with a wide range of topography. The latitude ranges from sea level to 5200 meters with extremes in temperature, rainfall, and humidity. Eighty percent of the 209 million plus population resides in rural areas. Maua, located in the Meru District of the Eastern Providence of Kenya, is situated at an altitude of 1750 meters in the rolling foothills of Mt. Kenya. Situated one degree north of the equator, the sun sets around 6 p.m. daily and rises 6 a.m. The average daytime temperature while we were there was 70 to 75 degrees. The district of Meru has a population of about 840,000 people, slightly smaller than the population of Rhode Island. The town of Maua is literally at the end of a road about 350 miles northeast of Nairobi. Maua is about 30 miles away from the district's main city of Meru and is the major town for a population of about 200,000 people. While the luxury of electricity is not available to the general community, MMH utilizes a generator for electricity for four hours each evening and for emergency surgeries. A clean water supply is a recent phenomenon and is intermittent at best. MMH is one of several hospitals which serves the people of the Meru District. The primary language in the area is Kimeru. Kiswahili, the national language, and English are taught in schools.

MMH, established in 1928 by the Methodist Church of England, has 130 beds and a very comprehensive health program throughout the Meru District. It is also the site of a three-year nursing school. The classes are taught in English and the hospital staff uses English as its primary language. The students at the nursing school are trained to be specialists in general nursing, community health, and midwifery.

The average perinatal death rate at MMH from 1982 to 1985 was 130 to 200 per year. Pediatric admissions have averaged about 2000 annually since 1985. From January through July, 1987, there were seventy-dive deaths reported on the pediatric ward alone. Six of these were the result of a measles epidemic that began in March.

The research question was: What are the attitudes of selected nursing students studying in Maua, Kenya, toward childhood death? Assumptions for the study were that the questions asked would be appropriate to gain the information I desired, and that the students would be honest in their responses.

METHODOLOGY

The population from which the sample was drawn was ninety-seven student nurses enrolled at MMH School of Nursing at the time of the study. Eighty-four students were accessible to participate in the project between July 1 and July 28, 1987, thirteen students being assigned off campus at the time. All students were Kenyans and English-speaking. Seventy-five percent of the total population were from Meru District, while 25 percent came from other areas of Kenya.

A systematic, probability sampling method was used whereby every fifth name on the roster of accessible students was selected for the sample until twenty-five names were chosen. The twenty-five students were informed of the study by their tutor, a nursing instructor from Great Britain, and were asked to pick up consent forms from the instructor if they were interested in participating in the study. Nineteen students picked up consent forms, twelve students forms were signed and returned. These twelve students thus constituted the sample for this study. The size of the sample was determined by considering what would be realistically possible to complete within the time frame that the researcher would be in Maua. The study was approved by the University of Wisconsin-Milwaukee's School of Nursing review board for the protection of human subjects and confidentiality was maintained for all participants.

A review of the demographic information of the sample reveals that there was an even distribution of males and females in the sample. The mean age was 21.7 years with a range of twenty to twenty-four years. Only one of the students was married and was the parent of a fifteen month-old child. The ethnic representation of the sample was similar to the ethnic distribution of the target population. All of the six classes of the students were represented except for one. Usually, one-fourth of each class is male, and a new class is enrolled every six months. All of the students interviewed indicated a Christian religious affiliation, the majority were Methodist.

An interview schedule was designed by the investigator with questions drawn from the literature. Discussions about Maua school of nursing faculty helped to improve the wording of the questions so they would be appropriate to the sample. Interviews were arranged through the class tutor at a time and place of convenience to the student. The interviews, which varied in length from 30 to 60 minutes, were conducted in private, and permission was obtained to tape each interview.

RESULTS

Upon returning to the United States, the tapes were transcribed and a content analysis was done. The content analysis included the review of several of the transcripts by an expert to validate the identification of themes from the data.

The interview guide consisted of twenty questions. Initial questions were asked to elicit demographic information about the subject. The rest of the questions fell into three categories. First, a series of questions was asked to determine what types of deaths the students felt to be most tragic. Second, the students were asked about their experience with childhood death, both within their own families and as student nurses. Third, questions were asked to elicit information about how they perceived their role as a nurse in relationship to childhood death. Finally, they were all given an opportunity to add information they felt would be of value but was not previously discussed.

Types of Tragic Deaths

In response to the first group of questions, eleven students indicated that male and female deaths were both as tragic. One student indicated a male's death to be more tragic. Also the students were asked to indicate which death was most tragic from a list of five specific age groups. The groups were identified as 1) an infant under one year of age; 2) a young child between one and five years of age; 3) a young person, six to twenty-five years of age; 4) a middle aged person up to forty years of age; and 5) an elderly person over forty years old. The age groups were established with consideration of the fact that life expectancy of Kenyans is fifty-five years. More than half of the students indicated that the death of a young person six to twenty-five years of age was most tragic. No one selected the infant under one year of age as most tragic. When asked to choose the most tragic death among the premature infant, a full term newborn and a young child, ten students felt the death of a young child to be most tragic.

The overwhelming response as to why the death of a young person was perceived as most tragic was related to that person's worth to the family and the community. This was especially true if the young person did not have an opportunity to marry and have children. At least half of the respondents specifically mentioned the lack of descendants as the reason why this death is considered most tragic. It was indicated that knowledge of the young person by the community made it harder for the group to accept death in this age group and that it was sad that the person who died at this age would not have an opportunity to—as one person stated—enjoy the pleasures of the world.

In response as to why a young child's death seemed more tragic than that of a premature infant or a newborn child, again, more than two-thirds of the responses were related to the young child's worth to the family and that the community would have had occasion to know the child. Four of the students felt that the mother was most affected by a young child's death, while one person indicated that this death was most tragic because there was no need for them to die. Another respondent called the death of a young child "a mystery" if sudden in nature which made it most tragic to this person.

Childhood Death Experiences

Even though all the students had experiences while in training with an infant's or young child's death within the last year, only five people had an infant or young child die in their own families. One of the students had been involved with an infant's death on the day prior to being interviewed. The majority of the deaths experienced by the students were caused by communicable diseases and three were the result of prematurity.

In discussing these experiences, most of the respondents commented that what made these deaths so difficult for them was that they had been involved with the care of the child, in many cases the child was improving and the death was sudden and unanticipated. One student commented that "I felt very bad. I almost cried and we were told that you should not be crying." As in the United States, the responses suggest that the death of an unexpected or preventable nature is difficult to accept, especially in situations where one has been intimately involved with the patient.

One definition of attitudes towards death is "the sum total of a person's inclinations, feelings, prejudices or bias, and convictions about death." This definition was operationalized for this study. To summarize the attitudes about childhood death of this sample, several themes were identified from the data. The themes are reflective of Martinson's description of how attitudes are formed [8]. She indicates that attitudes are formed by direct experience, explicit learning, and implicit learning. The themes are: 1) the student nurse's perceptions of the nurse's role following the child's death; 2) the student nurse's perceptions of the role of traditional customs in relationship to childhood death; and 3) the student nurse's perceptions of the role of Christianity in relationship to childhood death.

First, let's look at the respondent's perceptions about the nurse's role following the death of a child. When discussing providing support to the parents, the terms reassurance and comfort were most often used by the students. At least half of the respondents described emotional support as explaining why the child died, and that the death was no one's fault. Also, emotional support included explaining that God took the child, it was part of God's plan. One person stated, "God has decided to take the life of a child and we have done all the magic we can." In fact, two students referred to "magic" in their responses. Another referred to life as God's gift and he can take it anytime. Several students followed this with reassuring the parents that God will give them another child. The data also imply that it is important to the students that the parents do not blame the nursing staff for the death.

Role of Nurse in Childhood Death

The students were also asked about the role of a nurse in the community health program in relation to childhood death. The majority of the students indicated that if they did not know about a child's death prior to the home visit, it may be difficult to elicit information about the death as parents are unwilling to share this information or to talk about the death. Two respondents stated that the parents might even beat you or harm you for reminding them of something they chose to forget. Namboze has written that in the Kenyan culture, children are not supposed to be counted for fear that death may claim some of them [14]. This notion was reinforced by the student's responses. In addition, three of the students indicated that if the cause of death was preventable, their role would be to instruct the parents on how to avoid the problem in the future.

The second theme, the student nurse's perceptions of the role of traditional customs in relationship to childhood death, was addressed throughout the interviews by many of the students. Often, they would begin their responses by using the word 'traditionally.' Many of the traditions dealt with burial rituals. Several students commented that a mother is responsible for the burial of a newborn if the infant died at home. The father's role is limited to digging the grave. For the most part, if a newborn or a child dies in the hospital, traditionally the child is not taken home for burial, but instead is left at the hospital and buried there. This was also indicated as common when a young person died who was not married or did not have children. On explanation for this practice was that, especially in the case of a newborn, non one knew the child and therefore they had little importance in the community. Also, several persons mentioned that other children at home are not supposed to view dead bodies and are very often not even informed of a child's death. One opposing viewpoint came from a student who stated that it is good to get the death out of your mind, but not in that way, not by hiding it.

Naming practices were also identified as traditionally having significance. One person indicated that often children are not named at birth in case they may die. If a child is named and then dies, several students indicated that that particular name is not used again in the family. One respondent mentioned that the next child to be born in a family would be named after an animal and not given a "good name" for fear that that child will also die.

Two persons mentioned that parents whose child had died are traditionally expected to avoid other children in the community and that others do not go to the home or borrow anything from that home for some time. However, several students mentioned that other family members and people come into the home to cook for the family and provide support. I sensed that from some of the comments made, one reason for the isolation may be related to the potentially communicable nature of a large number of childhood deaths, and may be reinforced by the communities' repeated experiences with epidemic diseases. Only two persons mentioned that there are changes in the physical appearance of the parents following a child's death. Both commented that the mother removes her head scarf for a period of time and that neither parent is permitted to cut their hair. It was noted by one student that this was not the case in Christian families.

One person commented that traditionally, it was believed that the child died because it was "bewitched" and that the family would seek a witch doctor to learn about why the child died. Finally, three persons made direct statements about how tradition is changing especially in regard to burial practices and how nurses are viewed by society.

This leads us to a discussion of the third theme, the student nurse's perceptions of the role of Christianity in relationship to childhood death. One student commented on the impact of the presence of the British stating, "We are taking in a Christian way." This was indicated as a changing of traditional ways except in very remote places. One student suggested that although Christianity has created changes, many continue to practice traditional ways secretly. This student also appeared to perceive the presence of Christianity and the British as an intrusion.

In Christian families, at least half of the respondents indicated that the church was involved with the burial rituals, even for the unmarried person, and that some burials may occur at the church. When discussing Christianity, three students mentioned God's will as the reason for the person's death. For this reason, one of the students felt she should not feel bad about the death. Another commented that Christians do not cry a lot. Instead they accept death and pray. One found relief in the fact that when you die you go to a nicer place.

Lastly, two students commented on the recent change in how the role of the nurse is perceived. In the past, nurses were frowned upon because it was known that they were involved with touching dead bodies. It was taboo to touch someone who had died unless they were a member of your family. Now it is perceived as more acceptable for a nurse to be involved in preparation of the dead.

CONCLUSION

In summary, the data suggest that the attitudes of the twelve student nurses interviewed toward childhood death is basically fatalistic in nature. Although there were no attempts to draw conclusions from the data, the responses give some indication of the role of traditional customs and the impact of Christianity on this group of students. One may suspect, as Feifel suggests, that as infant and childhood mortality decrease in this society, the value of the child will increase and with it the impact of this death on the society will increase [15]. At this point in time, it is suggested that the students perceive the death of a child as part of God's plan and totally in his control. This was supported by my observation of a general "matter-of-fact" response by the nursing staff at the time of the child's death.

Finally, there are several issues related to the methods utilized in conducting this research I would like to point out. In retrospect, it would have been advantageous to spend more time in the community and to have had a more extensive knowledge of cultural practices and beliefs of this culture before conducting my research. Interviews were conducted with an enrolled staff nurse, the head nurse of the pediatric ward, the psychiatric nurse in the community health program, and a local Methodist minister in an attempt to further validate the data obtained. However, since there was no pilot study utilizing the interview guide, the potential for missing key data was increased.

As a student, I am grateful that I had the opportunity to pursue this project. I feel that I have benefited greatly from this experience and look forward to the time when I can return to Maua to conduct a more extensive research activity.

REFERENCES

1. *Statistical Yearbook: 1985*, United Nations, 1986.
2. M. J. Boylan, Kenya: Young Nation with Health Problems, *Journal of American Medical Women's Association, 35*:5, pp. 126-128, 1982.
3. A. Kaufman, D. Voorhees, E. Tabek, G. Perry, and D. Newman, Kenya: A Case Study in Third World Medicine, *Journal of Family Practice, 14*, pp. 609-610, 1982.
4. J. B. Kune, Some Factors Influencing the Mortality of Under-Five in a Rural Area of Kenya, A Multivariate Analysis, *Journal of Tropical Pediatrics, 26*:3, pp. 114-122, 1980.
5. W. M. Mwangi, and G. M. Mwabu, Economics of Health and Nutrition in Kenya, *Social Science and Medicine, 22*, pp. 775-780, 1986.
6. J. K. Van Ginneken and A. S. Muller, Maternal and Child Health in Rural Kenya: An Epidemiological Study, Croom Helm, London, 1984.
7. M. M. Leininger, Transcultural Nursing: Concepts, Theories, and Practice, John Wiley & Sons, New York, 1978.
8. I. M. Martinson, M. Palta, and N. V. Rude, Death and Dying: Selected Attitudes of Minnesota's Registered Nurses, *Nursing Research, 27*, pp. 226-229, 1978.
9. M. E. O'Brian, Transcultural Nursing Research: Alien in an Alien Land, *Image, 13*, pp. 37-39, 1981.

10. J. Clinton, Sociocultural Issues Relevant to Health, in *Health Promotion through the Life Span*, C. Liem and C. Mandle (eds.), C. V. Mosby, St. Louis, pp. 570-583, 1986.
11. T. A. Rando, Grief, Dying and Death: Clinical Interventions for Caregivers, Research Press, Chicago, 1984.
12. T. A. Rando, *Parental Loss of a Child*, Research Press, Champaign, Illinois, 1986.
13. R. Kalish and D. Reynolds, *Death and Ethnicity: A Psychocultural Study*, University of Southern California Press, Los Angeles, 1976.
14. J. M. Namboze, Health and Culture in an African Society, *Social Science and Medicine, 17*, pp. 2041-2043, 1983.
15. H. Feifel, *New Meanings of Death*, McGraw-Hill, New York, 1970.

CHAPTER 13

Spirituality and the Child: A Grandparent Death

Carol Irizarry

From 1985-1987 a study was conducted in Adelaide, Australia, on childhood bereavement. It was concerned with how children between the ages of eight and twelve responded when a grandparent died— what they thought about and what they experienced at the time of the death of someone so close to them. A second focus of the study was related to how children's ideas and attitudes developed within the support of the family—specifically how their parents interacted with them around their grieving.

The years eight to twelve were chosen because it is during this stage, while they are still largely under the influence of their parents, that children become socialized to the attitudes, norms, taboos and expectations of society. A grandparent death was felt to be significant because it is likely to be the child's first significant personal experience with death [1; 2, p. 206].

At the beginning of the research there was no overt intention to study the spirituality of children. Rather it was the experience in interviewing children and their parents which influenced investigation and thought in that direction.

Because of the researcher's own interest in religious education, questions were included in the interviews concerning attendance at religious services. This was an attempt to identify whether there were any noticeable differences in the ways children deal with death who lived in more religiously oriented families. But an awareness of the potential for children's spiritual lives emerged from thoughts and ideas the children themselves were sharing, rather than from direct questioning. It was as if the children were trying to raise other, equally important issues. This experience seemed to be similar to that of Robert Coles, who said in the introductory material to his book, *The Moral Life of Children*, "I am astonished at how stubbornly I turned my attention away from some extremely important messages I was being given by children, in order to pursue other matters" [3, p. 5]. Coles had spent years interviewing children in various situations of social or economic hardship during which time he had originally been inclined to dismiss or explain rather simplistically, the children's reports of religious experience which they felt had sustained them in the face of severe adversity.

This chapter discusses the data that emerged from the research, both from interviews with children and their parents; the findings will most likely have relevance to those interested in children and death. It presents and explores the idea that an opportunity exists at the time of death for someone close to children to help them understand and address spiritual concerns in themselves and to recognize that the most difficult questions being asked are related to the spiritual nature of humankind.

BACKGROUND OF THE STUDY

In examining the literature related to childhood bereavement the discussions about how children respond to death generally covered two areas of investigation. One was the cognitive understanding that children exhibited at the various stages of development. This cognitive research was based largely on Piaget's work and seemed to indicate developmental stages of understanding death which paralleled chronological development [4-8].

The other area related to the various emotional responses of children, particularly of those who manifested a 'problem' in continuing their normal lives after the death event. It was surprising how little empirical research had been conducted in the area of the emotional responses of children to death—research where the children themselves had been interviewed. Often information was obtained from the caretakers in the children's lives. The studies directly involving children were usually focussed on the death of a parent, an unusual and most traumatic death for a child; or the children studied were receiving psychological treatment at the time of the interview [1, 9, 10]. Although such studies did outline various reactions of children to the death, they seemed most relevant to an understanding of children who had experienced a death that posed a threat to their development. Thus it was felt that the responses of children in a more typical or common bereavement situation, such as a grandparent's death, had received inadequate examination.

THE RESEARCH STUDY

The review of the literature led to a decision to study normal children, that is, children who were not manifesting any overt social or psychological behavior problems and who had not experienced the death of a parent. In order to obtain such a population, it was decided to try to work through the school system, and after a great deal of patience the study began in a church-affiliated private school in 1985. During the two years of the study, three private and three public schools were used and fifty-six children from these various schools were interviewed. The interviews, which were audio-taped, lasted about one half to three quarters of an hour and consisted of 113 questions which covered the child's relationship with the grandparent before the death, the hearing about the death event, the mourning rituals, and reactions since the death.

After interviewing each child, the parents were sent a questionnaire requesting family information and a letter asking if they would be willing to be interviewed. After agreeing to the interview, the mother and the father were seen separately to obtain their personal memories of the death event. Nineteen couples, or thirty-eight parents, were interviewed, representing 34 percent of the children's parents. Table 1 illustrates the demographic characteristics of the population used in the study.

It was apparent that the study involved a very homogeneous, well educated population and certainly the parents appeared to be child-centered, involved, and deeply concerned about handling the death in the best possible manner. It was felt that a great deal could be learned from their interactions with their children.

CHILDREN'S DATA

First the analysis of the data obtained from the interviews examined the responses from the fifty-six children. This was done by identifying ten themes which frequently emerged in their conversations and then coding the number of children who expressed each of these themes. Some themes were quite predictable while others were surprising. The ten themes are presented below with a few illustrations included from the children's comments. Code names have of course been used.

Table 1. Demographic Characteristics of
Families Studied

Children Interviewed	Percent of Population	
56 children		
30 girls	54	
26 boys	46	
Ages		
8/9 years	29	
10/11 years	59	
12/13 years	12	
Years Since Death		
1 year or less	41	
2-3 years	34	
4 years or more	25	
Frequency of Contact with Grandparent		
Once a month or more	74	
Once a year	21	
Less than once a year	5	
Grandparent Relationship		
Mother's father	52	
Mother's mother	9	
Father's father	32	
Father's mother	7	
Parents		
Returned information on family data	59	
Agreed to be interviewed in person	34	— 19 couples
Tertiary education	76	— mothers
	82	— fathers
Australian born	94	
Protestant	58	
Roman Catholic	21	

Themes Prevalent in Children's Responses

(16%) **Theme A:** Children identify feeling differently from their parents because their parents have the ability to "get over" the death faster and go on with life.

Emily (9), "I don't think dad thinks about it as much as I can do. He can do something I can't do to put it out of his mind. He is a good reader and maybe he gets ideas from books on how not to think about it."

(36%) **Theme B:** Children try to protect parents by avoiding behavior which might contribute to their parents' sadness or worry.

Jane (11), "I didn't talk about Grandpa, because I wanted to make Dad less sad and I didn't want them to see me crying because then they'd worry about me."

Peter (12), "I didn't ask mom questions because she seemed really upset so I didn't want [long pause] I didn't want to upset her more."

(57%) **Theme C:** Children worry about how parents will act at the time of death. They fear unusual behavior from their parents or that something will happen to them.

Terry (11), "I was worried that my dad would go and kill himself to see his father in heaven."

Carol (9), "My parents had a fight. I thought they might get in the car and drive away and kill themselves by having an accident. If I told them, they would say I was silly."

(87%) **Theme D:** Children see parents as different people at the time of death—voice, tone, tears, different discipline.

Maryanne (10), "My parents were very upset; both of them cried when they talked about the fun times they had with my grandfather. They did not usually talk as much as they did when he died. They gave me more pocket money."

Rob (11), "On the phone my mom sounded half panicked and half normal. My father was lying down and he was more silent than usual."

(30%) Theme E: Children observe parents engaged in an unusual degree of conversation between themselves or with others.

(55%) Theme F: Children would have liked to have seen things done differently. They have suggestions and opinions.

Barry (11), "People shouldn't have laughed at the reception after grandpa's funeral. It upset my grandmother. I think that people were sad at the church and happy right after."

Maryanne (10), "I did not like the music at the service—it was too sad. I would have liked happy music. I also wanted to see inside the coffin."

(39%) Theme G: Children use exact words to explain death to another that they remember were used to them—even if they did not understand or like the phrase.

(55%) Theme H: Children want different kinds of information— more "details," more graphic explanation of the cause of death, effects of illness, moment of death, etc.

Sally (10), "I want to know: what did he die of, where did he die, how long ago did he die, how was he cremated, why was I not allowed to see him dead, what did he look like when he was dead, did he go blue?"

Sue (8), "I want to know how he died. People were too sad to tell me."

(7%) Theme I: Children develop explanations to fill gaps left by missing details.

Helen (10), "The sleeping pills she had been given may not have been the correct ones because normal ones don't make someone die. My dad was talking about it. My grandma had a cold and had gone to the hospital. She didn't want to go to sleep and was given sleeping pills and then she died. My father said it was 'old age.' "

(43%) Theme J: Recollections of death events seem so specific and detailed that they appear frozen in children's memories.

The responses of the children were deeply moving and several impressions emerged that were difficult to dispel. One was that so many of the children seemed mature or 'adult-like' in their comments. The literature related to childhood bereavement did not suggest the level of insight or self awareness that dominated the straightforward responses which were received. If the children felt confusion, it was often felt in relation to their parents' reactions, not their own. A nine year-old girl said,

> "When I woke up from a bad dream about my grandpa, my parents said, 'All you have to do is to get over it like we have to.' I thought they meant that if I kept getting upset the sadness would never go away. Father said he has sad feelings but he's over it."

A second impression which was gained from the initial analysis was that the children "wanted more," but at first only superficial ideas were formulated about what this longing in the children represented. It was thought that an analysis of the data from the parents' interviews might provide some understanding related to children's needs and indicate how parents were helping children deal with death.

PERSONAL DATA

The first analysis of the parents' interviews was based on a congruence of responses among the three family members who had been interviewed. The parents had each been asked twenty-seven of the questions that were asked of the children but from the perspective of what they felt their child was experiencing or thinking about the particular item. The aim was to determine the extent to which either of them could identify the same responses as their child. There were five possible responses: 1) all three could agree (child, mother, father); 2) mother and child could agree; 3) father and child could agree; 4) the parents could agree with each other (but not with the child); and 5) all three could have different responses. Table 2 shows the results of this analysis.

Table 2. Congruence of Child-Mother-Father Responses

Response Number	Percent of Response
1. Child and mother and father agreement	40
2. Child and mother agree	15
3. Child and father agree	9
4. Mother and father agree with each other (but not with child)	18
5. No agreement with child	18

This simple analysis of congruence shed some interesting light on parent-child communication. There was a considerable lack of awareness on the part of the parents regarding their children's thoughts and feelings around the death. (36% total no agreement with child.) Several factors stood out most clearly. Many parents did not realize that their child continued to think a great deal about the grandparent and the grandparent's death. They were largely unaware that their children had remaining questions about the death and they had little idea of what kinds of questions were still left unanswered. The strongest two factors were 1) that parents did not realize their child was worried about one or both of them; and 2) every parent felt that their child had someone in the family with whom he or she would discuss death.

Response Evolvement

A second analysis of the parents' material involved looking at changes in child and parent responses to death over time. This was done by charting the course of interaction between parents and child during three different stages following the news of the death. These stages were: 1) the news of the death; 2) the rituals surrounding the death; and 3) the return to normal life.

The news of the death — The disclosure proved to be a time of closeness and open communication for most families. All of the children were told immediately about the death and were told the truth. Parents openly displayed their own grief and the children shared in this moment. There seemed to be a great deal of physical contact and reassurance among family members and if at this point any of the children asked questions these were usually answered simply and directly. None of the children were sent away from the family. It emerged from the interviews that children and parents had similar, clear memories of when the death happened, how and by whom they heard the news, the way in which feelings were openly expressed, and the comfort that was given and received by all the family members.

The rituals surrounding the death — The stage following the news of the death was a period of participation in mourning rituals such as the funeral service, burial, family gathering or other death-related activities. The child had initially been given full access to his or her bereaved parent but during this next stage the bereaved parent seemed to withdraw from family life and the spouse, or non-bereaved parent took over the care-taking role in the family. This made the non-bereaved parent the central communication figure for the child with the result that much of the communication between the child and the bereaved parent was indirect. As Stephen (age 11) reported, "Dad told us to leave mom alone. He said to ask him things because she was having a hard time."

Understandably, the non-bereaved parent tried to provide comfort for his or her spouse and at the same time respond to the child's needs or questions. Most parents in this role worked very hard to reassure their child that everything was alright and that everyone was going to be fine. It was at this time that the child's questions were often answered with logical explanations such as the fact that everyone gets old and dies or that the deceased grandparent had enjoyed a full life and that it was now "time to die" or that death was God's will. The purpose of this kind of response to the child seemed to be to comfort him or her through reassurance. For the most part, the children found such calmness and reassurance at odds with their astute and accurate observations.

Charlie (age 10) reported, "My parents talked a lot and were sad when they were alone. When my brother and I were around they acted normal."

Mia (age 11) stayed home with her father while her bereaved mother went to the funeral. She asked her father what death really meant. She described his answer, "I can remember him going pretty pale and then he said, 'God will receive him.' I though he was upset talking to me."

Many children reported that a great deal of their energy was directed towards trying to understand what was happening. Maryanne (age 10) said, "I sat and watched and tried to figure out what mom and dad were saying. I liked them talking to me because then I could understand a bit more."

The children started to be concerned about their parents' welfare and to try to find ways to help them feel better. It was as if they were also adopting a comforting reassuring role. Seventy-five percent said they tried to be "especially good" during this time, 57 percent said they worried about their parents, 64 percent said they tried to help their parents feel better and 59 percent said they wanted to keep their parents company so they wouldn't feel so lonely. Interestingly, the parents did not seen to notice that the children were very concerned or worried about them or that children had questions which were not answered. Some of the children sought help from others such as friends or family members. They were clearly aware of whom they could speak to about the death. John (age 11) said, "I could talk to my cousin because my brother would think I was silly and my parents would think I was dumb. My cousin is good at talking about things like that."

The children appeared frustrated at times with attitudes exhibited towards them. "I thought mom and dad didn't try to explain it to me as they could another adult who didn't understand," commented Peter, (age 11). They also sometimes filled the gap left opening in their understanding with ideas they built themselves. Helen (age 10) concluded, "The sleeping pills nana had been given must not have been the right ones because normally they don't make someone die."

Many of the children were obviously reaching out for an engagement with the adults in their lives that was not forthcoming. In their own sadness and while trying to provide security, the parents narrowed, controlled and limited the communication between themselves and their child.

The return to normal life — The third stage following the death brought a return to normal life. This was the period when the public mourning rituals were finished and family members had begun to function in a way that more closely resembled their pre-death routines.

The child resumed a more direct access to the bereaved parent and it was felt that perhaps at this stage a more open communication would be established. For many reasons this did not appear to happen.

The children easily identified that when they raised questions about the death it had the effect of making at least one parent very sad again. The protection mode that the children had previously established towards parents continued and most children become convinced at this point that they could not initiate their concerns or questions. Almost 50 percent of the children reported they continued dreaming about the death or grandparent and some described this as day dreaming.

Nancy (age 11) "When I went to school I used to sit and not do my work and I'd get told off for not doing my work. I told the teacher at 'Show and Tell' but she still thought I was day dreaming."

Some children seemed confused as they continued to feel sad and they sometimes interpreted their parents return to work and normal life as an indication that these parents were now "over the death." Often this attitude was not understood and a number of children developed their own explanations for what was happening with their parents. Some of them thought that adults had special ways to overcome sadness while others suspected that their parents were still sad but were hiding the sadness. In postulating that adults "get over" death faster than children the statements uttered by children sounded remarkably like those often heard by adults who are attempting to interpret children's behavior.

Dana (age 8) explained it this way. "You see, adults live in a different world than we do. In their world, they know how to get over things like this."

Another boy Len (age 11) said, "Probably adults get over a death quicker than children because they can think in ways that can get over it. They have children and have to get on with life. Parents don't want to upset children."

It was in their struggle to interpret behavior that some of the most profound comments were made.

Nancy (age 11) puzzled about her bereaved mother's behavior. I wonder how mom doesn't think about it now when I do. She is grown up and is busy controlling children—doing what she has to do. Grown-ups don't show when they're upset."

Emily (age 9) said, "I don't think dad thinks about it as much as I do. He can do something I can't. He can put it out of his mind. He is a good reader and maybe gets ideas out of books about how not to think of it."

These comments and many similar ones had not been expressed before. They arose in the interview situation as children attempted to explain their own and their parents' behavior and to give reasons for what they saw as a gap in their own feelings and their parents return to normal. Many parents spoke about the fatigue of a long family illness followed by the activity of a funeral and the relief of being able to return to a daily routine. They appeared to feel sincerely that such an attitude was best for themselves, their family, and their child. They felt that the children were fine and had gotten over the death well, especially in view of the fact that there were no overt behavioral symptoms of distress exhibited by the children.

On the contrary, for the most part the children also appeared to "return to normal." They understood and accepted their parents need not to dwell on the death and kept their thoughts, feelings and questions to themselves. Occasionally, such as at a holiday celebration or a birthday, there would be a spontaneous shared expression of grief among family members and for a moment the parents and child again participated in the open communication of the earliest stage. None of the children presumed on this intimate moment to raise their own concerns. They were left alone with various thoughts and feelings which no adult helped them to express, identify, interpret or focus.

Richard (age 12) "I reckon it's good what you're doing because I haven't had a chance to talk to anyone except my best friend."

Adam (age 9) "I think of grandpa when I read the deaths in the newspaper while I'm looking for people I know."

Darren (age 11) "There are a few things I'd like to have said to him before he died. I did say how much I loved him but I'd like to have told him thank you for all the things he'd done for me, like taking me on rides."

Sally (age 11) "I thought about grandma missing concerts. She was always happy coming to tap dancing concerts. Now she will not hear my music again."

Spirituality

What started to emerge from the examination of these stages in family communication, in combination with the children's data seemed to be a picture of the child as immersed in and responsive to the family dynamics around the death. Understandably, parents in general were extremely concerned with reassuring their children that everything would be alright and that life was still safe and rational. There exists in nurturing adults a strong wish to protect the young from the pains of fear and grief. Few parents would deny sharing this exact feeling, especially at a time of great emotional stress, such as the death of a family member. But the information being collected from this limited study seemed to indicate that it just didn't work and indeed perhaps that such protective gestures made life more confusing for the children involved.

Speculations regarding the spirituality of children began when thinking about the gap between the kind of comments the children were making and the attempt by parents to protect them from the pain of death. For it is inevitable in facing death that every human being, regardless of age, meets the end of human explanations and understanding. One simply longs for more—whether in fear, or grief or anger, or simply curiosity—one reaches out to embrace the mystery of death. Nelly Morton, in her article on, "Risks in Dealing with Children's Reality" says, "We cannot use the word 'dead' because the child cannot understand it. Do we? On the other hand, we allow the child to experience painfully again and again—death as separation" [11, p. 80].

The separation that the children in this study experienced was from their parents' extensive range of emotions and reactions and this frequently also meant separation from a more sustaining level of comfort. Such an idea could not have been more poignantly expressed than by Nancy, age nine, when she gave me the following advice to pass on to parents.

> "You should tell parents to ask their children why they are sad. And if they are sad about it themselves, they should tell their child that they are sad, too. Then the child will know that she is not the only one."

This young child clearly did feel isolated with her feelings and reactions and, as with many of the other children, it seemed as if her responses were too sophisticated to be recognized or accepted by the adults in her life. Nancy and the other children appeared to have been dealing with death at a deeper level than adults are willing to attribute to children. Could the experience of death have been taken by children as a spiritual concern, one that transcended rational explanations and reassurances?

This thought inevitably leads us to a discussion of the definition being used for spirituality. Inge Corless, in her article, "Spirituality for Whom?" reviewed many different definitions of spirituality in an attempt to arrive at a useful one for people interested in the spiritual component of health care. Corless concluded that spirituality generally had to do with the inner life or with matters that transcend human experience. Spirituality was seen as distinct from religion or religious feeling, although most religions view spirituality as a baseline foundation for religious experience [12, p. 89]. Corless was influenced in her ideas by Donna Le Marie, who spoke of the work of this inner life as being "to be true to oneself." This is an important concept in relation to children [12, p. 89].

In her book, *Education for Spiritual Growth*, Iris Cully talks about the development of the inner life or spirituality as a continual rather than static experience. She says that spiritual growth is a process which implies, "formation, shaping and development, however open-ended the goal" [13, p. 23].

Accepting then a definition of spirituality as having to do with the "inner life," the ensuing question is the essential one. Can children be considered to have a spiritual life? In order to address this question in more depth, a systematic search was conducted on the subject of "spirituality and children." Surprisingly there was not much material on the subject. There was, however, strong indication in some of the recent literature that children's spiritual lives were being considered in a more serious light.

Robert Coles talks about the moment when he began to think of children's spiritual life, "as worth comprehending on its own merit with its own dignity and significance, rather than as a 'reflection' or 'consequence' " [3, p. 5]. He had obviously changed his interpretation of this matter over the years in which he had been interviewing children.

Edward Robinson, from the Religious Experience Research Unit at Manchester College, Oxford, wrote a unique and fascinating book on childhood religious experience called *The Original Vision* [14]. He surveyed about 500 adults regarding their memories of transcendent experiences and he became convinced of the authenticity of those reported experiences. For Robinson, "Childhood can best be understood as a dimension of life (not a chronological period) about which we can only become fully conscious in later life" [14, p. x.]. This view adds a new perspective to the developmentally oriented theories of childhood which are currently adhered to by educationalists—including those interested in religious education.

Using this concept as a framework, what were the kind of things that the loving and concerned parents in my research study had missed while trying to help their children with the family death that had occurred? The most obvious seemed to be that they did not search for their children's questions before supplying answers. The spiritual dimension, for most children, lay in the profound sense of loss at the death of a loved person and in the ensuing struggle that followed to make sense of their feelings—including worrying about the death of others whom they loved. The idea of such a struggle seemed unbearable to most parents. They could not accept the idea that "the capacity for wonder and horror go together" [14, p. 61].

Related to this need to supply answers and give reassurance to their children was the inability to express their own range of emotions for fear of frightening the children. How interesting that so many children knew that something was wrong with their parents and with what appeared to a reversal of roles tried to provide comfort to their parents. Nellie Morton remarked that, "Under the adult assumption that death as adults know it is shattering and traumatic for a small child, children are shielded from and ill-prepared for the one inevitable experience" [11, p. 80]. And Robinson concluded from his interview data that "the ways in which children show up the hypocrisy of adults and their attitudes to death is often entertaining or disturbing" [14, p. 121].

Possibly because death is such an incomprehensible event for everyone—adults and children—it is easy to build a view of the world which finds children incapable of struggling with life and death issues. When such issues are addressed seriously, they would appear to have a spiritual dimension.

At the time of a family death, there exists an opportunity to nurture children in their spiritual lives and development. They can be helped to begin to formulate questions which will remain with them the rest of their lives. In fact, their lives may be spent trying to supply answers to well-formulated questions. This philosophy stands in direct contrast to an approach that is based primarily on communicating reassurance to children. It assumes with Lifton and Olson, that learning how to live, "without overwhelming anxiety in the face of the uncertainty of death," [15, p. 69] is a basic and fundamental concern facing each human being. Does the reality of death make such questions real for children?

William Damon has recently written a book aimed at helping adults understand how to nurture children's moral growth [16]. He has developed the concept of "respectful engagement" with the child to describe a process of interaction which might also be helpful with topics like death. Only one parent of the thirty-eight who were interviewed had responded to a question concerning life after death by asking his son what his thoughts were. The son's response was to participate in a discussion on the subject in which he was free to try out his own ideas. The focus of the conversation was not on providing answers to a question but on communicating with the child on the subject of death. It was most fascinating that many parents who would use this approach with other topics, such as sex education, were unable to do so concerning the subject of death.

The reason is, perhaps, because this type of engagement carries the potential for generating feelings of insecurity. Iris Cully suggests that spiritual development should be perceived in the form of a quest. The goal of such a quest is not reassurance. "Life will not go according to plan," she ways, "but somehow it will be liveable." She added that people on this sort of spiritual quest "must be able to live with uncertainty. And this runs counter to all human need for security" [13, p. 37].

The need for security may never be greater than when one is faced by the losses encountered at death. The parents who were interviewed were dealing with the death of their own parent, usually a difficult and painful experience at any age. Many of them cried during the interview when speaking about the person who had been so important to them during their lives. It is easy to understand how difficult, if not impossible, it might well be to engage one's child in a meaningful discussion about death at such a time.

What is more difficult to understand and accept is the continued lack of engagement long after the death, the lack of engagement from other adults who could talk seriously to the child (relatives, teachers, clergy), and the frequently encountered rigid adherence to a view of children which labels their spiritual concerns as "immature" and awaits the development of "mature" ideas and feelings. Is it any surprise that such maturity in the realm of ethical, moral, religious and spiritual development is often not forthcoming? The simplistic and immature attitudes reflected by many adults regarding spiritual and religious ideas could possibly be readdressed by encounters in childhood with adults who are able to help them search out and explore their questions at the time of a family death and identify such issues as spiritual concerns.

When the study began and the children sat down at the small microphone to talk, it was initially surprising how pleased they were to be sharing their ideas and memories. Then the surprise stopped as closer attention was paid to their comments and advice. The words of Christine, age 10, became a guiding principle. She said, "For adults to understand how a child is thinking, they should talk normally as if the child was a person—and not too young to understand."

Perhaps it is the adults who must face the uncertainty of all of life and approach children with the simple reassurance that the spiritual dimensions, of all of life's most challenging and difficult questions, are worthy of quest. Sharing adult insecurities or hesitancies, not being able to alleviate all discomfort around death, and helping children formulate questions rather than supply answers too readily may in the end prove to provide the most lasting growth and comfort.

REFERENCES

1. E. Furman, *A Child's Parent Dies*, Yale University Press, New Haven, 1974.
2. E. S. Schneidman, *Deaths of Man*, Quadrangle, New York, 1973.
3. R. Coles, *The Moral Life of Children*, Houghton Mifflin Company, Boston, 1986.
4. J. Piaget, *The Child's Conception of the World*, Littlefield, Adams and Co., Totowa, New Jersey, 1967.
5. S. Anthony, The Child's Idea of Death and Grief, in *The World of the Child*, T. Talbot (ed.), Anchor Books, New York, 1968.
6. G. Koocher, Children, Death and Cognitive Development, *Developmental Psychology, 9*, pp. 363-375, 1973.
7. R. Kastenbaum, Death and Development through the Life Span? in *New Meanings of Death*, H. Feifel (ed.), McGraw Hill, New York, 1977.
8. B. Rafael, *The Anatomy of Bereavement*, Basic Books, New York, 1983.
9. G. Kilman, The Children, in *Understanding Bereavement and Grief*, N. Linzer (ed.), Yeshiva University Press, New York, 1977.
10. M. Van Eerdwegh, M. Bieri, R. Parrilla, and P. Clayton, The Bereaved Child, *British Journal of Psychiatry, 140*, pp. 23-39, 1982.
11. N. Morton, Risks in Dealing with Children's Reality, in *Risk and Reality*, Board of Missions, The United Church, Cincinnati, Ohio, 1970.
12. J. Corless, Spirituality for Whim? in *In the Quest of the Spiritual Component of Care for the Terminally Ill*, F. Wald (ed.), *Colloquin*, May 3-4, Yale University School of Nursing, 1986.
13. I. Cully, *Education for Spiritual Growth*, Harper and Row Publishers, San Francisco, 1984.
14. E. Robinson, *The Original Vision: A Study of the Religious Experience of Childhood*, The Seabury Press, New York, 1983.
15. R. Lifton and E. Olson, *Living and Dying*, Praeger Publishers, New York, 1984.
16. W. Damon, *The Moral Child*, The Free Press, New York, 1988.

CHAPTER 14

Looking Back to Help See the Future: A Proposal for the Use of Guided Autobiography with the Dying and Children

Craig E. Seaton

The term "life review" is generally associated with psychiatrist Robert Butler who has argued rather persuasively that as older people approach their own death they tend to have an evaluative, panoramic, replay of their life experience [1-3].

The idea of remembering and reviewing one's life experience during times of stress and crisis is not a novel idea of course. Folklore, literature and life experience testify to the commonality of "seeing my life pass before my eyes" in such diverse settings as near drowning, car accidents, falls from high places, and the like.

Within the behavioral sciences, one of the earliest reports of the occurrence of the life review process as an aspect of normal human development appears in the writings of Charlotte Buhler. She and her colleagues studied several hundred biographical works collected in the 1930s in Vienna. She noted several stages of progressive growth and characterized one of these stages as focusing upon retrospective evaluation and consideration of the future.

The writings of Carl Jung suggest that the entire "afternoon of life" is a period when the mature person is more inclined to be introspective, analytical and open to aspects of their own personality than they would have been earlier. He suggests, for example, that men become more aware of their feminine traits (nurturing, expressive, emotional) and women begin to acknowledge their male traits (assertive, systematic, goal directed) [4].

Erik Erikson has created a widely discussed theory which describes the process of human development across the life span [5]. His understanding of what is involved in development at different ages is premised upon the belief that each of eight general stages of development are characterized by crisis resolution experiences. Erikson believes that one must resolve each of these issues which are uniquely characteristic of the stages in a relatively successful manner before one is able to move forward in the developmental sequence. The last stage of human development, and the one characteristic of old age, is that which he labels "integrity versus despair." Erikson believes that this stage is intensely introspective and that the old person engages in an indepth life review. Studies of adult development have very frequently cited the life review process as a normative experience, though the age of occurrence seems to vary widely among the different studies [5-7].

A method called Guided Autobiography (GA) has been devised by James Birren to facilitate the life review process. Birren, a leader in psychological gerontology, developed a thematic autobiographical format which has been utilized profitably with a wide range of client groups. His usual procedure in the application of Guided Autobiography involves a theoretical overview of adult development, presenting stimulating material to enhance memory recall (see Appendix), solitary time for reflection and recording information, and small group sharing of one's personal biographical information [8]. A wide range of professional literature attests to the value of the utilization of life review methods with various client groups, particularly the elderly [9-29].

I have found GA to be a very powerful technique in connection with individuals of varying backgrounds and ages. These include university students, seniors project administrators, social workers, nurses, clergy and retired people. The potential benefits for participants have included:

1. the enhanced capacity to transcend current physical and social limitations;
2. a clarified sense of a personal philosophy of life or world view;
3. coping mechanisms have been identified and reinforced;
4. greater self-understanding and self-acceptance;
5. memory is stimulated and a sense of vitality is renewed;
6. intergenerational understanding is enhanced;
7. a legacy is provided for family and friends when material is organized and retained in writing or on audio or videotape;
8. it results in increased empathy for others; and

9. the activity has intrinsic merit as self-expression and recreational activity.

I believe that GA has great potential for use by professionals in their dealings with the dying and their survivors (i.e., spouses, children, adult children and grandchildren). It is apparent from the previous review of the literature that life review is a common experience and that this underlying process is a powerful process which may be enhanced through professional direction. Guided Autobiography provides a thematic structure that individuals readily identify with and find to be a useful road map to renavigate their personal life course. Nine themes have commonly been utilized including: branching points, family history, work history, the role of money, health and body image, sexual identity, experience with death, loves and hates, and life meaning.

What I propose is as follows:

1. Professionals who deal with the dying and their survivors should consider how the GA might be adapted for use with dying patients and their families.

   The thematic structure of GA, or parts of it, might provide a useful vehicle for discussion of the life experience of the dying patient. Since discussion with the dying is often strained and built around defending against terror and reality of death, for the caregiver, family member and/or the dying—the GA might open channels of communication and allow for expression of feelings.

2. Those who desire to support the bereaved survivors should consider how the GA might be adapted for use with support groups. I believe it could be useful in connection with self-help groups and for purposes of training for those who need to get in touch with their own life experience prior to working with the bereaved.

3. Those who desire to overcome lack of knowledge about and appreciation for the different generations might consider how GA might be utilized as a tool to create a product. This written or recorded material may be shared among the generations even after the experience with the dying person has been concluded. Whether because of geographic distance or psychological distance, or very different socialization experience, sometimes the dead person is not known as completely as the survivors would desire. The GA may serve as a mechanism for knowledge and family continuity that would otherwise not be possible.

APPENDIX

Thematic material to focus reflection and to guide the development of the "Guided Autobiography."

Theme Assignment: History of the Major Branching Points in Your Life.

Think of your life as a branching tree, as a flowing river which has many points of juncture, or as a trailing plant which puts down roots at various places and then grows one.

What is a branching point? Branching points are events, experiences, happenings in our lives that significantly affect the direction of flow of our life. Branching points are experiences that shape our lives in some important way.

Branching points may be big events (marriage, retirement, geographical move) or they may seem small and apparently inconsequential (reading a book, going on a hike). Big outcomes may have small beginnings.

From your point of view, what have been the major branching points in our life? What were the events, experiences, interactions with people and places that have had a major influence or impact on the way your life flowed?

Sensitizing Questions: (To guide but not structure your thinking about your personal history)

1. About how old were you? Place the turning point along a time dimension. The timing of an event is often very important. Did it happen too soon? Were you too young? Did it happen too late? Were you too old?
2. Significant people? Who were the important people involved in the turning point? Father, mother, spouse? You alone? Often people see that the same people are involved again and again in major life turning points.
3. Emotions and feelings then? What were the feelings, emotions you experienced at the time the branching point occurred? How intense were these feelings? (extremely elated, sort of sad, a little frustrated, very happy). Sometimes our feelings in reaction to an experience are mixed or are changeable. Don't be concerned if your feelings seem contradictory.
4. Emotions and feelings now? Sometimes our feelings about an experience or event change over time. Something that seemed a disaster when it happened, turns out to be a positive event later

on; and vice versa. What emotions do you experience as you think about the turning point now?

5. Personal choice? How much personal choice was involved in this branching point? How much personal control did you have? Was it something that happened that was completely out of your control? Who or what else as the influence?

6. Consequences? Branching points are branching points because they change our lives in one or many important ways. In your view, what are the ways your life was changed because of this branching point? What effect, impact, consequences did it have on your life? How would your life have been different if it had not occurred?

Theme Assignment: History of Your Family

What is your family? The history of your family includes your family of origin (grandparents, parents, siblings, uncles and aunts, etc.) as well as your family of adulthood (spouse, children, grandchildren, etc.)

The important family members in shaping your life should be mentioned, not just all the family members. Some have been more important in positive ways and some in negative ways in shaping your life.

What family members have had a major impact in shaping your life? Why?

What would another person have to know about your family in order to understand you and how you've come to be the person you are?

Sensitizing Questions: (To guide but not structure your thinking about your personal history)

1. Who held the power in your family? Why? Who made the decisions? How did you know?
2. Who offered support, warmth and nurturing? Why? Who did you go to for comfort? In whom did you confide?
3. To what major family member(s) have you been closest? Why?
4. What important family member did you know the least? Feel least close to? Why? Who should you have been close to but for some reason weren't?
5. Did you like your family? Why or why not?
6. What was the best about your family? Worst about it? What were (are) the strengths and weaknesses in your family?
7. Was there anyone in your family of whom you were afraid? Why?
8. Who were the heroes in your family? The family favorites? How did you know?

9. What was the feeling tone in your family? Happy . . . sad, crowded . . . spacious, noisy . . . quiet, warm . . . cold?
10. What were the major areas of conflict, problems, and issues in your family?
11. What were the rules in your family, the "shoulds" and "oughts?"
12. What events, experiences have torn your family apart, or made your family stronger?
13. Were you loved? How did you know?

Theme Assignment: History of Your Major Life Work or Career

What is a career? It is your major life's work. It occupies your energy, your activity, and your time.

A career, a life work, can have many forms. Usually we think of it as work outside the home for pay. A life work can also be found in being a husband, a wife, a parent, or in religious devotion, in play, in art, in education, in community service.

People can have a number of careers and/or a sequence of careers.

What has been your major life's work or career?

Sensitizing Questions:

1. How did you get into your major life work? How did you find it? Did you choose it because your family expected it? Was it because of a teacher you know? Did your appearance have anything to do with it? When did you begin your life work?
2. How early did you formulate your life career goals? What did you want to be when you grew up? How have childhood interests, passions, teachers influenced the path your life work has taken? How much choice did you have?
3. What has been the developmental course of your life work? Has it been continuous? Discontinuous? What have been the peaks, valleys? Have there been major or minor setbacks? Major changes in focus? Have you had a sequence or series of careers?
4. What have been the biggest influences in directing the path of your career once chosen? People, places, events, etc.
5. If you don't have a major life work (yet), what would you like to do? Why?
6. If you feel you have finished your major life work, how do you evaluate it?
7. How has your work provided new options? Limited them?
8. Are you "on time" in your career, or ahead or behind in terms of your expectations?

9. What have been (are) the challenges of your life work? Your successes? The problems? The failures?
10. If you have more than one life work identity, which of these has been the most important to you? Why?
11. What has been unique or special about your work experiences? Place of work? Travel? People?
12. What have you enjoyed most about your life work? Least?
13. If you had it to do over again, how would you develop differently along your life work path? Would you choose the same life work? Why or why not?

Theme Assignment: The Role of Money in Your Life

Money is one of the most important themes in life. It is both an obvious and a subtle influence. Money touches many aspects of our lives—family, education, career, health, relationships with others, and self-esteem.

Your attitude toward money has been shaped by many influences, both positive and negative.

Sensitizing Questions: (To guide but not structure your thinking)

1. What role did money play in your family? What were you taught about money? Was it scarce or plentiful? Were you poor or well-off?
2. How did your family's money compare to other people's money?
3. In your life, how important is it to make money?
4. Did money have any relationship to love in your life? How?
5. What was the first time you earned money? How did you feel about it? How did it affect your later ideas about money?
6. What have been your greatest financial successes?
7. What have been your worst financial mistakes?
8. How central is the role that money plays in your life?
9. Does money have any relationship to your self-esteem?
10. How much do you think about money? Do you worry about money?
11. Do you regard yourself as generous or stingy? Why?
12. Have you ever borrowed money? How did you feel about it?
13. Are you a good or poor manager of money? Why?
14. Do you ever give money away? How did you feel about it?

These Assignment: History of Your Health and Body Image

The image of your body and your health has many aspects, objective features and your feelings. In part, it involves an implied comparison with other persons, whether you were (are) more or less healthy, stronger or weaker, coordinated or clumsy, attractive or unattractive. We would like to know how you regard your body and health.

What has been the history of your health and body image?

Sensitizing Questions: (To guide but not structure your writing)

1. What was your health like as a baby? Child? Adolescent? Young adult? Middle aged adult? Older adult?
2. Were your considered a sickly child? If so, what were the consequences for your development?
3. Were you a fast-developing or slow-developing child? Where you ahead or behind in growth as an adolescent?
4. What health problems have you experienced in your life? How did you feel about each of these? How did you handle these problems?
5. How has your body reacted to games and athletic sports?
6. In what ways does your body react to stress? Has this changed during your life? What do you do in response to your body's stress signals?
7. What have you done during your life to help/hurt your health?
8. How would you describe your appearance or physical self as a baby? Child? Adolescent? Young adult? Middle aged adult? Older adult? (i.e., short, tall, thin, fat, attractive, ugly, poised, awkward).
9. What part(s) of your body do you like the least? Why? How has this changed over your life?
10. What part(s) of your body do you like most? Why? How has this changed over your life?
11. What have you done to alter, change, or improve your health and physical self during your life?
12. How do you regard your body in terms of female or male image?
13. If you could change your body in any way, how would you want it to be different?

Theme Assignment: History of Your Sexual Identity, Sex Roles, and Sexual Experiences

Sexuality includes our sense of ourselves as male or female (sexual identity), our ideas about appropriate sex role behavior, and our sexual experiences.

What has been the history of your sexual development, including the development of your identity as male/female, your concepts of appropriate sex role behavior, your sexual experiences?

Sensitizing Questions: (To guide but not structure your writing)

1. When did you first realize that you were a boy or a girl? When did you first realize that little boys and girls were different? How did you feel about that?

2. What toys, games did you play when you were a child? Were any kinds of play, toys, games forbidden? What clothes were you dressed in as a child? What significance did this have in the development of your sexual identity?

3. Were you a "tomboy"? a "sissy"? a "fraidy cat"? Did you ever wish you had been born the opposite sex? Why?

4. What did your parents, teachers, relatives teach you about what "good" girls and boys did and didn't do? What were the rules for being a boy or a girl? What were your parents' views about your sexuality?

5. Where did you get your sex education (parent, friends, books, school, religious training)? Where and when did you learn the facts of life?

6. What were your early sexual experiences? (doctor and nurse games, etc.)? Did you have childhood sweethearts?

7. Have you had any traumatic sexual experiences?

8. What have been your concepts or models of the "ideal" man, "ideal" woman? How have these ideas changed as you've grown up and grown older?

9. What are your concepts about the "ideal" relationship between two people?

10. How would you characterize yourself as a man or woman? How has this changed? What "traditionally" masculine or feminine aspects can you identify in yourself?

11. How do you relate to members of the opposite sex? How has this changed?

12. What has been the history of your sexual experiences? How have they changed as you've grown older? What factors (aging, health, menopause, retirement, etc.) have affected your sexual identity and sexual experiences?

13. How do you feel about your sexuality? Have your ideas about appropriate sexual behavior changed over time (i.e., attitudes towards homosexuality, etc.).

Theme Assignment: History of Your Experiences with Death and/or Your Ideas about Death

Death can affect you life in many ways. You may have experienced the loss of a beloved pet as a child; you may have lost parents, grandparents, dear friends, a spouse, child, a brother or sister. Maybe the death of a political hero affected you profoundly.

How have your experiences with death affected your life and your character? How have your reactions to death changed over the years? How have your ideas concerning your own death changed?

Sensitizing Questions: (To guide but not structure your writing)

1. How did you feel about death when you were a child? Did you lose an animal which was like a member of the family. What did you think when your pet died?
2. How was death talked about and treated in your family? Did it frighten you? How did you understand it?
3. When did you go to your first funeral? What did you think? How did you react?
4. What effect did the threat of death in wartime have on you?
5. Were you ever so sick you thought you might die?
6. What have been your close calls with death? Have your ideas about your own death changed over the years? How do you feel about your death now?
7. How have you grieved?
8. Do dead parents, grandparents, spouses, or others continue to have an effect on your life?
9. Do you feel guilty about anyone's death? Angry? Resentful? Abandoned? Have you ever felt responsible for anyone's death?
10. Have you ever killed anyone? How did you feel about it at the time? How do you feel about it now?
11. Did some great person's death have an effect on you? (i.e., Kennedy, Roosevelt, etc.).
12. Is death an enemy or a friend for you? Is it to be dreaded and fought or welcomed?
13. What kind of a death would you like to have?
14. If you could talk with a dead person, what would you ask him/her?
15. What was the most significant death you have experienced? How did it change you or your life?

Theme Assignment: History of Your Loves and Hates

Love is a strong emotional attachment to a particular person, place, or thing. Absence of the love object causes distress in the form of lonesomeness, anxiety, and longing. What have been the major loves of your life?

Hate is a strong feeling of dislike or ill will toward some person, place, or thing. What have been the hates or strong aversions in your life?

What major loves and hates of yours would another person have to know in order to appreciate and understand your development and uniqueness?

Sensitizing Questions: (To guide but not structure your thoughts about your personal history)

1. What persons, places or things aroused your greatest feelings of love when you were a child?
2. Who was your first love?
3. Who in your life made you feel loved and why?
4. Were you ever consumed by love? When and under what circumstances?
5. What has been the role of love in your life? How has it changed over time?
6. Why did your loves end? What happens when you lose a love? Did your feelings change or did you lose the object of your love?
7. How have your ideas about love changed during your life?
8. What have been the major hates of your life? What places, people, events, characteristics of people, objects, ideas, or kinds of behavior cause you to feel extreme dislike?
9. What were your major dislikes as a child? How did they change with time?
10. Have you ever hated someone so much you wished they would die?
11. How have you expressed your hatred?
12. Have you changed your hates over the years or have they remained the same?
13. If you could wish ill upon some person by voodoo or magic, who would it be?
14. Do you express your hate or keep it inside?
15. Do you have some strong unexpressed feelings of love for some person, place, or thing?
16. When you were growing up, what were you taught about love and hate? How have your ideas changed?

Theme Assignment: The Meaning of Your Life and the History of Your Aspirations and Life Goals

Questions of meaning, values, morality and religion are often elusive and difficult to articulate. Human life is characterized by moral complexity and ambiguity. Often the black and white of childhood, the simple delineation of right and wrong changes to large areas of grey in our adult lives. Questions of value and meaning, religion and morality, are often fraught with contradictions. Some people become moral gymnasts, stretching and bending with agility in the moral realm of life. Others find their home in a traditional religious philosophy and structure. Numerous people today claim to have their own religion, an eclectic synthesis of many diverse elements. Still others avow atheism or agnosticism. Secular humanism claims a large following in contemporary culture.

How do your life goals fit into your context of meaning and values? How have you set your life goals? What are they?

Trace the history of your moral and/or religious development. How has it changed through your life?

Do you have a philosophy of life? If so, what is it?

What does your life mean? What does human life in general mean?

Sensitizing Questions: (To stimulate your thinking in this area)

1. What kinds of different goals do you have—material, social, personal, universal, moral, religious—and how important are they to you? Have your goals always been the same?
2. Were there any religious traditions in your home as a child? Have you carried them on? Why or why not?
3. Have you ever had a religious experience? What were you doing and where did it happen? How did you react?
4. What symbols, either religious or secular, are significant for you? Why?
5. What are the principles that guide your life? What are your standards? What does it mean if you don't live up to them?
6. What has been your purpose in life? Have you had more than one purpose? How have they changed?
7. Do you find meaning in the idea of social justice, posterity, or brotherhood of man? How do you act on these ideas?
8. Do you want to emulate some great figure (Moses, Ghandi, Christ, Schweitzer, Eleanor Roosevelt, etc.)? Who are your moral heroes? Have they changed over time?
9. Were you taught not to be cruel to animals so that you wouldn't be cruel to people? What is your relationship to the natural world?

10. Have you ever found life meaningless? Did it fill you with despair? Did you come to some existential understanding?
11. Why be moral? WHY BE?

Note: All "Sensitizing Material" found in the appendix is based upon material presented by Dr. James Birren during the Gerontology Summer Institute—Summer 1982, at the Andrus Gerontology Center, University of Southern California.

REFERENCES

1. R. Butler, The Life Review: An Interpretation of Reminiscence in the Aged. *Psychiatry, XXVI*, pp. 65-76, February 1963.
2. R. N. Butler, Psychiatry and the Elderly: An Overview, *American Journal of Psychiatry, 132*, pp. 893-900, 1975.
3. R. Butler, Successful Aging and the Role of the Life Review, *Journal of American Geriatric Society*, pp. 529-535, 1979.
4. C. Jung, The Stages of Life, in *The Portable Jung*, J. Campbell (ed.), Viking Press, New York, 1971.
5. E. Erikson, *Childhood and Society*, (2nd Edition), W. W. Norton & Company, Inc., New York, 1963.
6. R. Gould, *Transformations*, Simon and Schuster, New York, 1978.
7. G. Sheehy, *Passages: Predictable Crises of Adult Life*, Dutton, New York, 1974.
8. C. Seaton, *Facilitating Personal Development in Adulthood through Guided Autobiography: Rationale and Procedures*, Monograph number one, Fraser Valley Aging Resource Centre, Langley, B.C., 1983.
9. P. Ebersole, Problems of Group Reminiscing with Institutionalized Aged, *Journal of Gerontological Nursing, 2*, pp. 23-27, 1976.
10. R. Georgemiller and H. N. Maloney, Group Life Review and Denial of Death, *Clinical Gerontologist, 2*:4, pp. 37-49, 1984.
11. M. Hala, Reminiscence Group Therapy Project, *Journal of Gerontological Nursing, 1*:3, pp. 35-41, 1975.
12. R. Harris and S. Harris, Therapeutic Uses of Oral History Techniques in Medicine, *International Journal of Aging and Human Development, 12*:1, pp. 27-34, 1980-81.
13. R. J. Havighurst and R. Glasser, An Exploratory Study of Reminiscence, *Journal of Gerontology, 27*:2, pp. 245-253, 1972.
14. G. Hughston and S. Merriam, Reminiscence: A Nonformal Technique for Improving Cognitive Functioning in the Aged, *International Journal of Aging and Human Development, 15*:2, pp. 139-149, 1982.
15. M. Kaminsky, Pictures from the Past: The Uses of Reminiscence in Casework with the Elderly, *Journal of Gerontological Social Work, 1*:1, pp. 19-31, 1978.

16. J. Kiernat, The Use of Life Review Activity with Confused Nursing Home Residents, *American Journal of Occupational Therapy, 33*:5, pp. 306-310, 1979.
17. C. N. Lewis, The Adaptive Value of Reminiscing in Old Age, *Journal of Geriatric Psychiatry, 6*:1, pp. 117-121, 1973.
18. M. I. Lewis and R. N. Butler, Life Review Therapy: Putting Memories to Work in Individual and Group Psychotherapy, *Geriatrics, 29*:11, pp. 165-173, 1974.
19. J. Liton and S. C. Olstein, Therapeutic Aspects of Reminiscence, *Social Casework*, pp. 263-268, 1969.
20. A. W. McMahon and P. J. Rhudick, Reminiscing: Adaptational Signifiance in the Aged, *Archives of General Psychiatry, 10*, pp. 292-298, 1964.
21. S. Merriam, The Concept and Function of Reminiscence: A Review of the Research, *Gerontologist, 20*:5, pp. 604-609, 1980.
22. P. Perrotta and J. Meacham, Can a Reminiscing Intervention Alter Depression and Self-esteem?, *International Journal of Aging and Human Development, 14*:1, pp. 23-29, 1981-82.
23. A. Pincus, Reminiscence in Aging and Its Implications for Social Work Practice, *Social Work, 15*:3, pp. 47-53, 1981.
24. V. Revere and S. Tobin, Myth and Reality: The Older Person's Relationship to His Past, *International Journal of Aging and Human Development, 12*:1, pp. 15-26, 1980-81.
25. M. Romaniuk, Review: Reminiscence and the Second Half of Life, *Experimental Aging Research, 7*, pp. 315-335, 1981.
26. M. Romaniuk and J. G. Romaniuk, Looking Back: An Analysis of Reminiscence Functions and Triggers, *Experimental Aging Research, 7*, pp. 477-489, 1981.
27. M. Ryden, Nursing Intervention in Support of Reminiscence, *Journal of Gerontological Nursing, 7*:8, pp. 461-463, 1981.
28. M. H. Spero, Confronting Death and the Concept of Life Review: The Talmudic Approach, *Omega, 12*:1, pp. 37-43, 1981-82.
29. M. A. Wolf, The Meaning of Education in Late Life: An Exploration of Life Review, *Gerontology and Geriatrics Education, 5*:3, pp. 51-59, 1985.

PART V

Social, Historical and Spiritual Issues

CHAPTER 15

Responses of Parents to Sudden Death

Mary Kachoyeanos and Florence E. Selder

Traditional grief theorists suggest there is a definite and orderly process that results in resolution of grief. In contrast, clinicians caring for bereaved parents report a different perspective. For parents, grief seems to be unending. The notion that parents may be maladjusted or have an underlying disorder if they do not pass through certain grief stages may be unfounded.

Even Sigmund Freud reassessed his original theory of grief after the loss of his beloved daughter. In a letter found in Freud's personal correspondence file, he describes the never-ending grief of a parent who has lost a child. Freud wrote [1, p. 353]:

> We know that the acute grief we feel after a loss will come to an end, but that we remain inconsolable, and will never find a substitute. Everything that comes to take the place of the lost object, even if it fills it completely, nevertheless remains something different.

A review of the literature yielded numerous studies on parental responses to the sudden death of an infant [2, 3]. Few studies were reported that examined parental responses to the sudden death of older children. Much of the work examining parental responses to the death of an older child has been with parents of children with life threatening/chronic illness such as cystic fibrosis and children who died from cancer. Additionally, many of the studies of parents of bereaved infants and older children were descriptive correlational studies, using some type of physical or life adjustment tool [4-7]. These studies provided an important contribution to an understanding of parental bereavement behavior. However, no studies were found which described parents' responses in their own words.

CONCEPTUAL FRAMEWORK

Life Transition Theory (LTT) as proposed by Selder is the conceptual framework for the study [8]. Life transition theory was developed from a series of clinical studies designed to investigate people's responses to disrupting events [8-10]. Life transition theory evolved from these studies.

Life transition is a way of conceptually describing the reported experiences of persons responding to a critical life event which has disrupted their current reality. Life transition is the bridging of an existing reality with an emerging one. The task or purpose of any life transition is to incorporate the experienced or "lived" event in such a way that it has meaning for the person.

Clearly, a parent's reality is fundamentally disrupted by the unexpected death of one's child. The terminus or closure of the life transition is the point when the disrupting event no longer has primacy.

This chapter is based on research conducted for the purpose of describing responses of parents to the sudden unexpected death of a school-aged and older child. Major findings of the study are related. Not all data are reported, rather examples have been selected from the data that are representative of the findings.

MATERIALS AND METHODS

Subject Selection

A convenience sample of parents whose child died suddenly was initially recruited through a local Compassionate Friends Support Group. Parents were approached, the study explained, and informed consent was obtained. All deceased children were considered healthy prior to their deaths, none suffered from chronic or life-threatening illness.

Criteria for subject selection were: 1) at the time of death the child was school aged or older; 2) the child had been dead a minimum of six months; and 3) parents were not currently in therapy to resolve the child's death.

Research Approach and Instruments

A descriptive qualitative approach was utilized for the study. Data were collected through an indepth interview. An interview guide was developed based on a review of the literature and with consultation of experts in the field of bereavement. The interview was pretested with one parental dyad. The interview guide was then redesigned for clarity and sequencing of topics. Questions were grouped as to events around the death, parental and family responses and present circumstances. Sample questions were: Tell me how you first heard of your child's death? What was the funeral like? What do you miss about your child? What are things like now? How do men and women differ in their reactions? What things were helpful and what were not helpful? The interview was tape recorded. The average interview was one and a half hours. The interview took place in the subject's home and/or a place designated by the subject. All couple interviews were conducted in their home. Couples were interviewed at the same time. In order to assure couple responses that were independent of each other, each of the partners were interviewed by a separate interviewer and in different parts of the house.

The interviewer opened the interview with, "Tell me how you first found out about your child's death." The interview guide was used to assist the parents in the unfolding of their story. The parents conversation flowed naturally or steadily. Rarely was it necessary to use the probe questions in the interview. At the end of the interview the interviewer checked to see that all the areas in the interview guide had been addressed. Demographic data regarding the child's age at death, cause of death, time since death, and parental occupations and religious affiliation were recorded on separate data sheets.

DATA ANALYSIS PROCEDURES

The tape recorded interviews were transcribed *verbatim* and then erased. Interviews were coded. Processes and themes were identified. Transcripts were first coded independently by the investigators who subsequently convened to resolve any differences in the deviation of the codes until .99 agreement was achieved.

⸱ RESULTS

Sample Characteristics

A total of twenty-seven parents were interviewed, eleven intact couples and five mothers, two of whom were single parents. Twenty-six of the twenty-seven parents interviewed were Caucasian and within the low-middle to middle socio-economic group. Subjects' occupations

Table 3. Causes of Death

Causes
—Aspiration from a foreign substance
—Drowning
—Fall from a hill
—Fall from a porch
—Hit by train
—Car accident (drunk driver)
—Lost control of car
—Fulminating viral infection
—Boating accident
—Bicycle accident
—Industrial accident

included housewives, blue-collar workers and professionals. They represented the Catholic, Protestant and Jewish religions.

Ages of children at time of death ranged from four years, four months[1] to twenty-four years. Time since child's death ranged from two to fourteen years. Causes of death are listed in Table 3.

Accidents were the primary cause of death. Two children died within forty-eight hours after acquiring a fulminating viral infection.

FINDINGS: EVENTS AROUND THE DEATH AND FUNERAL

Being Informed

In response to "How did you first hear of your child's death?", parents whose child was killed in an automobile accident were personally informed by police who came to their home. The parents of children killed out of town were telephoned by police. The parents felt the police tried their best to be empathetic but were obviously uncomfortable in their role. An interesting finding was that fathers were asked to go to the morgue to identify the body. Mothers were discouraged from accompanying them. One mother said, "I wanted to go (with father), I thought

[1] Prior to the interview it was assumed the child was school-age; at the interview it was determined that the child was of pre-school age. Since the parent's responses were similar to other parents, the subject was included in the study.

I should but the detective said it was better I didn't." In retrospect, most parents felt they would have liked to have been together when viewing the dead child in order to support each other. As one father said, "No one should have to do that alone."

Parents who were called to the emergency room for their child described a process of depersonalization. One mother reported, "First they came out and said, 'Joan[1] is in very poor condition but we're trying everything we can do to save her.' Next the doctor said, 'I'm sorry, we did everything we could to save your *child*, but we weren't successful.' Then the nurse came out and asked, 'Have you decided which funeral home to send the *body* to?' In a very short time our beautiful daughter, Joan, became merely, a body." Parents found the depersonalization very painful and report it as still painful to recall.

Conversely, a mother related a supportive experience with emergency room personnel. "The doctor came out of the room, looked at me and said, 'I'm so sorry, there was nothing we could do to save her,' then he cried. I knew he really cared, even if he couldn't do anything."

Viewing the Body

Parents reported that seeing the body was helpful. They also responded that they encouraged their other children to do so. Seeing the body served to prevent later ungrounded fantasies as to the nature and extent of the damage to the body. For instance, parents said, "It was bad, but not as bad as I would have imagined." In contrast, a few of the parents who, either because of special circumstances or advice, did not view the body reported being haunted by fantasies of mutilation of the body. In these cases, the parents were unable to limit their fantasies. Fathers who didn't view the body reported they had failed their child as they perceived themselves lacking the courage to do the "manly act."

Parents who reported it was important to view the body sometimes did not have an open coffin for the wake. These parents wanted others to remember the child as they were prior to death.

Funeral

As a tribute to their child, parents made an effort to create a special meaning in the funeral experience. Further, parents were concerned about the effect of their child's death on their friends and classmates. There was an attempt to engage many others in the planning and the design of the funeral. Frequently, the principal of the child's school and

[1]Children's names have been changed to guarantee anonimity.

classmates participated in the ceremony. In addition, the siblings wanted others to really know their brother/sister. To achieve this, they created collages of pictures and other memorabilia that accurately portrayed their brother or sister.

Parents wrote letters to be included in the coffin. The letters conveyed all the unsaid and unshared feelings. This was also an opportunity to forgive and request forgiveness for real or imagined transgressions.

Attempts of relatives and friends to invoke the will of God in the child's death were met with anger and disbelief. A mother's comments reflected the feelings of most parents. "At first, for a long while I wondered why God hadn't stopped the guy from killing my child (killed by drunk driver). People would tell me it was God's will, I don't believe that. Because if God wants our children, why doesn't he just let them go to sleep and take them that way?"

During the period of the funeral, parents were advised to give away the child's belongings. Those who acquiesced, later expressed resentment at being urged to dismantle their child's room and discard their belongings. Parents who kept their child's belongings intact report that it is difficult if not impossible to enter the child's room for several months. Some parents stored the child's possessions. For some, it was years before they relinquished the child's things. When parents finally parted with the child's possessions it was to someone meaningful to the child. Parents were pleased when friends asked for a memento (such as a sweater) and saw the request as a tribute to their child. All parents kept something special of their child such as a frozen fish caught by the child, a pressed corsage from graduation, funeral flowers and a favorite sweatshirt.

After the Funeral

After the funeral, feelings of isolation and abandonment were commonly reported. Parents were surprised and hurt when good friends distanced themselves. They desperately wanted people to phone, to visit and to acknowledge their grief. Their friends' actions were best explained by "I don't know, I guess it's because they're afraid it might happen to them." Many old friendships were never recaptured.

A continuing need of parents is to have people talk about their child, to use the child's name. Parents yearn to hear stories about their child as they derive a great source of comfort from reminiscing. Things or acts parents found helpful and non-helpful are listed in Tables 4 and 5.

Table 4. Actions Parents Found Helpful

Actions
—Openly acknowledging the child's death
—Talking about the child
—Reminiscing about the child
—Using the child's name
—Receiving help with funeral arrangements
—Others taking the initiative to "do" for the parent
—Friends continuing to maintain active friendships
—Expressing affection, hugging the parents
—Writing notes on the anniversary of the child's death and birthday
—Writing poems and letters to their dead child
—Planting trees, creating scholarships in memory of the child
—Collages of the child's accomplishments
—Keeping some prized object of the child in close proximity, such as a locket

Table 5. Factors Parents Found Non-Helpful

Non-Helpful Actions
—Telling the parent you understand their pain
—Suggesting they'll get over the death
—Encouraging parents to dismantle the child's room
—Not engaging in conversation regarding the dead child
—Friends not visiting
—Suggesting the parent have another child
—For those parents who had other children, reminding them of their good fortune

DIFFERENCES BETWEEN MEN AND WOMEN

Parents' reports confirmed that expectations for male and female behavior are based on age-old stereotypes. Women were considered fragile and expected to cry. Men were expected to be stoic and to be strong for the mother.

In contrast, women were expected and encouraged to grieve. There seemed to be an underlying assumption that women suffer the loss of a child more than men. Invariably, concerns for the mother's welfare were directed to the father. Rarely were fathers asked how they were doing. As a consequence, the grieving process might be delayed for males. Paradoxically, women were given permission to cry, yet were expected to function as hostess to the other mourners. Mothers reported being in a daze as if on "automatic pilot" throughout the funeral. In some ways they felt disconnected with their bodies. As one mother said, "I remember hearing someone laugh and wondered who it was. Then I realized it was me. It couldn't be: mothers aren't supposed to laugh when their child dies."

Though fathers felt part of the funeral itself, mothers and fathers agreed that men were often ignored. Condolences tended to be paid more often to the mother than father. When asked why they thought this was so, several fathers said, "I suppose it's because the woman carries the baby inside of her. Somehow there is a closer tie."

A major finding of the study was the differences in how mothers and fathers wanted to express intimacy. Fathers saw intimacy as the sharing of sex and relationships. Mothers found the sexual act abhorrent, one was not supposed to enjoy oneself when your child lay in their grave. Mothers wanted to talk about the child's death, they wanted to be reinforced that they'd been a good mother. Fathers wanted to put the death behind them and move on. Parents identified this difference in their perception of intimacy as the greatest cause of marital discord. A summary of differences in male and female responses is presented in Table 6.

LIFE TRANSITION THEORY

A transition is initiated after the death of a child. The purpose of the transition is to find meaning in the event bridging the disrupted reality with one of several possible new realities. The major characteristic of the transition is uncertainty. As information decreases uncertainty, a common method to reduce uncertainty is to give and obtain information. However, in this study, there is no type or amount of initial

Table 6. Men and Women's Grief
Reactions and Responses

Reaction and Response Differences
—deference
—language
—expectation
—intimacy

information that will reduce the parents' uncertainty. Parents report being in a fog for at least one year. They report going through the motions of daily living. Some parents withdrew totally from engaging in activities. One mother quit her job so she could take time to think about her son. For another parent, it was five years before she "entered" the world again. "Each morning I'd awake and contemplate ending it all, then one day I awoke and decided either do it [commit suicide] or get on with life. I opted for life."

In order for parents to move through the transition and construct a new reality, they must become aware of the impact of the child's death on their present and future. Awareness informs the parents of the irrevocability and permanency of the disrupted reality brought about by the child's death. The process of identification of missed options enables parents to become aware of the extent and depth of their loss.

Missed options are events the parent will never experience or characteristics of the child the parent will never again be able to recapture. Characteristics of the dead child such as their humor, their laughter, and even their temper were things that parents wished they could again experience. All parents commented on never having the grandchildren of the dead child. This presented a large void in their life even if the parents had other children and grandchildren. Missing future events in the child's life such as school plays, graduation, and marriage were sources of sorrow. After reading his deceased daughter's diary, a father expressed sadness that she never experienced the joy of sex and an intimate relationship.

A second process that continued to make parents aware of the irrevocability and permanency of the child's death is reactivation. Reactivation is an awareness of thoughts, feelings, and sensations reminiscent of the loss. These thoughts are triggered by some environmental stimulus. An example of reactivation was reported by a mother whose daughter died in an automobile accident two years earlier.

> A few weeks ago my husband and I were getting out of our car in the parking lot of a shopping center. Suddenly, I heard [but did not see] brakes screeching, a loud crash, and then glass breaking. I froze. Suddenly I thought of Karen. I imagined, how horrible those last few minutes must have been for her. I started to shake violently. My husband put me back in the car and we drove to my mother's. Once there I couldn't get myself out of the car. I must have sat there for over an hour before I was myself again.

Sometimes memories evoked during reactivation are painfully nostalgic. A mother recalls such an incident.

> It was near Christmas and I was getting ready for a party and needed a wrap. I recalled that Susan (dead child) had a fur cape. I went up to the attic to retrieve it. As soon as I picked it up I saw a single strand of her long blond hair. I started to cry, buried my head in the cape. The aroma of her perfume was intermingled with the fur. I don't know how long I sat there savoring her memory, the tears coming and coming.

Parents' reports substantiate that in our society there is an implicit mandate to "be strong and get on with life." Yet parents impart not knowing how to act, not knowing if they will survive, not knowing if the pain will diminish.

For all parents there is a point in the transition when each took some self-initiated action to minimize their uncertainty. Support groups provided the parents an opportunity to normalize their feelings. Parents did this through a process of comparative testing. Knowing that other parents had experienced similar feelings and reactions, parents were able to verify their sanity. Parents were able to meet others whose child had been dead longer and had survived. This gave them hope that they, too, would survive.

Parents generally agreed that the support given by those having similar experiences was unique, and in many ways more therapeutic than that provided by either clergy, counselors or friends. As a mother who went to a support group in desperation said,

> I was disappointed in the reactions of my friends. Shortly after Jane died, I attended a luncheon given by my bridge club. I was having difficulty sleeping and eating and generally suffering from depression. Several of the members commented on my appearance. They asked if I'd had the flu. Nobody acknowledged the fact that my child had died, that I must be suffering a terrible void. I wanted to say, 'I look bad because I've lost my child. How do you expect me to look?' I felt like they were saying, 'Come on now it's time to shape up.' People at Compassion Friends knew exactly how I felt. It was a relief to know I wasn't crazy. It was so helpful to know that a parent like Sara, who'd lost her daughter three years earlier, was doing well. It gave me hope that I too would get through this terrible pain.

Another way parents minimized their pain was to presence their child. Presencing is indirectly manifesting the essence of their child which is no longer directly accessible. Methods parents used varied. Several invented stories. For a father it was "pretending James was on a fishing trip and he'd be coming home." A mother's story making took place everyday when her child was due home from school. "For months

I'd hear footsteps up the back stoop and I'd think 'Randy is coming home from school, then I'd quickly remember Randy is never coming home again." A few parents reported spending inordinate amounts of time viewing videos and home movies of the child and listening to tape recordings of the child's voice.

Another parent relayed that each time he went on a business trip he would pretend his daughter was at home and imagined her in activities she enjoyed. He said this was not denial, that he was very aware his child was dead, but his pretense helped to ease his pain. There was no specific timeframe when these events occurred or disappeared. The common factor was that many parents engaged in this behavior.

The mother in the sample whose child had been dead the longest (14 years) produced a diary describing the experiences she and others had in which the child's presence was felt. Some reports were of dreams while others were feelings of the child being in proximity. When asked, "How long has this gone on?" the mother replied, "Always, but now Rhea only appears occasionally." 'Efforts to conjure up her presence were often futile. "I'll say 'Rhea, why don't you come, I need you.'" When asked why she thought Rhea did not presence herself as often, the mother stated she believed Rhea was becoming content.

A persistent fear for all parents is that the child's existence and contributions will be forgotten by others. So parents engage in activities to keep the child's memory in the awareness of others. Examples are having the child's portrait painted from a picture and displaying it in a prominent part of the home, burying the child's ashes in the yard of their home, establishing scholarships and other memorials in the child's name.

The Future

A child's death challenges the parents' view that there is a timeless future. The child's death is a declaration that this is not true, that the future is time limited. Parents become aware that life is uncertain. Parents relay that they no longer make long-range plans. A shift occurs in their view of the passage of time. Parents convey their view of the future as "I don't think of the future. I take it one day at a time." Taking one day at a time reduces uncertainty. It is a way of structuring a reality that is predictable and a way of dealing with the ambiguity of life. Thus, parents begin to shape their realities within a collapsed timeframe.

Summary, Recommendations, Area for Further Study

Parental responses to the sudden death of a child were described. The information has value for health professionals. Professionals who are in early contact with parents whose child died suddenly need to keep the child as a person in the forefront. Using the child's name and talking about the child are necessary interventions. Parents need to be guided to services that will assist them, such as support groups. Parents can be reassured that their thoughts and feelings are normal; that they may question their sanity and that, with them, their experiences of reactivation of the loss will become less intrusive.

Professionals must gain an awareness that the death of a child is not readily resolvable and has long-lasting consequences. It is vital that mechanisms be instituted to follow-up parents whose child died suddenly in the hospital or emergency room.

The study findings reported in this chapter are based on interviews with parents who used the support of Compassionate Friends. Therefore, conclusions can only be applied to this sample. Additionally, a study comparing parents whose child died suddenly and those whose child died from a chronic life-threatening illness is suggested.

REFERENCES

1. G. Pollack, Mourning and Adaption, *The International Journal of Psychoanalysis, 42,* parts 4-5, pp. 341-361, 1961.
2. M. S. Miles, S.I.D.S.: Parents Are the Patients, *Journal of Emergency Nursing, 3*:3, pp. 29-32, 1977.
3. T. A Helmrath and E. M. Steinitz, Death of an Infant: Parental Grieving and the Failure of Social Support, *Journal of Family Practice, 6,* pp. 785-790, 1978.
4. M. S. Miles, Emotional Symptoms and Physical Health in Bereaved Parents, *Nursing Research, 34*:2, pp. 76-81, 1985.
5. Videka-Sherman, Coping with the Death of a Child: A Study Over Time, *American Journal of Ortho-Psychiatry, 54*:4, pp. 688-698, 1982.
6. M. Lauer, R. Mulhern, J. Wallskog, and B. Camitta, A Comparison Study of Parental Adaptation Following a Child's Death at Home or in a Hospital, *Pediatrics, 71*:1, pp. 107-112, January 1983.
7. I. Moore, C. Gilliss, and I. Martinson, Psychosomatic Symptoms in Parents Two Years After the Death of a Child with Cancer, *Nursing Research, 37*:2, pp. 76-81, 1988.
8. F. Selder (Schmitt), "The Structuring of a Life Transition Following a Spinal Cord Injury," unpublished doctoral dissertation, University of Illinois at the Medical Center, Chicago, Illinois, 1982.

9. K. M. Stecker, "Life Transition: Family Responses to an Adult with End-Stage Renal Disease Receiving Hemodialysis," unpublished master's thesis, University of Wisconsin-Milwaukee, Milwaukee, Wisconsin.

10. M. Van Riper, "Life Transition: Parental Responses Following the Death of an Infant with Down Syndrome," unpublished master's thesis, University of Wisconsin-Milwaukee, Milwaukee, Wisconsin.

CHAPTER 16

View of Life in Bereavement and Loss

Kjell Kallenberg

It is interesting to note the growing interest in issues and questions concerning ethics, the meaning of life, and one's view of life during the 1980s. At the same time, 20th century western society has also undergone a vast secularization [1]. In our modern society norms and values seem to be certified statements and secular values rather than divine laws and religious beliefs. One such example is that health has become an intrinsic value in itself. To be young and healthy has become more and more important. In our technocratic culture, we are taught that problems can be handled and dealt with in a rational way, perhaps with the rare exception called death, which remains an irritating human factor in our society.

What happens if our health is seriously threatened? What happens in a crisis when life suddenly and significantly changes for us? Grief can be seen as a typical example of a psychological crisis which at some time or another influences everyone's lives. When life involves pain, questions about one's view of life become more important. But if secularization has changed the individual's view of life in the post-Christian society, we may ask what type of view of life helps people in the difficult situations such as life crisis or bereavement and loss? What characterizes a view of life which provides help and comfort and offers a constructive way of dealing with trauma? The answers to these questions may be found by scanning either the contents of a view of life or by its traits and qualities (e.g., degree of integration or a combination of both). An example of a component in the content of one's view of life of significance to individuals in bereavement could be the belief in life after death. Others may find comfort in believing that there is a higher meaning in what has happened. Other examples of traits and qualities in a view of life may be its openness or closeness or its internal saliency and ego involvement. The interest in these concepts in connection with a view of life implies that it may be related to personality and it is important to identity [2].

WHAT IS A VIEW OF LIFE?

A view of life brings to mind ideological systems concerning the eternal questions relating to life and death. Various religions and philosophical traditions have attempted to provide answers to these questions. Investigations indicate that people are indirectly influenced by these ideological systems [3]. Most people would probably say that they have no special view of life, as they would associate the term to a pretentious and demanding ideological system. Still, it is obvious that people do have answers concerning existential questions. In the tradition of Robert Lane [4], it could be stated that constant patterns of beliefs and values are found among most people to the extent that these may be defined as a view of life. One's view of life is the personal way one answers questions concerning the meaning of life, what does or does not exist, and what is or is not fair in human relations. But it may also be something a person has in common with other people in the same culture which, in the language of experience or in the expression of art and drama, forms the identity of the culture.

In order to understand people's view of life, it is necessary to start at a concept broader than religion which could make it possible to investigate the interplay between values and theoretical views of man and the world.

In a more strict sense, view of life is defined as those theoretical and evaluative assumptions that make up or are of vital importance in forming an overall view of man and the world, creating a central system of values which are expressed in a basic attitude [5, 6]. It may, therefore, be proposed that there are three interrelated components involved in a view of life. The first component consists of *general theories concerning man and the world* (i.e., theories relevant to the origins of the universe, the ultimate character of reality, the difference between human beings and other living organisms and the process of death and life after death).

The second element, *the central system of valuation,* consists of central values and norms related to these theoretical ideas about reality. This type of system indicates for the individual basic rules necessary to follow for human beings to live together.

The third element of the view of life refers to an *individual's mood* as being either hopeful and trusting or full of anguish and mistrust. Basic attitudes color the individual's life which is manifested in different ways. An individual's view of life is not merely cognitive or verbal expressions which may be empty phrases on occasion. To quote Shakespeare, "mere empty words, signifying nothing." An evaluation of the individual's behavior and strategies of action must also be taken into account and the interplay between these strategies and evaluations as well. Thus, the concept of view of life springs from the assumption that personality is in some way mirrored in a person's view of life and that this personal view of life also expresses one's personality.

AN EMPIRICAL STUDY OF VIEW OF LIFE AND GRIEF PATTERNS

To design an empirical investigation of an abstract entity, such as view of life among people in general, naturally entails substantial methodological problems. In the present study nineteen individuals were investigated during a period of one year with the purpose of obtaining a description of the process of grief and the significance of the view of life. The criterion for participation in the study was the experience of a sudden and unexpected death of a close relative. Sudden and unexpected death is defined as the deceased being under sixty-five years of age at death and previously enjoying a good state of health. The individuals interviewed were between twenty-five and fifty-five years of age, born in Sweden and of Swedish parents. The study entailed ninety-four interviews with eight to ten hours devoted to each participant. Three sessions per individual were taped and transcribed. Protocols were made during the remaining sessions. A set of seventy-four questions was used as a guide for the dialogue-sessions. Some of the questions could be categorized as purely existential, others concerned previous life-experiences, circumstances before the trauma and self image. The final interview took place a few weeks after the first anniversary of death, ". . . so that we would not trigger anniversary-reactions but might learn about them if they had occurred" [7, p. 24].

The interviews were supplemented by observations and two psychological tests and a self-assessment inventory. With the help of the tests, interpretation of the interviews were validated. Initially, the process of grief was investigated. In spite of the fact that all participants in the study had undergone similar traumatic experiences, their reactions differed in significant ways. Some individuals expressed their grief strongly and over an extended period of time while others did not appear to react at all. Several individuals seemed to work through their grief in a constructive manner. From the results of this study, four different patterns of grief could be discriminated:

1. boundless grief;
2. spontaneous grief;
3. delayed grief; and
4. indifferent coping.

The first and fourth reactions to grief were the simplest to recognize. The first reaction was contradictory to the fourth. Boundless grief was judged as extremely intense and the immediate reaction judged as immensely strong. Even after several months, the persons in this category continued in what was described as a very difficult situation. For these individuals, the past was constantly present and dominating their lives. They were unable to go back to work for several months and they used significantly more drugs and alcohol as compared to the persons in the other three groups.

A quite different picture was shown in the fourth group. No one was, of course, untouched by this sudden death; however, the individuals in this group showed minimal expressions of grief in words or otherwise. The death appeared to be more or less a parenthesis in their lives, not significantly upsetting reality. "Life must go on" was a typical phrase used by the individuals in this category. It was not surprising that recovery appeared to go very well for this group. Nothing had actually changed in their ways of life.

Categories 2 and 3, spontaneous and delayed grief, are possible as a pair to discriminate from 1 and 4, boundless grief and indifferent coping. Boundless grief and indifferent coping could be characterized as involving small changes in reaction. For both spontaneous and delayed grief, the opposite was true. Both reactions were characterized by changes and progress which only differed in the first stage of bereavement. The spontaneous grief was typically described by the words "shock," "reaction" and "coping" followed by a positive orientation toward the future.

Let us now turn to the existential questions. In a crisis situation, individuals ask questions evident of a desire to create meaning and order from the circumstances which have just radically changed for them [8]. An important part of the early bereavement is to recapitulate what has happened. It is important for the individual to create a clear chronological order and structure the events relevant to the trauma. One dominating question common to most of the individuals in this study is why this should happen to them. Whether or not the individual has a religious faith, the idea that life itself should be fair and just is commonly expressed. It was common to hear, for example, that it is unfair that children should die instead of old people or that "good" people with high moral qualities should die. The subjective experience of a sudden and unexpected death of a loved one is typically a reaction that it is wrong and unfair.

The individual's view of life also differs in these four categories. What distinguishes each group were not philosophical, religious or political opinions. But rather critical issues were those relating to one's self image, view of society, the individual's social reality as a whole and the person's ability to influence his/her life. Both spontaneous and delayed grief express an attitude which may be described as trusting, while the attitude in the boundless grief and indifferent coping may be indicative of mistrust. This basic attitude, which has previously been defined here as the third component in this study's view of life, may be combined with almost any established view of life or ideology. In the spontaneous and delayed grief the self-image is more positive. The respondents in these two groups were typically active in society and believed that it was possible to change society. In constructive grief there may be a trait which could be called trust. Trust implies that these individuals, even in difficult and painful situations, show a confidence, almost a knowledge, that there is a way through the dark. The pain they experience is not judged as less for those individuals in the other groups, but they perceive themselves as able to cope with it. Life was typically viewed by the individuals in these groups as not so much a struggle but a gift.

DISCUSSION

The results of this study demonstrate that there appears to be a relationship between the process grief and the view of life for these participating individuals. This relationship may be further understood by referring to the concepts of trust and mistrust. As mentioned earlier, an individual's basic attitude is one of the essential features of one's view of life. View of life expresses varying degrees of totality, meaning and coherence within a basic attitude which is described either as one of trust or of mistrust. Trust and mistrust are established early in life. These concepts have been described by Erikson in connection to the first stage in his theory of personality development: the eight ages of man [9]. Trust or mistrust are the basic ingredients in early childhood when identity is being formed. Subsequently, the basic experience of trust or mistrust learned as a child carries over in all stages of life.

Each individual's view of life contains both trust and mistrust. Even the view of life characterized by basic trust holds reasonable parts of mistrust. But the individual judged as having obtained basic trust responds to a negative or painful experience as being temporary. For both the individuals in the spontaneous and delayed grief groups, it could be said that trust was stronger than mistrust generally. It appeared that trust was strong enough to endure the presence of mistrust. Generally speaking, trust requires the presence of mistrust to preserve a balance of realism for the individual. Unlimited trust in an individual is often judged as naive and unrealistic. On the other hand, pure mistrust in an individual leads often to depression and despair. It could be proposed that a view of life characterized by basic trust sets the stage for a confident attitude toward the future even in the face of crises and turmoil.

If a trustful view of life is characterized by the individual's capacity to balance trust and mistrust, with trust dominating generally, the opposite could be said about a view of life characterized by mistrust. However, it is important to note for the clinician that the phenomenon of mistrust is often disguised as an expression of trust. It appears that the greater the mistrust, the more obvious is the compensating character of trust expression. The compensating trust can be seen as a defense against the dominating mistrust.

In summary, the investigation presented here has attempted to provide preliminary answers as to whether there exists a relationship between a person's view of life and his/her way of coping with grief. It could be said that a view of life is a synthesis of the characteristic words and actions of an individual. This synthesis expresses, in turn, a central system of values and a basic attitude. The basic attitude can express primarily trust or mistrust. From the results of this study it was also shown that an individual's view of life rarely conforms to established ideologies in the society. It seems that individuals' views of life contain bits of ideas and ideological elements which form a very personal pattern. It was also found that the religious component did not necessarily provide a view of life characterized with basic trust. However, when view of life is characterized by basic trust, then the presence of religious components or faith reinforces its interpretative capacity. Thus, the extent to which an individual's view of life interprets difficult life events in a meaningful way is related to the resources within the personality. A person with a basic trust appears to have a greater capacity for adapting to the significant change in the life situation caused by the trauma of a sudden and unexpected death.

REFERENCES

1. R. Ingelhart, *The Silent Revolution: Changing Values and Political Styles among Western Publics,* Princeton University Press, Princeton, New Jersey, 1977.
2. D. Batson and L. Ventis, *The Religious Experience: A Social-Psychological Perspective,* Oxford University Press, New York, 1982.
3. P. Converse, The Nature of Belief Systems in Mass Public, in *Ideology and Discontent,* D. E. Apter (ed.), Free Press, New York, 1964.
4. R. Lane, *Political Ideology: Why the American Common Man Believes What He Does,* Free Press of Glencoe, New York, 1962
5. A. Jeffner, Att Studera Livsaskadningar, in *Aktuella Livsaskadningar,* del 1, Brakenhielm et al (eds.), Karlshamn, Uppsala, 1982.
6. A. Jeffner, *Livsaskadningar i Sverige,* stencil, Teologiska Institutionen, Uppsala, 1987.
7. C. M. Parkes and R. S. Weiss, *Recovery from Bereavement,* Basic Books, New York, 1983.
8. A. Antonovsky, *Health, Stress and Coping: New Perspectives on Mental and Physical Well-Being,* Jossey-Bass, San Francisco, 1979.
9. E. H. Erikson, Identity and the Life Cycle, *Psychological Issues,* Vol. 1, Norton, New York, 1959.

CHAPTER 17

The Paranoid Society: The Health Craze and the Fear of Death

Tadini Bacigalupi

When Elisabeth Kubler-Ross first published *On Death and Dying*, she outlined five stages of dying: denial, anger, bargaining, depression, and acceptance [1]. People who have been diagnosed as having a terminal illness progress through these stages over time. Not all people go through every stage, nor is the progression necessarily linear. The stages of dying, however, provide a framework to understand the progression from life to death. Americans are now living in two stages of dying—denial and bargaining.

Americans' preoccupation with health and the avoidance of death is evident in a variety of articles in newspapers and advertisements on television. Using recent issues of *The Denver Post* as a source of information [2-12], health related articles ranged from cholesterol as a massive public health threat to the relationship between cancer and electromagnetism. Included in that time period's articles were the deadly threats of boiled and decaffeinated coffee, radon, and the risk of getting up at night (I assume to go to the bathroom). It appears Americans' fear of death has gone to extremes.

Using the more generic, as opposed to the clinical, definition of paranoia, we can see numerous indicators that Americans are paranoid about death. To say Americans are becoming a nation of worrywarts [13, pp. 66-67] is not an exaggeration. It is common to see Americans out running from early morning to late at night. But why? I intend to show that people are not "running toward" health as much as they are "running from" death. In addition, other questions will be addressed. Where did this fear of death come from? Why has it resulted in a health craze? And what are the ramifications for society?

BACKGROUND

Americans are taking up a variety of health practices: exercise, eating healthy (more fiber, less cholesterol, less fat, etc.) wearing seat belts, and avoiding smoking, excessive drinking, etc. But why?

In order to understand the health fanaticism of Americans, it is important to understand the reasoning behind their actions. People do not go about changing their lives for no reason at all. People need to be motivated to change.

The answer goes back to Thomas' definition of the situation, that things believed to be true are true in their consequences [14]. People are being taught to believe certain practices will prolong life. The driving force behind changing habits is some form of motivation. One form of motivation is fear; and one of the most potent fears, for Americans, is death [15-17].

The development of this fear of death is a long historical process. Americans' attitudes are rooted in the culture of the era, but the cultural message is one that has developed over time.

Rando has suggested there are three types of societies: death accepting, death defying, and death denying [12]. The first is illustrated by primitive, nontechnological societies where death is seen as a natural part of the life cycle. Death defying societies are those where the dead attempt to take their earthly possessions and status with them to heaven, and thus defy death. Egypt is the best example of this type of society. Death denying is exemplified by those societies that "refuse to confront death" and instead see death as unnatural and "antithetical" to living. The most obvious example is the United States [19], though Aries suggests the English are even more death denying than Americans [20].

Through the Middle Ages, the cultural context of human life suggested that death was the pathway to a new existence with God [17]. Early Christian doctrine promoted the belief that humans' reward was in heaven. Belief in the afterlife, which was better, gave death the descriptor of "good." If death lost this "good" definition, then people would probably wish to avoid it.

The evidence suggests that the people of the Middle Ages were, for the most part, a death accepting society. People met death in their homes and died simply. The aged knew when death was near and prepared for it. Death was a ritual, organized and presided over by the dying. It was a public ceremony shared with parents, friends, neighbors, and children. The dying awaited death lying down on their backs with their faces turned toward heaven [15, pp. 7-12, 20]. But only functionalist societies remain stable over long periods of time; in time, attitudes and beliefs began to change.

Boyle and Morris show that even in early Christian beliefs, as evidenced in the Bible, the fear of death was present [21, pp. 43-54]. Job tells us death is the "king of terrors" (Job 18:14) and the Jews believed long years were a blessing from God (Job 18:43). Death was conceived of as a land of "thick darkness, an awful pit, or a walled city covered with dust" (Job 18:54). While the sermon from the pulpit in the Middle Ages told people that death was better than life, that death led to the resurrection and, paradoxically, triumph over death, people still feared death. This fear grew with the Black Plague in the late 1300s, during which various estimates suggest that over a quarter of the world's population died in a painful manner [21]. Few families were left untouched.

At the same time, church doctrine was changing. Death brought judgment and the weighing of souls [15, 21]. By the 15th century, church doctrine made it known that not all would make it to heaven. As the afterlife became no longer universally good nor obtainable, it is not surprising that attitudes began to change and death was viewed as something to be feared.

However, it was not just church doctrine which formed western attitudes toward death. The concept that life can be prolonged through healthy living is equally important. Roger Bacon, a Franciscan friar (1214-1294), wrote that old age is "an evil to be defeated, a progressive disease that could be counteracted," and expressed the view that life "could be prolonged by therapeutic intervention" [21 pp. 79-80]. A similar position was taken by Luigi Cornaro (1469-1565) in *Discourses on the Sober Life*. His position was that all people could live a long and productive life if they practiced a healthy regimen [21]. Descartes (1596-1650) added one more element to the model that suggested life could be prolonged through healthy living, and that was the mechanistic metaphor, "It will hardly seem strange . . . [to] think of this body as a machine created by the hand of God" [21, p. 87].

In other words, if the body is a machine, it can be repaired and maintained. This leads to a conclusion that death can be postponed or perhaps even defeated. With the developments in medicine that soon followed during the Enlightenment, it is not surprising to find physicians suggesting the goal of medicine as the "preservation of health and the extension of life" [21, p. 108].

DEATH IN AMERICA

These two European influences—church doctrine and the belief that life can and should be prolonged—have obviously had an effect on how Americans view both death and health. Authors agree that society in colonial America was basically death accepting [15, 20-22]. Death was common and normal. Death took place at home with the dying surrounded by friends and family. Coffin notes that the dying person had long before prepared for their death by setting aside a lamb and liquor for the funeral feast [22, pp. 73-75]. Some families even had the liquor put aside for the funeral at the time of a child's birth. The funeral was a time for the whole community to express their grief and renew their solidarity [21, p. 145].

The Victorian era began to bring changes in how death was accepted. Under the influence of the romantics, death became more grievous. Death wrenched man from life. The funeral became more passionate and more familial [21, p. 145]. Death was no longer a community event, but instead became a family event. Passionate sorrow and hysterical grief became the way of mourning the loss of a loved one [15, p. 67].

As the 19th century drew to a close, a new wrinkle was added to Americans' outlook on death. Aries, along with Boyle and Morris, notes that, in an effort to spare the dying the knowledge of his/her fate, death was no longer discussed. The dying were not told the seriousness of their condition. This brought about another change, the replacement of the word "Death" with euphemisms.

The beginning of the 20th century brought a variety of other changes to American society. Technology brought the automobile and, with it, a certain freedom. The United States, already a mobile society, became more mobile. Children suddenly had the freedom to cross the nation in search of better-paying jobs. One result, in terms of dying, was that children were no longer necessarily around to take care of sick or dying parents.

Contemporaneously, medicine was beginning to make great strides in its ability to save lives. With people beginning to have more faith in medicine, it was only logical that the dying patient should go to a hospital, where the best professional care was available. By the 1930s it was becoming common for the dying to be taken to the hospital [15, p. 878]. This step was not only intended to give the dying the best care, but to spare the living, those surrounding the sick, from having to cope with a dying person. This removal of the dying from the presence of the living further exacerbated the trend to remove death from life. With the establishment and growth of the nursing home, the transition from a death accepting to a death denying society was completed. No longer did the family need to deal with the person who was even potentially dying. Death had been removed from common life.

At the same time that death has been removed from the home, medical technology has advanced. Many formerly fatal diseases have been defeated or cured. Polio is no longer a problem. Many forms of cancer are treatable. Heart attack deaths (according to the American Heart Association) have been reduced from 500 to 350 thousand per year. Today, with life support, human beings can be kept alive indefinitely. The evidence is mounting, in the mind of Americans, that death can be defeated.

But the removal of death from life has consequences. People are no longer capable of dealing with death as a social and normal reality. Because it is not a common part of life, Americans have become afraid of death. Feifel has said [17, p. 4]:

> ... death no longer signals atonement and redemption as much as man's loneliness. . . . [man's] fear of death reveals less concern with judgement and more with total annihilation and loss of identity. . . . A principal consequence of our defiance of eternal time and the corollary acknowledgement of time-limited life has been a specious denial of death. . . . We have expelled death from common experience and lost the 19th century domestic technology of how to deal with a corpse.

Thus, through changes in church doctrine, technology, medical science, social conditions, and patterns of dying, Americans have reached the point where, seemingly, death can be denied as a "basic condition of life" [17, p. 5]. It is this belief, that death can be denied, that has had important ramifications for living.

ON LIVING

Another piece in the puzzle of death is that, if death is medically defeatable, then how do humans die? The answer lies not so much in how people die, but what is the cause. Obviously, people die of accidents, murder and a variety of other causes, but if we examine causes of death on death certificates, the most common cause is disease. In the past, people died of "natural" causes. Now people die of some disease, and, medical ideology assures us, disease is curable. Thus, the medical definition of why someone has died influences Americans' beliefs about death, making it seem less inevitable.

In the medical profession the concept of death is a concept of failure [1, 15, 20, 23, 24]. Doctors view death as a personal affront. This means that physicians often will do anything (heroic efforts) to prolong life, even to the point of going against a patient's stated wishes. At the same time, physicians, nutritionists, health experts, and a variety of others are working to get Americans to change their habits in order to achieve the profession's goal of prolonging life and consequently avoiding failure through death. Lost in this confusing array of prescriptions and proscriptions is the concept that death is normal, death is natural, and death is a process all humans will experience.

Several pieces of the puzzle are fitting together: 14th century changes in church doctrine, 17th century beliefs about the prolongation of life, advances in medical technology, and a medical definition of the situation that death is a failure. But whose failure? It is unlikely that it is the physician's failure, as s/he has used all the power of medical science to prolong life; therefore, it must be the patient's failure.

W. I. Thomas said that if something is believed to be true, it is true in its consequences. If physicians believe death is preventable, then they must do something about those who can prevent it. The result has been that those who die are blamed for bringing on their own death. The medical profession is engaged in a model that "blames the victim" for dying [25]. The implication is "long life could have been yours, if only you'd behaved correctly." And, while the medical profession blames the victim, the family does the same thing. The evidence is seen in the grief process, where one of the stages of grief is anger, and much of that anger is aimed at the deceased.

Therefore, in order to prevent failure, the medical community has engaged in a public campaign to place the blame for a person's death squarely on the shoulders of the deceased. ABC News, for example, has Dr. Timothy Johnson explaining how taking an aspirin every other day will help prevent heart attacks, and how important it is for women to do a monthly breast examination to prevent cancer. The American Heart Association conducts a campaign to reduce cholesterol in Americans' diet; and the American Lung Association is working to keep people from smoking. Every possible thing a human can do to prevent death is reported so that Americans will know what not to do. The lists are long. Don't:

be bald	*The Denver Post*	(3/31/90)
have five children		(3/31/90)
be even mildly overweight		(3/29/90)
live in a smoggy environment		(3/28/90)
smoke		(3/28/90)
let your children eat high cholesterol foods		(3/12/90)
skip regular exercise		(3/12/90)
use fluoride		(1/26/90)

forget your vegetables	(1/17/90)
eat high cholesterol foods	(1/17/90)
be constantly angry	(1/17/90)
live near electromagnetism (power lines)	(11/30/90)
drink drip coffee (only filtered)	(11/23/89)
drink decaffeinated coffee	(11/14/89)
get up at night	(11/14/89)
live with radon	(10/24/89)
go out in the sun	
drive without seatbelts	
etc.,	
etc.,	

This is just a sampling of the restraints that Americans are supposed to live with in order to prevent death. Other things Americans should do is eat oat bran (maybe), eat tofu, drink juice, do 20 minutes of aerobic exercise at least three times a week, reduce the amount of meat eaten, and a host of other things.

But it should not be forgotten, as Barsky has noted, that in these health practices, there is also the element of capitalism [16]. See your doctor before you start an exercise program ($), eat right ($), use the right running shoes for you ($), buy the right exercise equipment ($$), go to the health club ($$), and be sure to have the best radon detector, etc., ($$$$$$$). Industry and the medical profession are making a profit from the health consciousness of Americans, so it should not be surprising to see a continuation of the capitalistic exploitation of Americans' fear of death well into the future. As both Parsons and Marx have noted, vested interests are going to work to maintain the *status quo*.

A variety of complex factors have come together to promote Americans' health craze: changes in peoples' beliefs about death and its desirability, a philosophical belief that death can be postponed, medical successes over disease and capitalism have all combined to teach Americans to deny and fear death. In denying and fearing death, it has now become almost a duty for Americans to postpone death or prolong life. Despite what former Colorado Governor Dick Lamm said, that "Older Americans have a duty to die," the medical profession has been teaching Americans to live, and to realize they are at fault if they die.

However, in the rush to prolong life, the issue that has been forgotten is that death is normal [17, p. 12].

> Death comes not to the dead, but to the living. To deny or ignore
> it is to distort life's pattern. . . . As Paz . . . has insightfully stated,

'a civilization that denies death ends by denying life.' . . . To die—
this is the human condition; to live decently and to die well—this is
man's privilege.

But because death is seen as abnormal, everything must be done to
prevent it. Americans seem to have embraced this concept. Healthy
practices are meant, therefore, to prevent the inevitable. In this
manner, these beliefs express a form of paranoia. Unless Americans'
perceptions of death change, it can be expected that the paranoid
pursuit of health will persist into the future.

REFERENCES

1. E. Kubler-Ross, *On Death and Dying*, Macmillan, New York, 1969.
2. *Denver Post*, 1989 Advertisement for Radtrack Quick-Screen Radon
   Detector, p. 11A, 10/24/89.
3. *Denver Post*, New Heart Risks: Getting Up at Night, Decaffeinated Coffee,
   p. 2A, 11/14/89.
4. *Denver Post*, Study Clears Filtered Coffee, 11/23/89.
5. *Denver Post*, Study Links Cancer in Humans, Electromagnetism, p. 2A,
   11/30/89.
6. A. Landers, Lets Clear the Air on Health Matters, *Denver Post*, p. 3C,
   1/17/90.
7. *Denver Post*, Researchers Tie Fluoride to Bone Cancer in Male Rats, p. 4A,
   1/26/90.
8. K. Duggan, Museum's Fitness Fair Shapes Young Minds, *Denver Post*,
   p. 3B, 3/12/90.
9. *Denver Post*, Soybeans May Deter Tumors in Breasts, p. 6A, 3/28/90.
10. *Denver Post*, Mice Research Suggests Smog Can Hasten Cancer, p. 2A,
    3/28/90.
11. *Denver Post*, Overweight Women Increase Risk of Heart Disease, p. 2A,
    3/29/90.
12. *Denver Post*, Bald Men at Risk for Heart Woes, 2/31/90.
13. D. Brand, A Nation of Healthy Worrywarts?, *Time Magazine*, pp. 66-67,
    July 25, 1988.
14. W. I. Thomas, Definition of the Situation, in *Sociological Theory: A Book of
    Readings*, (5th Edition), L. Coser and B. Rosenberg (eds.), Waveland Press,
    Prospect Heights, Illinois, pp. 189-191, 1989 [1922].
15. P. Aries, *Western Attitudes toward Death: From the Middle Ages to the
    Present*, Johns Hopkins University Press, Baltimore, 1974.
16. A. J. Barsky, *Our Troubled Quest for Wellness*, Little Brown, Boston, 1988.
17. H. Feifel, The Meaning of Death in American Society, in *Death Education:
    Preparation for Living*, B. R. Green and D. P. Irish (eds.), Schenkman,
    Cambridge, Massachusetts, 1971.
18. T. A. Rando, *Grief, Dying, and Death: Clinical Interventions for Caregivers*,
    Research Press Company, Champaign, Illinois, 1984.

19. E. Becker, *Denial of Death*, Free Press, New York, 1973.
20. P. Aries, *The Hour of Our Death*, Vintage Press, New York, 1981.
21. J. M. Boyle and J. E. Morris, *The Mirror of Time: Images of Aging and Dying*, Greenwood Press, New York, 1987.
22. M. Coffin, *Death in Early America*, Thomas Nelson Inc., Nashville, 1976.
23. R. H. Coombs and P. S. Powers, Socialization for Death: The Physician's Role, in *Toward a Sociology of Death and Dying*, L. H. Lofland (ed.), Sage, Beverly Hills, 1976.
24. M. L. Kothari and L. A. Mehta, *Death: A New Perspective on the Phenomena of Disease and Dying*, Marion Boyars, New York, 1986.
25. W. Ryan, *Blaming the Victim*, Vintage Press, New York, 1974.

CHAPTER 18

Implications of Societal Change on the Role of the Funeral Director and Clergy

Vernon F. Gunckel

PARAMETERS

The basis for this chapter is centered around personal experience and observations within the context of a relationship between the church and the funeral industry over the past eleven years. Data that have been gathered reflect a specific geographical area of Canada, primarily Toronto, Ontario, and are limited in their perspective according to peculiar demographics and identity. It is recognized that there are many variables operational in attempting to identify these data as being representative for the purpose of drawing conclusions. While a certain amount of data gathered may not be consistent due to a number of factors with other findings, there are some implications, seeming to confirm information received from several studies in recent years, that may be more generally applied.

Variables include a recognition of certain distinct differences between Canadian and American societies. While there are a great number of shared aspects of the two societies, there are also marked differences in identity.

Canadians tend to be more conservative and traditional in their approach to life experience and less likely to take risks than their American counterparts. The majority of Canadians who profess religious belief are to be found within the stream of the so-called "mainline tradition."

The Canadian experience is also being identified with the concept of multi-culturalism as a central part of the country's mosaic.

Much of the material shared is viewed from the urban point of view and may not necessarily reflect what is to be found in other settings throughout North America.

The central purpose of this chapter is to share information from one point of view and to stimulate an exchange of knowledge so caregivers can better meet the needs of those to be served. It is not meant to offer a prescription for behavior or to dictate a dogma for procedures in approaching those who grieve. It is understood that various theological perspectives will condition some of the ideas and concepts expressed within a framework of personal and religious doctrinal positions.

CHANGES IN SOCIETY IDENTIFIED

Funeral directors and clergy have a tendency to speak of "community" in terms of a specific geographical location and conceive of it as an identifiable entity. In recent years the concept of "community" has taken on a broader and, at the same time, narrower definition.

Many smaller communities within an urban setting and with past historic identity have become incorporated within a larger geographical region. With the increase of population the boundaries of these former communities have vanished, thus bringing about a merger of previous villages and townships.

The expansion of the high-rise condominium life-style has led to greater anonymity. People today are also more mobile. Gone are the days when the neighbor next door lived there for thirty or forty years. This was a neighborhood where families saw their children grow up and get married; they shared in each other's joys, anxieties and dreams. On one given day I met a family that had lived in the same house for thirty-eight years. Later that same day I met a young couple who had moved seven times in the last three years.

The concept of a home as a place where one would raise a family has now become focused as an item of investment and a commodity, thus influencing an attitude about the purpose of a "house" as opposed to a "home" in the traditional sense.

An individual tends to identify with a number of "communities." It may be that a person's community is centered around one's ethnic background and activity, an interest group, a professional organization or institution or a combination of these. The concept of "family" has been radically altered. As with the idea of community, funeral directors and clergy tend to use the term "family" as they had in the past. Part of this comes from not knowing what other term or terms to use in referring to those whom they serve.

How one lives life may be centered around a particular lifestyle. Gay couples are asking for recognition as family, especially those who have adopted children. There is an increase in single-parent families. In the past the emphasis was couple-oriented in traditional marital settings. Many families are not close due to geographical as well as interest differences. There has been a reexamination of "values."

Younger people today appear to be less prone to organized institutional religion. This does not necessarily mean that they have denied the aspects of the spiritual, but desire to express their beliefs in other contexts. What may have been identified as "traditional ways" of doing things has given way to the "less traditional." The influence of these factors, among others, are being reflected in the funeral practices and rituals of today.

My experience with the funeral home where I am affiliated, has been that there is an increase in the number of people who come to us with no specific religious identification. Only when asked to give such identification, will individuals feel it necessary to supply one for the purpose of finding a clergy to conduct the service and for that reason only. The funeral director encourages this practice, in part, because of the perceived limitation of alternatives available.

There are three chapels in the organization where I work. One serves a specific ethnic community while the other two serve a broader diverse population. Data gathered from these chapels over a twelve-month period have confirmed the effect that societal change is having relating to individual option selection.

Of a total of 1,417 "calls," the following is noted:

Eight percent opted for immediate disposition. Most of these had no period for visitation or a service. This figure seems to be increasing. In the last year, a funeral firm in Toronto has presented itself as a specialized service in offering immediate disposal at a modest price. It is my opinion that we will see an increase in this type of service.

Thirty-seven percent had chosen cremation rather than burial or entombment.

Twenty-seven percent had the funeral in a church. The chapel that serves the ethnic community accounted for the highest number of church services. Of the 27 percent, 22 percent were held in that chapel. Of the 27 percent who had services in a church, 20 percent were either Roman Catholic or Greek Orthodox.

Seventy percent had the funeral in the funeral home chapel.

Three percent held services elsewhere—in the home, graveside, at the cottage, etc. Of this percentage, a few had asked for a time of visitation but had no service.

Visitation time, if held at all, could be limited to one day, one evening, or one hour before the funeral. In other days, we would see two or three days for visitation, but this seems to be less practiced today. The time for visiting may be determined according to the specific geographical region with which one identifies. For example, Ontario and eastern Canada are seen as more traditional for set visitation times whereas Western Canada, visitation would be held primarily on the day of the funeral with little or no visiting prior.

Other recognized trends can be seen in specific requests made by individuals. Young people tend to opt for a closed casket. With a greater mix of faiths and inter-marriage, individuals seek a more inter-denominational approach to the funeral recognizing the needs and individual differences. More "complete" services are held in the funeral chapel with people no longer going to the cemetery.

These changes in the societal milieu in which we live today have had a major impact on the role of the funeral home and funeral director as well as the church and clergy.

HOW THESE CHANGES IMPACT ON
THE ROLE OF THE FUNERAL HOME
AND FUNERAL DIRECTOR

The funeral industry in North America is becoming a major corporate business. In the United States, as well as in Canada, many family owned and operated funeral homes have been sold to large corporate conglomerates. These big businesses may have: 1) assets in the millions of dollars, 2) employees in the thousands, 3) additional owner-ship, and 4) where permitted by law, monument companies, cemeteries, florists, and related businesses.

There has been an increased emphasis on "Pre-Need" arrangements which encourage people to preplan, and often prepay, funerals. A number of funeral homes in Toronto have recently opened Centres for Pre-Need Planning.

Many funeral homes are becoming involved in "Post Funeral Care" or "Follow-up" which consists of everything from the sending of a card or letter to the bereaved shortly after a service, a personal phone call, inviting the bereaved to attend a seminar or workshop, sending a quarterly newsletter, building a resource center within the funeral home for reference materials, offering educational programs in the "community" for both professionals in the field of bereavement work and the general public, and establishing self-help groups and referral programs.

Societal change has expanded the role expectations of the funeral director. More personal involvement is asked for. This does not mean that nothing was done in the past. The needs of those who have grieved had been met in a number of ways through the attention and care given by the funeral director.

However, in recent years there has been a change in the dimension and scope as to what is expected of the funeral director today. Research from the Clarke Institute of Psychiatry in Toronto has indicated a dramatic change in where people will go for help in meeting their grief needs. When asked where they would turn, the funeral director placed high at the top of the list, well above clergy. While funeral directors are not being asked to become "grief counselors," more demands are being placed upon them in relation to assisting individuals with the aspect of grief and grief recovery, thus necessitating a more thorough knowledge of the grief process. For a number of funeral directors, this is causing some concern and feelings of uneasiness. A funeral director recently commented to me, "I am being asked to address issues I personally feel I am not prepared to meet." Funeral directors are becoming more personally involved with those whom they serve and sharpening of their interpersonal communication skills becomes necessary.

A study funded by the National Research and Information Centre in Evanston, Illinois, an organization affiliated with the funeral industry, concerned itself with the implications of those who help the bereaved [1]. Several implications were drawn in relation to how the funeral director conducts himself/herself during the bereavement ritual.

In dealing with the bereaved in the early days after the death, the study pointed out that the funeral director can best help the bereaved by communicating to them by word and action his/her total concern for them and their sorrow and needs.

> Realize that you may be one of the few people who will have the opportunity to deal with the whole family and the support system together. While you should recognize individual differences, the family and support system themselves form a system and should be responded to as such [2, p. 196].

The bereaved surveyed in the Evanston Study had indicated pleasure when they felt the funeral director was unhurried and that this service was his/her primary activity of the day. On the other hand, the study pointed out that various bereaved expressed disappointment for those occasions when the funeral director seemed preoccupied or rushed or seemingly going through routine during the preliminary discussions and arrangements.

Therese Rando cautions funeral directors that "respect must be shown at all times for the deceased and for their survivors" [2, p. 197]. She goes on to say, "While you may have buried numbers of mothers before, it is a first-time occurrence for the mother's survivors and sensitivity about this must be maintained at all times" [2, p. 197].

The funeral director is being asked to take note of his/her nonverbal as well as verbal communication skills which includes improving one's listening ability. In meeting these needs, some funeral homes have implemented an ongoing program of professional staff development within the organization where staff can learn and practice these skills. The funeral home and funeral director are also being asked to provide viable alternatives to traditional practice. There are those mourners who feel that their individuality has not been acknowledged nor their personal needs met. Expectations as to what the funeral director "thinks is best" for them may influence any decision-making on their part.

In conversations with a number of people, the most often received comments revolve around the structure of the funeral service itself. Many have said that they were somewhat uncomfortable when making arrangements and given no opportunity to depart from the "norm" as the funeral director saw things.

It has been suggested that rather than assuming what the mourners need or want, the funeral director might approach individuals with the question, "What do you want this service to mean to you"? Traditional practice may not be appropriate in all situations.

This is not to say that tradition is bad. Some people need tradition. It is for many, an old friend you can count on and lean on. Some traditional things can help a great deal. However, within reason, perhaps there is a need to restructure an approach which includes alternatives.

The Evanston Study found that what families desired most was that "the wishes of the bereaved for the service should be observed wherever possible." Doug Manning said that the primary question every funeral director and clergy must ask of themselves is, "Do we help people get over their grief?" In relation to changes, he goes on to say [3, pp. 25, 32],

> Change simply for change sake isn't acceptable. Changes should be approached with caution. We must be sure that our efforts at improving are not, in reality, efforts to deny the fact of death. But we must be open to other ways of doing things.

As indicated earlier in this chapter, a number of funeral homes have become involved in bereavement support programs of various types.

As a funeral director, an effective approach has been to offer the basic message, "We are here to offer what resources you may require if you need them." In the development of a Bereavement Support Program where I have been affiliated, the funeral home staff was involved in the beginning with the organization and planning of the program. Frequent meetings are held to improve the approach where changes are identified.

At the time funeral arrangements are discussed, each person with whom arrangements are being made receives a *portfolio*, or what we call a "survival kit," containing the funeral contract, a brochure outlining the services provided, and a booklet entitled, "Where Do I Go From Here?" identifying pension plans, insurance, legal matters, community services, and bereavement support help programs.

Within a month following the funeral, unless a person requests otherwise, each person who had made the arrangements will receive a personal phone call ascertaining as to how they are doing and inquiring how we can be of any further help to them.

The response received from this post-funeral follow-up has been most affirmative and readily accepted by most as a genuine expression of caring. Forty-seven percent of those called went beyond the pleasantries of simply saying, "Thank you for calling." Of the 47 percent:

> Twenty percent talked for a time exceeding 20 minutes. They have talked about their feelings, family situations they need help resolving, suggestions for resources for meeting specific needs, just to name a few.
>
> Ten percent had specific questions about a number of concerns and were referred to various sources which could respond to those concerns.
>
> Ten percent asked for a personal visit. Of this number, 2 percent required an additional visit from a staff member at the funeral home.
>
> Seven percent asked for further bereavement support materials to be sent.

These services are not intended to take away from the ministry of the clergy. They are offered as supplemental to their efforts. Clergy are involved in a number of ways in the program.

The church and funeral home have enjoyed a close relationship over the years and should attempt to continue a close liaison of cooperative effort.

HOW THESE CHANGES IMPACT ON THE ROLE
OF THE CHURCH AND CLERGY

It has become increasingly difficult to define the role of "The Church" in North America due to the diversity of theological perspectives. In recent years we have witnessed a resurgence of a more conservative and evangelical approach to religious faith. This has been noted more in the United States than in Canada where the mainline traditional churches contain the larger number of adherents.

Nevertheless, in the midst of this individuality and diversity in a religious approach to death and dying, several consistent themes seem to emerge.

A number of churches have attempted to address the needs of those who mourn in various ways. Seminars, workshops and study groups on death and dying have been offered. Lay visitation programs have not only assisted clergy with their busy schedules but have added a greater dimension to the concept of ministry of the laity.

Churches have not only made facilities available but have also sponsored self-help groups for widows and widowers. THEOS (They Help Each Other Spiritually) is a nondenominational organization founded in Pittsburgh in 1962. The organization has expanded to include chapters throughout the United States and Canada.

The church has a unique opportunity to meet the needs of mourners in the very context of the hope it offers. There is however, considerable variance as to how the effectiveness of the clergy is perceived in relation to meeting the needs of those who grieve.

I conducted an independent survey to identify how people felt about the role of clergy in meeting their needs at the time of their loss. Data were collected from 1,350 individuals. Of this number, 1,116 responded. While the survey has its limitations, it pointed out some important implications as to how people in the Toronto area viewed the caregiver role of clergy.

Of those who had returned the survey:

Sixty-eight percent indicated that they had not received a phone call or a prefuneral visit from clergy and that for many who were not affiliated with a church, met clergy for the first time a few minutes before the service.

Two percent said they had been extremely satisfied with the funeral service conducted by the clergy.

Five percent said they were very satisfied.

Sixty-two percent said they were satisfied.

Eighteen percent indicated that they were somewhat dissatisfied.

Ten percent indicated that they were very dissatisfied.

Three percent gave no response.

Eighty-two percent indicated that they did not receive a phone call, follow-up letter, visit or any contact with the clergy or member of the church following the funeral service.

Recognizing the limitations of the survey and its inadequacy as a proper research document, it nevertheless points out some serious concerns. Under comments, many had written about their experience and offered suggestions for improvement. Some had voiced their belief that clergy should recognize the importance of the funeral service as a means of facilitating grief-work. There were those who responded by saying that on occasion some clergy had assumed an almost flippant attitude toward the funeral and treated it as a matter of routine. Individuals expressed their feeling that the funeral should address the immediate needs in trying to understand, accept, and cope with their grief.

A large number of respondents indicated a greater desire to personalize the service. They believed that the service should be more than offering prayers and reading a few selections of scripture. While they may accept the religious aspects of the service, a significant proportion of the bereaved indicated that they would appreciate both the name of the deceased to be mentioned, and when mentioned to be correct, and some life experiences recalled.

Another implication for the clergy suggested by the survey was to involve the bereaved in developing plans for the service. Many pointed out that they were not trying to tell the clergy how they were to conduct the service, but expressed appreciation for those who had contacted them for any favorite poem, scripture or materials they might desire to be included in the service.

The hurt of the bereaved was most striking concerning visitation. Numerous times respondents expressed their feelings. "The minister never came." "There wasn't so much as a phone call. I understand that due to a busy schedule the minister couldn't come by but surely he could have at least called." "The night my husband died, the minister called and asked if I wanted him to come by. I wish he had just done it." "He promised he would call, but he never did." "The priest never talked to me before the service or after."

The implication from the survey for the clergy is clear: visit with the family before the funeral and with the bereaved in the weeks and months following the funeral. Assisting in the crisis of death is one of the most important ministries that clergy are called upon to perform. If any one message stood out in this survey, it was the importance of ministering to the bereaved as they adjust to their sorrow and grief.

Based on the comments from a number of respondents, the second strongest suggestion regarded what they had referred to as the clergy's inability to deal with grief. It appears that a grasp of grief psychology is lacking among many clergy. Several responded by saying that clergy appeared ill at ease and unsure of themselves in dealing with grief—especially in complex grief situations.

In order to fill what appears to be a gap in this area of ministry, several funeral homes in the Toronto area have presented clergy seminars in which speakers and workshops have been conducted. Toronto is not alone in this effort. Many other cities in North America have done likewise.

Independent organizations and consultants have offered special programs for clergy outside the jurisdiction of the church and the funeral home.

In looking at the curriculum of a number of theological schools on the continent, this aspect of ministry remains to be developed in greater depth than simply spending a short time within a course on Pastoral Care. It is not receiving the attention it deserves and requires.

There were a number of positive comments that were made about those clergy who came to visit and expressed in genuine ways their caring.

Respondents referred to clergy warmth, friendliness and words of comfort and support at the time of visitation and during the service. "The minister not only came by the evening before the service, but spent a good part of the day with us before and after the funeral." "The priest has been by several times as well as members of the parish and I'm not even a member of that church." "The thoughtfulness expressed by the minister during the service will always be appreciated. She made us feel better."

It should be recognized that none of the implications should be construed to imply a general negative evaluation of the clergy's efforts. The implications are simply suggestions of ways the clergy might be a greater benefit in the funeral ministry. While some implications are based on comments made by only a few respondents, they are worthy of consideration by the clergy in their efforts to provide even more effective service to the bereaved.

The funeral director and clergy have a significant role to play in meeting the needs of those who mourn. As caregivers we must constantly ask ourselves if our efforts are truly meeting the grief needs of those whom we serve.

REFERENCES

1. R. A. Kalish and H. Goldberg, Community Attitudes toward Directors, *Omega, 10*:4, 1979-80.
2. T. A. Rando, *Grief, Dying and Death: Clinical Interventions for Caregivers,* Research Press Company, Champaign, Illinois, 1984.
3. D. Manning, *Comforting Those Who Grieve: A Guide for Helping Others,* Harper and Row, San Francisco, 1987.

CHAPTER 19

Spiritual Care in Hospice*

Dorothy Ley

> Questions of value-belief lie at the heart of the human experience
> and existence, of life and death. . . . Our contemporary Utopian
> movements are truculently secular and scientific. There was a time
> when angels walked the earth; now we doubt that they are even in
> heaven.
>
> *Herman Feifel* (1986) [1]

The following is an overview of spiritual care—in particular
spirituality and spiritual care in hospice. I am a physician—one of
"those doctors." My perception of care and perception of the spirituality
in care is probably somewhat different from that of the generations
that I've taught and the generations that lie ahead. One's concept of
spirituality is both intimate and personal—and so it should be, no
matter one's age. We are spiritual beings deep within ourselves.

SPIRITUAL CARE IN HOSPICE

There are those who might think this an unnecessary subject for
discussion; after all, spiritual care runs through hospice care like a
thread. It is one of the pillars of hospice. Or is it? Are we assuming that
after the narcotics and the nursing, after the counseling and the initia-
tion of bereavement follow-up, after the service on the hospice floor,
spiritual care just falls neatly into place, particularly if the padre has
been involved in the final days or hours of care and has had a chance to
talk to the family and their friends. And so we go on our way to the next

*Presented in part at the Seventh International Conference on Death and Dying,
London, Ontario, 1989.

dying person. However, ninety-four percent of American hospice programs failed to demonstrate adequate spiritual care when surveyed. Only 5 percent of Canadian Hospice programs have a chaplain as part of the team.

Why? What is it about hospice that we have failed to recognize? What is it that we do not do, or that we do?

To understand the nature of spiritual care and the role of spirituality in hospice care, we have to go back a long way—to the meaning of spirituality and the roots of hospice. What is spirituality? The dictionary defines "spiritual" as "that which concerns the spirit or higher or moral qualities, especially as regarded in a religious aspect." But one must make a distinction between religion and spirituality. We do not always do that. Religion could be defined as an organized set of practices that surround a traditionally defined belief in the existence of a God or divine, superhuman, ruling power. These practices are set down in sacred writings or declared by authoritative teachers. There are other definitions. Religion is, if you like, a set of tools that one uses to express or practice one's beliefs.

Spirituality, on the other hand, subsumes religion. It may be (and hopefully is) a part of religious belief or practice, but religion may or may not be part of one's spirituality. Sometimes we forget that, particularly those with strong religious ties. Spirituality is our relationship with the infinite and with our fellow man. It has been said that it integrates our identities. It is the essence of self. It is the I. It is the God within each of us, the part that can commune with the transcendent. Our spirituality is what we seek when we search for meaning in our lives. It underlies our capacity to forgive, to create, to love, and to accept love. It frequently is intensified by approaching death.

Both Christian religion and spiritual care have been at the heart of hospice from its beginnings in the 4th century A.D., when Fabiola established a Christian hospice for pilgrims from African pagan Rome. The tradition of the knights hospitaller was based on the injunction of Christ in the 25th Chapter of the Gospel according to Saint Matthew, "Inasmuch as you have done it unto the least of these my brethren, you have done it unto me." The medieval hospices, whether the great fortress-hospital at Rhodes, the elegant hospice of Beaune, or the myriad of small hospices associated with monasteries all over Europe—were dedicated to the care of the sick and the dying—and the Christian burial of the dead. Whether the traveller was a knight on the journey to Jerusalem, or a poor beggar on the journey of life, the ancient hospice was a way station, a resting place, a place of care and concern for both the body and the spirit.

But the world changed. Society changed. With the waning of monastic influence and changing social patterns, the number of hospices, in the old sense, decreased. A different pattern of care developed—the hospital. Gradually, a society developed that increasingly valued order, efficiency, and social discipline and ultimately came to regard a human being as an economic unit. Hospitals increasingly became the repository of those who were unable to contribute to an industrialized society and a place to repair its damaged human tools—our modern hospitals.

At the same time a change in attitude toward death was taking place. From an event in medieval times accepted as the completion of life to be shared with family and friends, it came to be seen as a violent disruption of living, calling forth grief, a profound sense of loss and intense fear.

In the 17th century, in the midst of these societal changes, Descartes enunciated the dualism of mind and body. The Church assumed responsibility for a man's mind (and soul) and science (or medicine) for his body. It made it relatively easy for the emerging science of medicine to obtain cadavers, for example, because they did not have to be concerned about the soul. It was the responsibility of the Church.

This philosophy has had a profound and lasting effect on the practice of medicine and ultimately on both society's and medicine's attitude toward death and dying. We today are still caught in the dichotomy that Descartes enunciated so long ago, the separation of mind and body. Scientific medicine became increasingly intrusive in the process of dying, so much so that Ivan Illich coined the phrase, "the medicalization of death," to describe a society in which death had become faceless, secularized, institutionalized and robbed of its humanity [2]. Aries subsequently wrote that the hospital is the only place where death can hide [3].

The scientific explosion of the 20th century combined with rapid urbanization to isolate people from normal birth and death. The locus of care shifted from the community to "high tech" institutions. The role of the physician changed from a family friend and confidant to that of a distant, authoritative, scientific figure. The new technology and the increased availability of medical care as a result of universal or private health care insurance plans justified the public's belief that health was a right and fostered the illusion of medical infallibility and the indefinite deferment of death.

We became a death-denying society cared for by health professionals who saw the maintenance of life and not the quality of that life, as a measure of competence and turned away from death as a measure of failure. The stage was set for the modern hospice movement. Hospice, in the 20th century, began as a revolt against medical attitudes and practice and rigid institutionalized bureaucracy that reduced dying people to the state of a disease in a bed.

The social evolution of the 1960s rejected establishment power, including medical power, and questioned the validity of the Cartesian philosophy of the separation of the mind and the body. Cicely Saunders, in Great Britain, developed the hospice as an alternative form of holistic care for people dying difficult deaths with cancer [4]. Kubler-Ross, in America, conceptualized a series of stages in coming to terms with dying and fostered dying at home surrounded by family and friends. It was a return, philosophically at least, to the medieval view of dying.

There is a strong spiritual core to the philosophy of hospice as declared by both these women. St. Christopher's Hospice is a declared medical and Christian community, uniting modern pain and symptom control, the social sciences, and the psychiatric approach to the management of loss and bereavement with an avowed Christian commitment to care. Cicely Saunders herself is a devout Christian espousing the concept of the wounded healer, the victory that is won through pain and suffering and the paradoxical power of helplessness. Kubler-Ross eloquently articulated the need for disposing once and for all with the Cartesian separation of mind and body and for a holistic consideration of the needs of dying people, including the need to help them find meaning in their living and in their dying. Spirituality was and is a component of modern hospice care.

No discussion of spiritual care in hospice would be complete without a consideration of the concept of total pain and the meaning of suffering. Total pain is made up of different components: physical, social, and spiritual. Pain involves the whole individual. To deal with total pain one first has to care for the body. We have a growing expertise in relieving physical pain, in managing symptoms so we can maintain not only the activity of the individual, but a degree of independence, their self-esteem, and something of a normal life within the framework of their dying.

If hospice is to care for the person, for the whole person, then the family and the community must be included, because all are part of a family. In modern society the family unit may differ from the so-called "nuclear family"—but it exists nonetheless. One of the fundamental principles of hospice is that the unit of care is the person who is dying and their "family." "No man is an island," said John Donne. We cannot live apart from our relationships with other human beings. An essential part of hospice care, of spiritual care, is to recognize the community, and help them to come to terms with their own fears. Then they must be helped to mobilize their strengths and resources so they can help the person who is dying.

It may be necessary to re-establish communication. There is a tendency on the part of the people who are dying and their families, friends and caregivers, to withdraw from each other. When I was a child we used to play a game with a string with a button on the end that we swung around. I sometimes think of family, friends, community, and hospice as being like that game. Each gets out on the end of their own string and as long as they don't touch each other they can keep going. If they touch each other the strings get tangled up. As hospice caregivers we have to get the buttons off the ends of the strings without getting all tangled up. We have to re-establish communication. We have to help in the process of reconciliation. In many families there is a lot of reconciliation to be done. Every family has some. When we are about to go on a journey, we make our farewells and tie up loose ends, sometimes successfully and sometimes not. Death is "a journey into a new country." The goal of hospice is to facilitate reconciliation and help the dying to make their farewells. "It isn't a salvage operation," Saunders says, "it is an opportunity for creativity" [4, p. 29].

When we care for a person who is dying we must find out who they are. Who is that person? What is their essential being? There is a tendency in modern society to think of ourselves in terms of what we do. We consider a person to be manifested in their work, their interests, their accomplishments, but a person is more than that. Who are we deep inside ourselves? What are our inner concerns, our values? How can we make sense of it all at the end? How can we find meaning in our living and in our dying. That surely is the spiritual dimension of a person. For some, their religious values and their practices provide deep support and allow them to come to terms with their lives. For them, the chaplain in a program is an absolutely essential part of the team. Others may have no relationship to a religion, or may have a sense of guilt, or unease, or a feeling that they were never able to measure up to the expectations of their family, their church or their God. The sermons, the sacraments, and the services don't reach them. As hospice caregivers, we must reach them, whether we wear our collar backwards, wear a white coat or a nurse's cap, or a volunteer's smock, or push a broom as a housekeeper. Because death is a spiritual event it generates a desire to identify what is valuable and true in one's life. We want to tidy up the ends, to put first things first. The inability to do so in a person's life may generate a desolate feeling of meaninglessness.

To me this is the essence of spiritual pain, to feel that one is meaningless, or that one's life has been meaningless. In Victor Frankl's book,

Man's Search for Meaning [5], he writes that if there is no way out of suffering then we have a responsibility for the attitude in which we suffer. In *Why do Bad Things Happen to Good People?* [6], Kushner makes much the same point, that the pain is the reason and out of the pain and suffering comes the understanding, comes the answer. Kushner also reminds us (as Job learned) that God does not ask us to do things that He does not give us the strength to do.

Frankl also reminds us that no one can tell another person what the meaning of his life should be. Sometimes we in hospice care tend to sermonize about death and dying, but we do not have the right to tell dying people about the meaning of their life. The key is to give them the opportunity and the time to work through and solve their own problems—to find their own meaning. We may need to be no more than a presence—to be there. There may not be any answers. The dying ask only that we watch with them. There is a strange analogy between Gethsemane and hospice. Christ was asking for some meaning in what he had to do. He was asking that it not happen, but if it did, He would be able to endure the pain and the suffering that He knew lay ahead. How often our patients say to us, "Watch with me. I know I'm dying and I don't want to die and I don't want to be in pain, but if you help me, then I can do it." We should remember what Christ said to the disciplines, "Could you not watch with me one hour?" How often we are asked "Watch with me." And the bereaved also—"Watch with me," they say, "help me endure the pain, be there." You cannot die for them, you cannot give them a good death. You can walk with them, but you can never walk in a dying person's shoes, it is their death. All we can do is walk beside them. Life is not fair, it is not just, but we must help them find a way to acceptance and peace. We may learn about courage, about endurance and about laughter. Spiritually is not all "gloom and doom" and unhappiness. It is also laughter. We must share their pain and their suffering, but we also have to recognize and share their humor.

The concept of the wounded healer is so important in hospice care. We understand because we, too, are wounded; because we, too, have pain. We understand because we are and because we have come to accept our own mortality. We must dig down deep inside ourselves and integrate the scattered parts of ourselves to be able to respond with any degree of adequacy to a dying person's needs.

How do we help others? We caregivers are so diverse. We come from different backgrounds, different beliefs, from different religions or no religion at all, and we are not dying. It is said that no one can imagine their own death. This means that when we are caring for dying people we cannot really imagine what they are going through, except that we can feel suffering, we can feel pain, we can feel loss. What can we do? We can give them freedom and space by controlling their pain. We can listen. We may not have answers, but we can listen. We can do what is called "active listening"—listening in such a way as to help them find their own answers. And the gift of listening belongs to everyone on the team.

What is suffering? There are many definitions. Cassel writes eloquently about it, and has focused new attention on the interrelationship of pain and suffering. We suffer when we perceive an impending threat to our personality, to our personhood. Suffering and helping people deal with their suffering is part of spiritual care. Part of the recognition of suffering as distinct from pain is overcoming that dichotomy between mind and body [7].

There are a number of issues that affect spiritual care in modern society. There are global reasons for the current awareness for the need for spiritual care. Lifton presents some interesting and challenging material in his book, *The Broken Connection* [8]. Our sense of immortality depends on the link between life and death. In modern society our concept of that link is so often destroyed. An obvious cause of such destruction is nuclear war. We think of our own immortality in terms of the world we leave behind. If there is not going to be any world, then what do we do about our immortality? Our world has been struck by a series of natural disasters, where hundreds of thousands of people have been killed in the last few years. Chernobyl had an international impact because suddenly as a world we were faced with insidious death over which we had no control. We could not see it, and we could not anticipate it. The death of the seven astronauts on television was seen by millions of people and shook our faith in science and our sense of control. There is an increased impetus in our modern world to question the meaning of our lives. It is appropriate at this time to contemplate spirituality and spiritual care in hospice.

AIDS is a world pandemic that has generated a sense of hopelessness and fear and an increasing perception of helplessness and human frailty. Organized religion in the Western world has not been at the forefront of care for people with AIDS because AIDS first appeared in two marginalized groups in western society, homosexuals and drug users. That is not true in Africa. There is an HIV pandemic in Africa. Sixty percent of the population in some parts of Africa are infected. It is a disease of poverty, social dislocation and changing lifestyle. The church in Africa, as the church in the world, is being called to look at its role in providing pastoral care for dying people and for caregivers who may become infected. The church is being called to look at its role in promoting change in lifestyle and chastity. An African said, "the church and Christians are going to have to start walking with sinners and prostitutes. It is unchristian to walk always with Christians." The face of AIDS in Africa, is not gay rights, and it is not middle class western promiscuity. We are not free in Western countries from the implications of what's happening in Africa. We must recognize the spirituality of infected people, although it may be different from ours. Those of us who are Christian are going to have to examine some of the ways we treat not only our fellow Christians, but others. AIDS is calling on the church to look at itself in a way it has not done for centuries.

Another issue that is facing hospice and spiritual care in hospice is the rapid increase in the number of elderly in North American society. By the year 2000, there will have been a 130 percent increase in the number of people over eighty-five in this country. There is a generation gap between the people who are dying and their caregivers, sometimes of two and three generations. In caring for the terminally ill elderly, we must recognize the differences in the nature of the losses and in the perception of spirituality and relationship to religion. The elderly are concerned about the quality of their lives, not the length. They are afraid of being abandoned. We must reinforce their personhood and give them back the control that we take away from them so easily when we put them in institutions.

There are ethnic differences facing hospice. Hospice began in a white, Anglo-Saxon, Protestant, Christian community in Great Britain. We now live and try to practice hospice in a multi-cultural world. We now try to care for people from different ethnic and religious backgrounds and we, the people who are caring, come from different beliefs and have different spiritual concerns. There is compassion and concern in the Buddhist teaching. There is compassion and concern in the Jewish belief. Humanists are concerned with social justice and abiding commitment. All can and do provide spiritual care in hospice.

Spiritual care has been described as the "unfinished revolution in palliative care." Spirituality is difficult to describe and even more difficult to define. Norman Cousins states the problem facing hospice care most eloquently in his book, *The Anatomy of an Illness*: "Death is not the ultimate tragedy of life. The ultimate tragedy is de-personalization—dying in an alien and sterile area, separated from the spiritual nourishment that comes from being able to reach out to a loving hand, separated from hope" [9],

In answer, hospice says, "We are here. We will be with you in your living and in your dying. We will free you from pain and we will give you the freedom to find your own meaning in your own life—your way. We will comfort you and those you love—not always with words, often with a touch or a glance. We will bring you hope—not for tomorrow but for this day. We will not leave you. We will watch with you. We will just be there."

REFERENCES

1. H. Feifel, Foreword in, *In Quest of the Spiritual Component of Care for the Terminally Ill,* F. Wald (ed.), Yale University Press, New Haven, 1986.
2. I. Illich, *Medical Nemesis,* Random House, New York, 1976.
3. S. P. Aries, *The Hour of Our Death,* Alfred A. Knopf, New York, 1981.
4. C. Saunders, Spiritual Pain, *Journal of Palliative Care, 4*:8, pp. 29-32, 1988.
5. V. Frankl, *Man's Search for Meaning: An Introduction to Logotherapy,* Beacon Press, Boston, 1962.
6. H. Kushner, *When Bad Things Happen to Good People,* Avon, New York, 1983.
7. E. J. Cassel, The Nature of Suffering and the Goals of Medicine, *New England Journal of Medicine, 306,* pp. 639-645, March 18, 1962.
8. R. J. Lifton, *The Broken Connection,* Simon and Schuster, New York, 1979.
9. N. Cousins, *Anatomy of an Illness as Perceived by the Patient: Reflections on Healing and Regeneration,* Norton, New York, 1979.

PART VI

Bioethical Issues

CHAPTER 20

Personhood and the Question of Neonatal Euthanasia

Brian E. Woodrow

The author has chosen two tasks in this chapter. First, to discuss the concept of personhood; and second, attempting to relate personhood to the critical subject of euthanasia with respect to newborn infants with severe abnormalities. The landmark decision of the British Columbia Court of Appeal in July of 1988 which ruled that a human fetus is not a person, triggered a heated controversy across Canada and focused the attention of academics, politicians and citizens at large on the same question that has vexed scholars since the genesis of recorded thought—what is a person?

A favorite topic for philosophers over the ages, personhood is of particular interest in the contemporary field of biomedical ethics as the British Columbia decision bears witness. Quite apart from the issue of fetal rights, the meaning of personhood is a factor in many sensitive areas involving ethical decision making and in itself becomes a fundamental and agonizingly difficult problem. But it is the realm of the amazing technological progress of contemporary medical science that has forced humanity to look at itself and attempt to uncover what is the difference between biological and personal existence. In the minds of many thinkers, for instance, the continuation or cessation of medical treatment hinges on the vital question of personhood.

In no area of biomedicine is this problem more compelling than that of neonatal euthanasia with respect to newborn infants with gross abnormalities.

THEORIES OF PERSONHOOD

The common English word "person" is fraught with difficulty. Its meaning is certainly in the eye of the beholder. The Oxford English Dictionary defines "person" as

> . . . a mask used by a player, a character or personage acted, one who plays or performs a part, a character, relation or capacity in which one acts, a being, having legal rights, a judicial person; in late use, a human being in general.

Thus, there seems to be several different uses of the word "person" related to various areas of endeavor and only loosely connected to one another.

Common usage, however, dictates that "person" equals human being and is used to differentiate between people and "things." This distinction has carried over from common philosophic usage, and we find Immanuel Kant stipulating [1, p. 110]:

> . . . that persons, as contrasted with things, are of an unconditional worth and that respect is an attitude which has application to persons only and never to things. . . . They are . . . "ends-in-themselves and sources of value in their own right."

In the same way, John Locke equated "person" and "self" in a definition of personhood which depends on consciousness for its validity. In the rational tradition, Locke defined "person" as [1, p. 111-112]:

> . . . "a thinking, intelligent being, that has reason and reflection, and can consider itself as itself, the same thinking thing, in different times and places; which it does only by the consciousness which is inseparable from thinking, and seems to me essential to it." . . . For him, identity of person was simply identity of consciousness, so that I remain the same person if I am conscious of being so, even though my body should change drastically and be diminished through age, disease, or amputation.

These descriptions of personhood, and many others in the same vein which could be noted, all reflect in infinite variation the ancient dictum "Man is a rational animal" and presuppose to some extent the Platonic dualism which sees the human divided into a material body and immaterial soul. In this view, the tendency is to interpret personhood as a metaphysical entity, bodiless and hidden, an instrument of pure reason.

Such notions of personhood held sway until the contemporary age when dualism fell out of favor due to the development of science and a changed view of the relationship between humanity and nature. Rather than having human activities directed by the rules of natural law, scientific experimentation indicated a very close bond between humanity and nature. Homo sapiens is a product of nature and yet can change nature. We are both object and subject.

From this school of thought, colored by evolution, biology and the social sciences, probably the most influential contemporary thinker on the question of personhood is P. F. Strawson. He has adapted the term "person" in a sense which comes close to the common usage that every human being is a person. To Strawson, a person is indeed distinct from a material body, that is, in contrast to a thing.

Strawson denies, however, that this necessitates a human to be an immaterial entity. He states that terms applicable to material bodies are also applicable to humans as "persons." There are, he says [1, p. 112]:

> . . . two classes of terms, M-predicates and P-predicates, applicable respectively to material bodies and to persons; but there is an overlap, in that some M-predicates (perhaps all M-predicates) are applicable to persons, although there are some P-predicates that we "would not dream of applying" to material bodies (among the latter would be ascriptions of states of consciousness).

Strawson goes on to contend that persons cannot be reduced to their components any more than can material bodies; therefore, it is not enough to identify persons through M-predicates. In the same way, P-predicates cannot be identified according to M-predicates and are not to be reduced to them. Strawson concludes that an individual cannot be identified as a person until at least one P-predicate has been correctly ascribed to him [1, p. 112].

Strawson seems to have developed a theory of personhood which is intelligent and utilitarian and remarkably consistent with the common usage. But in stating this, it must be said that this theory of personhood, like most others, is not capable of empirical verification, and therefore adds to the quandary of defining personhood rather than helping to solve the problem. Strawson's contention that at least one P-predicate is essential for personhood could be of inestimable value in the field of biomedical ethics in deciding such questions as removing life support systems in terminal situations and initiating them in the case of newborns with gross defects. One weighty problem remains however: who decides what is a P-predicate?

In an important series of addresses printed under the general heading "The Beginnings of Personhood," the meaning of the term is discussed from an interdisciplinary perspective. A theologian, Albert C. Outler, says of personhood: "It is the human organism oriented toward its transcendental matrix, in which it lives and moves and has its human being" [2, p. 30]. Andre E. Hellegers, a physician, states that biological terms such as "human" should not be confused with unscientific terms such as "personhood," "soul," and "value" because the latter denote societal attitudes toward biological life, and science is restricted to describing biological facts, therefore terms like personhood ". . . have no meaning in biology" [3, p. 11].

Howard J. Taubenfeld agrees with Hellegers from the field of law: "I have to confess that many . . . terms which are used . . . have no specific legal content, just as they have no specific medical content. . . . The concept of person . . . is itself societally oriented" [4, pp. 16-17].

Lastly, a medically trained philosopher, H. Tristram Engelhardt, Jr., brings the argument full circle when he asserts [5, p. 20]:

> In the beginning, it should be remarked that this is a uniquely philosophical endeavor. Until one decides philosophically what will count as a human person, it is useless to expect that empirical sciences can devise operational criteria for the identification of instances. One has to know what one wants to measure before one can attempt to measure it.

It seems, then, that we are forced to consider two possibilities: 1) the meaning of personhood is beyond human comprehension at this time; and 2) the meaning of personhood is incredibly simple.

Perhaps the field of religious studies can assist us in examining these possibilities. The Holy Bible is a corpus of literature that can often cast some light on difficult questions concerning the human condition since it reflects humanity's search for ultimate meaning and truth over a period of many hundreds of years.

A cursory glance through the Old Testament indicates that the concept of personhood is unknown as a meaningful category in its inventory of ideas. Humanity is clearly fashioned in the image of God, therefore innately good, but its nature is entirely dependent on its relation to its creator. Humanity is granted the spirit of life (*nephesh*) as a gift from Yahweh, being made by Yahweh and for Yahweh, establishing thereby a relationship between God and humanity. This relationship is unique and carries with it duties and responsibilities, in particular, obeying the will of Yahweh. In return, the Creator promises to be ever faithful, ever present with these special creatures. To the Old

Testament writers, this concept of humanity is considered corporately, applying to the whole people of Israel, and it is alien to their thought to consider the individual as such. In effect, any notion of personhood that can be gathered from their beliefs must be inferred from collective notions of what it is to be a people in unique relationship to God. But a major inference can be made, quoting Kenneth Vaux [6, p. 13]:

> Hebrew anthropology locates man's uniqueness in his possibility. Heschel says, "To animals the world is what it is; to man this is a world in the making, and being human means being on the way, striving, waiting, hoping."

The New Testament continues to see "personhood" as a gift of God in the Old Testament sense and is firmly entrenched in the notion of humanity being divinely created in the image of God. There is virtually nothing in the Gospels, Epistles, or Revelation that contributes new data to a study of personhood, and even the teachings of Jesus as reported in the New Testament reflect Old Testament thought. But certainly expanded in the New Testament is the concept of the possibility of humanity. Implicit throughout is the insistence that human beings have supreme value in the eyes of God and must be treated with dignity and respect by their fellows; and, as life itself is a gift from God, men and women must be totally responsible concerning it. It is this kind of stewardship that will allow humanity to achieve all that it is possible for it to achieve.

A WORKING DEFINITION OF PERSONHOOD?

It is evident that running through all the arguments previously mentioned there is a common denominator, a basic awareness, an instinctive intuition, that there is more to personhood than the purely physical or the purely "spiritual." There is, it seems, an ontological factor involved in personhood. There is a growth process involved in which a person has the capacity to "become" more of a person through the very experience of life itself. As Harmon L. Smith states [7, pp. 114-115]:

> For to be a human person is not a matter of statically being a certain kind of substance, but a matter of becoming personal through temporal duration. And this means that personal being and becoming is a matter of variable degree which is referable to one's being more or less fully and intensely personal.

This is true as far as it relates to those who have the potential human resources to grow in their personhood, to dynamically engage in the process of becoming even marginally, but what of those individuals who do not have the resources? What of the anencephalic infant or the patient in irreversible coma? Because they lack any potential or any "possibility," does this mean that they have lost their status as persons? It is here, in these extreme cases, that we come face-to-face with the dilemma of personhood.

Perhaps it is impossible to define a person with any certainty, given the present level of knowledge. One can consider the problem from several viewpoints including one's own limited intellect, and can amass a considerable amount of expert opinion. All seem to be in general agreement that no one in all of history has satisfactorily defined a person. Researchers can feel that they are in very good company with their frustration over this topic, but it does not go away, because the notion of personhood is so crucial to the contemporary scene, especially in the area of medical care and bioethics.

It may be true that the crux of the problem can be explained in theological terms, looking again to the Old Testament concept of humanity being fashioned in the image of God. The essence of God is unknowable, it is a mystery. We can ascertain certain truths about the Creator through the acts of creation, but the center of God's being will be forever hidden. Humanity being in the image of God suggests that some characteristics of humanity must also remain a mystery for of necessity there is always a direct relationship between the image and that of which it is an image. Perhaps the characteristics of personhood, the central core of humanity, may be a hidden element.

And so we end where we began, with a question. But not quite. There is a concept in the Old Testament which may assist us by offering an insight into the fundamental meaning of personhood. The Hebrew idea of *nephesh* mentioned previously would seem to be a criterion for personhood. Although the term has variants of meaning, each expresses a particular aspect of life. The substance of *nephesh* describes the spirit of life, the life principle, the breath of Yahweh blown into the creature image Adam to cause life to begin. It is, according to Walter Eichrodt [8, p. 135]:

> . . . not a case of an abstract concept, but of a substantial entity which might almost be described as the stuff of life. . . . First and foremost the word means 'life', and what is more, . . . life bound up with a body.

Nephesh applies to both humans and animals but, states Edmond Jacob [9, p. 159]:

> . . . there is an important difference between man and other living beings: man alone receives the vital breath in his nostrils direct from Yahweh, which is proof that Yahweh considers him an individual, whilst animals are created in conformity with . . . the species.

George Knight has written that *nephesh* is also used to describe the seat of the intellect [10, p. 35]:

> . . . as a substitute for the word 'brain,' for which Hebrew has no equivalent. But once again it may stand for the life force in man as such that can ebb and flow in potentiality according to whether the person is sick or well.

Converting that concept into the contemporary scientific age, it is plausible to define the minimum qualification of a person as a human organism that demonstrates the spirit of life, that is, that indicates by some means that life is present, life being interpreted to mean that intellectual action can occur, intellectual action being interpreted to mean that cerebral cortex activity is possible.

Offering this definition is like walking on eggs for it is fraught with difficulties not the least being the meaning of its terms. Surely we must agree with Arthur Danto when he says that "understanding our language is not an inauspicious beginning for attaining philosophical truth" [1, p. 113]. When exploring a subject like "personhood," one gathers sympathy for linguistic analysis.

With this problem in mind, it will be prudent to describe "cerebral cortex activity" as this is the critical term in my definition of personhood. The cerebral cortex or neocortex comprises the outer portion of the two hemispheres of the cerebrum, the upper 80 percent of the human brain. It is responsible for the psychological properties and capacities of a human being. In the words of Arthur Earl Walker in his book, *Cerebral Death*, cerebral activity "involves high level faculties such as perception, voluntary movement, ideation, memory, etc., that underlie the general state of awareness referred to as consciousness" [11, p. 18]. These faculties are in contrast to the lower automatic coordinating and integrating functions of the body controlled primarily by the cerebellum and brain stem. Thus, in my definition of personhood, it is assumed that the cerebral cortex is extant and capable of at least marginal functioning,[1] regardless of spontaneous activity in the other systems of the body including the heart and lungs. Cerebral cortex activity can be equated theologically by utilizing the Aristotelian-Thomist notion that "the soul is the form of the body." According to Thomas Aquinas, the soul is an individual spiritual substance, the "form" or intrinsic determining principle of the human body which gives it its human condition. Body and soul functioning together comprise the unity of the human being. Robert North states: "Insofar as the soul is form of the body, God's creation of the soul must be regarded as an aspect of his creation of the body" [12, p. 227]. The soul is, of course, a metaphysical concept but it is possible to identify it with the organizational mode of the body, that is, as the "form" or determining principle of the body's intellectualization. Thus, if there is insufficient evidence to demonstrate that a marginal level of "soul-organizing principle" exists, then it is safe to conclude that personhood is not present in the human organism [12].

Regardless of the perplexities and issues surrounding the exact meaning of personhood, it is possible to fall back on the common usage that states every human being is a person. This definition takes care of most situations that are encountered in life and is the criterion recognized by criminal law, for example [13, p. 34]. It is always dangerous to place people in categories and we must resist the temptation to classify them rather than treat them as individual beings. As Whytehead and Chidwick have written, particularly in the medical sciences [14, p. 18]:

> We should reject any attempt to reach a rigid definition of a person or to make decisions easy and routine. Such an approach would degrade and depersonalize decisions which must always be individualized and reached after loving, concerned consideration of the circumstance of the unique person.

Another direction has been proposed to assist unraveling the mystery of personhood. This theory states that perhaps a single definition of personhood is impractical if not, indeed, impossible at the present state of our awareness. It may be that a polyvalent definition is possible, that is, one that applies itself differently to various disciplines. In other

---

[1] There are rare medical situations where a patient will mimic the signs of a completely dead brain including complete paralysis of all muscles, fixation of the pupils and isolectric (flat) EEG. Such patients, unable to communicate in any way, may be alert. Such conditions are known as locked-in syndrome. However, "a careful neurological examination, supplemented by laboratory and radiological examinations, will enable a diagnosis to be established" [11, p. 16].

words, there would be a legal definition, a medical definition, a theological definition, etc., each one referring to that field's particular "goods." Embracing these levels there would be an operational philosophical definition in synthetic terms. The shape of this model might well resemble Joseph Fletcher's fifteen famous or infamous "Indicators of Humanhood" from 1972 [15, pp. 1-4], but would have to be far more flexible and sensitive with the synthetic definition capable of recognizing the specifics of problems relating to particular disciplines. This may be the shape of things to come.[2]

I cannot help wondering if there are fundamental differences relating to the understanding of "person" on cultural and class lines as well. Do middle class Canadians define personhood (supposing that they do) in the same way as Indian and Inuit? What about orientals and occidentals, the rich and the poor? This is another facet of the study of personhood that warrants attention.

Let us hope that our natural curiosity and search for truth will continue to bring fresh insights into the colossal problems surrounding the simple question: "What is a person?" Even if we never discover the whole truth, the search will reap benefits in human relations throughout the world as we learn more about what it means to be a person and about our duties and responsibilities as persons, to ourselves and to one another.

THE QUANDARY OF EUTHANASIA

Before I attempt to apply my so-called "working" definition of personhood to the question of neonatal euthanasia, it might be wise to lay some groundwork.

In this discussion, I am concerned solely with the direct killing of patients in "hopeless" circumstances, that is, true euthanasia in the contemporary meaning of the word. Although it means, literally, "good death," *de facto* it means death without pain administered through lethal injection. It only clutters the issue to introduce categories of euthanasia such as "active," "passive," "voluntary," "involuntary," "direct," "indirect."

Let us call a spade a spade and deal with the ramifications of true euthanasia, the direct killing of a human being by medical means.

---

[2] This model was suggested by Prof. John Flynn of the College of Emmanuel & St. Chad, Saskatoon. In his address "The Beginnings of Personhood: Philosophical Considerations," H. Tristram Engelhardt, Jr., seems to be pointing in the same direction: ". . . There is a possibility that 'person' involves a heterogeneous family of concepts rather than a clear and distinct genus with definite species" [5, p. 20].

Is killing a person ever justified? A scan of the literature indicates that many scholars see no relevant moral distinction between killing a terminal patient in the last stages and removing life support and allowing the patient to die. Peter Black has declared [16, p. 90]:

> If (the doctor) feels responsible enough for his patient, killing the patient and letting him die are equivalent for him. . . . They are, in any case ethically identical, for his involvement in the outcome is total.

In effect, the end justifies the means when the end, death, is the merciful and desired end. And yet, some ethicists are very leery about the possibility of allowing physicians to be more active in this area. Richard McCormick quotes Gerard Hughes for instance, who while maintaining that the "distinction between killing and allowing to die . . . will not bear the weight which has often been put upon it" argues that it would undermine the general moral climate if doctors took more active steps, and that "the real importance of the distinction is its inculcation of a moral and legal climate which we cannot do without" [11, pp. 105-106]. Underlying these assertions there seems to be a fear that if euthanasia were more accepted, it would be discovered to our sorrow that the medical profession, family members and others with vested interests might, in certain cases, put aside any moral scruples they have, and seek their own selfish goals.

As a matter of fact, the traditional distinction between killing and allowing to die, although it is extremely difficult to analyze in moral terms, is felt to serve as a safeguard for the needy and the vulnerable in our society. And rightly so. It could be a short step from a lethal injection for a patient in irreversible coma to a possible "solution" to severe retardation, the increasing geriatric population and the economic crisis of medical and hospital care [18, pp. 14-17].

It seems evident, then, that euthanasia is not justified, either at the behest of patients, families or the medical team. The risks are too great, the comprehension of the dying process too limited, and the spiritual significance of the process too profound.

Are there any exceptions to the rule against euthanasia? Of course, there are exceptions to every rule, but it is a struggle to describe any in this context. They must be individual cases of rather unique circumstances, for example, a situation where a person is suffering excruciating pain and no effective analgesics are available for one reason or another. The standard should be firmly based however—hesitating long and hard before allowing any exception to the moral principle against killing human beings [18, p. 17].

EUTHANASIA OF NEWBORNS WITH
GROSS ABNORMALITIES

We turn now to the specific question of neonate euthanasia and, in particular, new born infants with gross abnormalities. There are several syndromes and defects which could be mentioned. Suffice it to say, we include here profound spina bifida (myelomeningocoele), anencephaly, cerebral agenesis, Niemann-Pick disease, and cri du chat and Lesch-Nyhan syndromes. Myelomeningocoele is a hernial exposure of the spinal cord and nerve roots through a defect in the spinal column; anencephaly is a congenital absence of the cranial vault with the cerebrum completely missing or reduced to a small mass; cerebral agenesis is an absence of the cerebrum due to lack of appearance in the developing embryo; Niemann-Pick disease is rare and hereditary and occurs chiefly in Jewish children. There is massive enlargement of the liver and spleen, discoloration of the skin, and nervous system dysfunction; cri du chat syndrome is a hereditary congenital condition characterized by an increased distance between the eyes, a tiny head, severe mental deficiency, and a plaintive catlike cry; Lesch-Nyhan syndrome is a hereditary disorder with physical and mental retardation, compulsive self-mutilation of fingers and lips by biting, ceaseless jerky or writhing involuntary movements, cerebral palsy, and impaired kidney function.

These newborns have been on the increase in recent years largely due to the development of newborn intensive care units. In days gone by, most of these babies would not have survived the initial hours *ex utero*. Now, thanks to medical research in obstetrics and pediatrics, these newborns can be maintained and given life support and their conditions may be vastly improved through surgery. Some may live for a few years, a few may live for several years. But this progress is only in the physical realm, and does not begin to correct the massive abnormalities of these neonates. Most are born grossly retarded and some have little or no brain function to speak of. They may be technically "alive" but whether they are "living" is a moot point.

These infants raise very delicate moral problems, and we can never forget the emotional [19, pp. 9-14], for we are dealing with babies, and it is always unsettling to discount the potential of a child. Certainly it is true that some of these newborns far exceed their potential at birth in both quality and quantity of life, and develop keen self awareness and meaningful relationships [20, pp. 13-15]. But others can never possibly attain actual personhood or meaningful life in any sense because of constant suffering and torment and immature cerebral cortex or both. To force them into a lengthy course of treatment, perhaps including extensive surgery, is to inflict upon them an additional burden and serves no purpose whatever unless it has a training value for pediatric residents and nurses who would surely have a better learning experience caring for more responsive children. In truth, these latter infants cannot be considered persons. Referring to my definition of personhood, such neonates cannot demonstrate in any way that they can perform an intellectual act, therefore the spirit of life is not extant, therefore they are not persons. In other words, they do not have any potential for life whatsoever, they can never be aware of themselves as "I," and certainly can never relate to anyone or anything else. The only thing they might be capable of is to feel pain [20, pp. 16-17]. The humane action is undoubtedly to assist them to peace through death.

But how? Certainly few would object to allowing such neonates to die. Indeed many are born dying already. Others are not helped to breathe at birth when it is apparent how grossly deformed they are. But there are some who breathe spontaneously and are cared for but not given extraordinary treatment. Quoting Whytehead and Chidwick [14, p. 43]:

> The usual practice is not to place the infant on a regular program of feeding, but only to give sugar and water when it appears hungry. However, some of these infants cannot swallow, and in any case such administration of fluids only serves to prolong the intended progress to death which results from inadequate nutrition, insufficient fluids, and perhaps infection. While the decision not to preserve life would likely be generally accepted, the means of attaining the end seem inhumane and unmerciful. Would . . . euthanasia be more compassionate?

A very good question! And one that, although not easy, is possible to answer. For this practice is not one of allowing to die, but rather killing by starvation. This is not letting nature take its course, for as Stanley Hauerwas suggests [21, pp. 228-229]:

> . . . it is no longer clear what nature means in such contexts, as nature has become an extension of our technology's ability to keep us alive. . . . If, for the "normal" child, "nature to take its course" means with the aid of all the technology we can muster, it can mean no less for the defective child.

Certainly a quick death by injection is better than a lingering one by starvation and is just as much "letting nature take its course." There are times when maintaining a life subverts the reverence for life.

A voice from the practice of law expounds a different argument without, characteristically for a lawyer perhaps, actually declaring himself for or against euthanasia. Arval A. Morris says [22, p. 144]:

> Properly understood, euthanasia is a matter of deciding in favor of death on the ground that death is in the better interests and is preferable to life for the one who is to die. . . . Euthanasia is administered solely and exclusively for his sake, and for no one else's. . . . It merely expresses . . . that life itself is not always a good, irrespective of its nature. . . . This view of the matter rules out administering nonvoluntary euthanasia to severely defective infants 1) because they are not "persons"; 2) because they would cause greater suffering to others . . .; 3) because they would be an economic or social burden. On this humane and proper view of euthanasia the question whether it can be administered . . . turns exclusively on whether one can reasonably say that it is being administered for his own sake; that is "would he be better off dead?"

This is a potent argument and worthy of consideration. To a certain degree it bolsters our position if we answer "yes."

Be that as it may, we have still rejected euthanasia as being contrary to the human spirit and potentially dangerous to the survival of the defenseless and weak in the culture. But we have also allowed for exceptions, and these unfortunate babies could undoubtedly count as exceptions. Absolutely nothing is gained through their lingering death by starvation. Indeed, despite Morris's comments, additional suffering is caused by the anxiety of the parents and the nursery staff and is an important consideration. In these cases, there is a definite distinction between killing and allowing to die—direct killing is by far the most humane and merciful act for it hastens the inevitable when time means nothing but pain. But even if euthanasia is rejected in these instances, it may be entertained for another reason. Euthanasia is suspect to many because it involves the direct killing of a person, but we have established, despite Arval Morris again, that infants with gross defects cannot be considered persons.

Subscribing to this argument is difficult, however, for a comatose patient on a respirator who has suffered brain death is also not a person according to my definition and yet many would hesitate to recommend euthanasia in such a case even though, emotionally, they would like to recommend it.

A WORD OF CAUTION AND A WORD
OF CHALLENGE

I want to hold to the contention that killing is justifiable in the case of grossly deformed neonates but I am also apprehensive, not about my conclusion, but about the possibility of abuse. The question of controls is of paramount importance.

This need has been recognized for many years and not least by the legal profession. Although we may not agree wholeheartedly with their conclusions, their reasoning is sound. John A. Robertson has some succinct comments [23, pp. 194-195]:

> Although the law clothes the defective infant with a right to life . . . many people think that that right ends when it conflicts with the interests of the parents, the medical profession, and the infant's own potential for full development. The law in action is likely to reflect this view, and, if the law in theory differs, this difference probably will be ignored. . . . The attending physician is a partial check . . . (but) the peculiarities of his role, the risk of conflicting interests, make the physician an unreliable protector of the infant. Since the power to cause the death of the defective newborn is an awesome one, it is essential that such decisions be carefully confined by law.

And as Thomas Oden stated in the 1970s in a wider cultural context, there was and continues to be, a general drift in our society toward the cheapening of the value of life, permissive abortion and the ethics of utility. He calls for Jewish and Christian ethics to offer correctives based on their historic understanding and wisdom. Oden writes [24, p. 89]:

> Most urgently this will take the form of a firm determination to protect those whose lives are least protected—I am referring especially to infants who are judged by guardians to be defective, worthless or subpersonal, and to the terminally ill who are thought to have little usefulness to society amid the "meaningless" process of dying.

Richard McCormick agrees and he also appeals to theology. Addressing himself to the field of neonatology, he states [25, p. 123]:

> In summary, these decisions are being made, sometimes perhaps abusively. And they are being made in terms of human judgments expressed by the medical profession in a variety of ways: e.g., "viable baby," "no realistic human future," "functionally

incompetent," "meaningful life," and so on. It is clear that such terms contain a whole value system. It is the task of contemporary theologians, in interdisciplinary dialogue, to lift up those value systems and test them in light of the value perceptions of the Christian tradition.

It is significant that the wise have been calling out for moral theologians to ponder and pronounce on the problems of euthanasia and related topics in the biomedical world. Surely no tradition knows more about death and dying than the Judeo-Christian, and certainly Christians understand through the sacrifice of Christ that death is both friend and enemy. Medical science desperately needs the advice and counsel of learned, open minded religious ethicists. Its practitioners may not fully realize it, but the roots of that unawareness may lie in the mistrust and ignorance which still persists to a certain degree between medicine and theology. It is through dialogue and cooperation between these two disciplines that progress will be made in understanding and, in part at least, solving the enormous moral and ethical problems which abound in biomedical science and which will continue to expand in the future.

REFERENCES

1. A. C. Danto, *The Encyclopedia of Philosophy*, 1972.
2. A. C. Outler, The Beginning of Personhood: Theological Considerations, *Perkins Journal, 27*, p. 30, Fall, 1973.
3. A. E. Hellegers, Medical Considerations, *Perkins Journal, 27*, p. 11, Fall 1973.
4. H. J. Taubenfeld, Legal Considerations, *Perkins Journal, 27*, pp. 16-17, Fall 1973.
5. H. T. Engelhardt, Philosophical Considerations, *Perkins Journal, 27*, p. 20, Fall 1973.
6. K. Vaux, *Biomedical Ethics*, Harper and Row, New York, 1976.
7. H. Smith, *Ethics and the New Medicine*, Abingdon, Nashville, 1970.
8. W. Eichrodt, *Theology of the Old Testament*, Vol. 2, SCM Press, London, 1967.
9. E. Jacob, *Theology of the Old Testament*, Harper and Row, New York, 1958.
10. G. A. F. Knight, *A Christian Theology of the Old Testament*, SCM Press, London, 1959.
11. A. E. Walker, *Cerebral Death*, Urban and Schwarzenberg, Baltimore, 1981.
12. R. North, *Teilhard and the Creation of the Soul*, Bruce Publishing, Milwaukee, 1967.
13. Law Reform Commission of Canada, *Euthanasia, Aiding Suicide and Cessation of Treatment*, Law Reform Commission of Canada, Ottawa, 1982.

14. L. Whytehead and P. Chidwick, (eds.), *Dying: Considerations Concerning the Passage from Life to Death*, Anglican Book Center, Toronto, 1980.
15. J. Fletcher, Indicators of Humanhood: A Tentative Profile of Man, *Hastings Center Report, 2*, pp. 1-4, November 1972.
16. P. Black, Killing and Allowing to Die, in *Infanticide and the Value of Life*, M. Kohl (ed.), Prometheus, New York, 1978.
17. R. A. McCormick, Notes on Moral Theology, *Theological Studies, 37*, pp. 105-106, March 1976.
18. S. Post, History, Infanticide, and Imperiled Newborns, *Hastings Center Report, 18*, pp. 14-17, August/September 1988.
19. S. Callahan, The Role of Emotion in Ethical Decisionmaking, *Hastings Center Report, 18*, pp. 9-14, June/July 1988.
20. D. A. Shewmon, Anencephaly: Selected Medical Aspects, *Hastings Center Report, 18*, pp. 13-15, October/November 1988.
21. S. Hauerwas, The Demands and Limits of Care-Ethical Reflections on the Moral Dilemma of Neonatal Intensive Care, *American Journal of the Medical Services, 209*, pp. 228-229, March/April 1975.
22. A. A. Morris, Law, Morality and Euthanasia for the Severely Defective Child, in *Infanticide and the Value of Life*, M. Kohl (ed.), Prometheus, New York, 1978.
23. J. A. Robertson, Involuntary Euthanasia of Defective Newborns: A Legal Analysis, in *Death, Dying and Euthanasia*, D. J. Moran and D. Mall (eds.), University Publications of America, Washington, D.C., 1977.
24. T. C. Oden, *Should Treatment Be Terminated*, Harper and Row, New York, 1976.
25. R. A. McCormick, Notes on Moral Theology, *Theological Studies, 36*, p. 123, March, 1975.

CHAPTER 21

Euthanasia: The Dying Decision

Gerry R. Cox and Ronald J. Fundis

Medical personnel face the question of dying with dignity, not only while trying to treat patients to save them, but also while allowing patients to die to give them some sense of dignity in death. The right to life as a fundamental right leads to decisions concerning the right to end life. For many, they dread the future that may force them to decide to end a life, whether their own or that of a loved one. Physicians also agonize over the decision of whether or not a patient has passed over the point of no return to a meaningful life, and then having to decide how long to prolong the patient's dying. Families often ask physicians to perform heroic lifesaving efforts on patients who are beyond saving. At what point should the physicians allow the patient to die? At the other end of the continuum would be the family who wants nothing done for the patient when their survival was quite possible. Should the physician allow a patient who could recover to die because the family wants them to die? Questions about the decision to die or let live fall within the topic of euthanasia.

Euthanasia comes from the Greek word "Thanatos" which means death and from the Greek word "eu" which means easy or good. Hence, euthanasia means good or easy death. For many, euthanasia is commonly thought of as mercy killing. Killing is a softer word than murder. A person can be killed in an accident, but the word murder implies a moral wrong was committed. From this view, euthanasia is viewed as the practice of painlessly putting to death persons who have incurable, painful, or distressing handicaps or diseases. Such euthanasia can be voluntary or involuntary. In voluntary euthanasia, the choice of death over life is made by someone else.

Once the decision for death has been made, there are two types of euthanasia. One is active and the other is passive. Active euthanasia means that the death of a person is directly and deliberately caused by another person. Passive euthanasia suggests that no extraordinary action is taken to keep the person alive. The decision to "pull the plug" as in active euthanasia or to never "plug in" the dying person is not as simple as it seems.

THE MEDICAL DECISION

The question of whether or not to choose to practice euthanasia is often looked upon as a medical decision. Physicians or other medical staff are frequently asked to decide whether or not the patient's health has deteriorated to the point where further treatment is useless. Doctors have expertise in the field of medicine; therefore, they are the best qualified technical judges of when to continue or to end medical treatment. Such a position, however, puts physicians in a compromising situation ethically. By the Hippocratic Oath, they are obligated to preserve life. If they aid a patient to find a means to die, are they violating their oath? If they do aid the patient to seek death, will they be prosecuted for murder? If they simply let the patient die, are they violating their oath? By letting the patient die, will they be sued? What if the diagnosis for the patient was in error? Often the patient is not well known to the physician. How could the decision be made to do what is "best" for the patient? Generally, the physician has three choices: 1) the patient could receive all possible treatment to prevent dying at any cost; 2) the patient could be actively terminated; or 3) the patient could be allowed to die with no efforts initiated to prolong life. Which choice should the physician make? Unfortunately, Hippocrates did not have the problem that doctors face today, or did he? Even Hippocrates must have had to make life and death decisions even though the technology was crude by comparison. Modern euthanasia decisions have been compounded by the advances in technology; however, it does not matter how sophisticated the technology is by comparison, a decision to use or not use the technology must still be made by the physician.

Physicians normally make life and death decisions in the course of their daily practice of medicine. The normally less lethal interventions such as risky surgeries, inoculations, and so forth simply do not have the same ethical dilemmas attached to them. Socially, questions of the ability to pay to receive treatment may have greater ethical considerations. Care is at least to some extent given to those with the ability to pay in preference to those who cannot pay. Without wanting to sound either elitist, patronizing, or insensitive, one author concludes that poor patients may actually be more fortunate than the rich in that they are more often left to die in peace [1]. Such decisions may be a more passive form of euthanasia.

The elderly, upon whom most euthanasia decisions are made [2] were born at a time when the automobile was just beginning to make its place in society. In their lifetimes, the changes in health care have been staggering. Medical technology has become more technical and more successful. Life spans have increased as new means of fighting disease and illness have been developed. Ways to keep people alive with mechanical devices now exist that can preserve "life" indefinitely for persons who actually have no hope of recovery or rehabilitation. The definition of death has not kept pace with this technological growth. At what point does one "pull the plug" if one cannot determine when the person is actually dead? It is also difficult to determine when a person has no hope of recovery when the technology exists to allow people to recover who would have had no hope in the past.

DEFINING DEATH

The definition of death has not always been a major question in the area of euthanasia. When death was determined by the absence of spontaneous respiration and heart beat, one could rather easily define death and when it occurred. With the development of technology to artificially pump blood for the individual, the question of defining death has become exceedingly complex. Death is a process and not a single moment in time. The body is composed of cells, and these cells die continually. Even when a person has been declared dead, part of the body remains alive. For transplants or donation of body parts to another person's body to take place, it is essential that the part to be donated is alive. Ethically, is the person really dead when "live parts" are taken for donation? To try to answer this question, death must be defined.

A person is declared dead when clinical death occurs. That occurs when spontaneous respiration and heart beat ceases. At what point does death occur? It is possible to resuscitate many individuals who are clinically dead allowing them to recover and to be restored to "normal" life. Heart attack victims, for example, often respond to resuscitation and make recoveries. Death would seemingly occur at a point beyond which resuscitation is impossible. That point is, unfortunately, not easily definable.

Brain death is usually defined as anoxia or a condition of oxygen deprivation in the brain cells. The brain cells begin to die in four to six minutes. The most highly evolved part of the brain, the cortex, dies first. This part of the brain controls memory, thought, and voluntary action. The midbrain would die next followed by the brain stem. If the cortex and the brain die and the person survives, the person would probably lapse into an irreversible coma. He or she would need to be intravenously fed; however, "life" could continue indefinitely (see Appendix I).

Biological death occurs when the organs and organ systems of the body die. Different organs die at different rates. The brain may stop functioning while the heart continues to beat for some time. A person may ventilate or breathe and sustain body parts for a time even after the brain has begun to die. If the ventilation stops, the brain will probably survive for several minutes until the oxygen deprivation destroys it.

Brain death is the method of determining death that is most widely used in technologically sophisticated societies. This is generally observed by a flat electroencephalogram (EEG) reading, unresponsiveness, lack of reflexes, no movements or breathing, and unreceptivity. Thus determining death is a combination of criteria and not a single measure. The current emphasis upon transplants requires that organs must be taken as soon as possible after the blood ceases to flow. An exact legal definition is needed to prevent homicide. With a respirator and pump oxygenating and surging blood through the body, it is now perhaps impossible to precisely determine the exact moment of death. Generally, the decision is made by the physician. The physician would be expected to do what he or she thinks will benefit the patient [3].

MEDICAL EUTHANASIA

What is the physician to do when the person is being supported artificially with no hope for recovery given present medical knowledge? Should the physician forego heroics to unnecessarily prolong a life that for all practical purposes has already ended? Should the physician simply allow nature to run its course? Such inaction is passive euthanasia. While saying that life should be cherished despite disabilities or handicaps, the American Medical Association suggests that the primary considerations should focus on what is best for the individual patient and not the avoidance of a burden to the family or to society [4].

Physicians will, at times, determine that a patient is medically dead and terminate life-supporting machines and permit nature to run its course. Instructions not to resuscitate are entered on the patient's chart. Typically, the relatives of the patient or the patient would have already been consulted and their approval given as well. The decision is made on the basis that the continuation of the patient's life serves no useful purpose because the individual has assumed the status of a vegetative organism without an active mind or ability to perform any tasks whatsoever. A physician generally would suffer little, if any, sanction or penalty for practicing passive euthanasia that is motivated by compassion for the patient and his or her family. As evidence of this, there have been only a small number of malpractice cases involving euthanasia in the United States and none ended in the verdict of guilty against the physician [5].

Active euthanasia involves the physician terminating a life. Such acts place the physician in jeopardy of being prosecuted for homicide. To intentionally kill a patient has been rejected by the American Medical Association [4]. Physicians have generally taken the position that passive euthanasia is acceptable, but they have also taken the position that active euthanasia is not acceptable. According to American Medical Association official policy, it can be ethical for a doctor to cause a patient's death by stopping treatment. Like the Catholic position, the American Medical Association opposes taking positive action to hasten death, but favors passive euthanasia which allows patients to die [6].

Yet physicians may be practicing active euthanasia more widely than they have been thought to be. A common method of active euthanasia is to over-drug the patient. By giving larger amounts of a pain-killer, the patient does not suffer as much physically and death may occur sooner than it would be allowing nature to run its course. This ends the suffering of the patient and the family [1, 7]. It does not run up needless medical bills either. Certainly, the practice of euthanasia does have an economic basis. To allow a hopelessly ill patient to run up substantial medical bills that would devastate the family that survives would not be a wise use of the family's or perhaps of society's limited medical resources. Certainly, the state could save billions by use of euthanasia [8].

Often the patient asks for the physician's help in dying. Certainly the mainstream Christian position could not be against the prudent use of pain killers. But the Congregation for the Doctrine of the Faith suggested that to deliberately cause the death of a person is wrong and is murder [4]. The Jewish, Lutheran, Presbyterian, Methodist and all other Protestant denominations that have acted on this issue take similar positions [8]. The real issue here is why are the pain killers being given in such high dosages? Is the intent to render the patient unconscious with the eventual result being to die sooner? Or is the intention simply and humanely to relieve pain with the consequence being a somewhat accelerated dying process? Some physicians are finding it difficult to draw the line on what is ethical or unethical in this area.

THE LAW AND EUTHANASIA

At what point in the euthanasia process does the person involved with euthanasia become criminally responsible? The law seems to be indifferent to letting a person die. It is clearly against the law to murder someone. In most cases, the law seems to be strongly against killing as well. It is clearly against the law to murder or even to kill another person. To simply let another die is seldom a legal problem. In practice, it is not so simple. Choosing not to resuscitate is acceptable legally without any serious challenge [6]. When someone eliminates intravenous feeding or does not perform routine simple surgery to correct minor problems such as connecting the esophagus, is this killing or letting one die? When babies struggle for two weeks before starving to death in a hospital due to lack of nourishment, is this killing or letting the child die? Under some circumstances, should the physician prescribe drugs to ease the pain and hasten the infant's death? Is this any different than physicians aiding deaths of those in concentration camps in Nazi Germany? The courts certainly view aiding an individual's death out of compassion as being quite different than what occurred in the Nazi euthanasia experiment [9].

There have been numerous court cases dealing with the question of euthanasia in the United States. The courts often acquit or reduce the sentences of those who murder/kill with the motive of euthanasia. Occasionally, the courts take a more serious view of such deaths (for an examination of such cases, see [10]. Euthanasia has also been a motive for suicide. At what point should those who cooperate in aiding another's suicide potentially be charged with murder?

For euthanasia to be considered as murder, certain legal conditions must be met. There must have been an act that resulted in a death. Death must be the intended result. The death must have been deliberated or thought about prior to the act. The individual must have malice afterthought or have ill feelings toward the victim prior to the act. Certainly, euthanasia involves most of these conditions. The intent is to cause death, the act is deliberated, and a death does result from the act (see Appendix II for examples of such laws). Those who commit murder for euthanasia would not have malice aforethought. In the case of euthanasia, motive assumes importance as a legal factor. In most cases, motive is not of great importance. If the individual can demonstrate that the act was committed out of compassion for the victim and for the circumstances that the victim faced as opposed to personal gain, then the courts are inclined to show leniency. Whether or not the individual requested the act does not seem to be a major factor [2].

Practicing euthanasia for utilitarian purposes has not fared well in the courts. The utilitarian doctrine of the greatest good for the greatest number figures in discussions of euthanasia. The Nazi programs under Hitler exterminated those who were nonproducers. While the Jewish people were the major group exterminated, other "unproductive" people such as the disabled, the sick, and the elderly were also exterminated. The courts did not look favorably upon the Nazis who practiced extermination to rid society of the "less desirable" people. While similar types of euthanasia may be occurring in the United States, the courts have not been favorable to the elimination of any peoples [9]. The legal system has also attempted to define patient rights. Some argue that the patient has a right to die. Perhaps the most famous case in the United States is the Karen Ann Quinlan case. She became comatose in 1975 and was placed on a respirator. Karen was not legally dead though her brain was damaged beyond recovery. The family asked the physician to remove the life-support machine. The physician refused initially. Her father went to the courts to be appointed her guardian in order to get the power to make the decision to have her disconnected from the machine. The court refused. On appeal, however, Mr. Quinlan was able to get approval. The court reasoned that the removal would allow Karen to die a natural death. Karen did not die until 1985. In her case, the life-support system that was seemingly keeping her alive for the first year was apparently not the only thing that was keeping her alive.

The legal relationship between the dying patient and the physician is not as precise as many would like. Physicians commonly administer analgesics which shorten the patient's life. This is apparently not illegal [8]. Even though death occurs, the desire to control the pain is paramount. The right to die also includes the legal right to refuse treatment. But what should the physician do when another member of the family refuses treatment? This is particularly a problem in the treatment of minors, comatose patients, and the mentally incompetent. The disease itself may affect rational thinking on the part of the patient. Drugs or guilt over hospital costs or whatever may cloud thinking. Since all patients are eventually going to die, it would seem natural that some would indicate a willingness to die.

While death itself is natural, the decision to die does affect survivors as well as society. Ethically, is it wrong to want to die if one's quality of life is threatened? If one can rationally make a choice to die, then the issue of one's right to die becomes important. If one is not rational due to drugs or because of the overwhelming fear of destroying one's family financially, then a decision becomes more difficult ethically. Refusal of treatment for various reasons has led to the development of living wills.

The living will is a request that if the person has no reasonable expectation of recovery from a life-threatening or quality-reducing situation that the person be allowed to die. In some cases, individuals have requested that their lives be ended by active euthanasia as well. Since the middle 1930s, several states have proposed legislation to legalized euthanasia under the living will concept. Typically, the legislation calls for life-support systems or life-saving treatments to be withdrawn if the patient has no likelihood of recovery. Some proposals call for the administration of a lethal injection or other methods to end the patient's life. California was the first state to pass a right-to-die bill in 1976. States who pass such laws must have safeguards to protect against legalized murder to obtain estates, financial gain, or to rid oneself of an unwanted spouse and so forth.

MORAL DECISIONS

The decision to practice active or passive euthanasia is a moral decision as well. All of the major religious denominations in the United States have given approval to passive euthanasia, i.e., allowing the terminally ill person to die. As mentioned earlier, few, if any, have taken a stand in favor of active euthanasia. Most have taken strong positions opposing active euthanasia (see [8] for a discussion of various religious views on passive and active euthanasia). The Jewish religion views any form of active euthanasia as strictly prohibited and condemned as plain murder. At the same time, the Jewish position sanctions the withdrawal of any factor which may delay death [11].

The Catholic Church seems to have one of the most complete literatures on euthanasia [8]. The Catholic Bishops of the United States issued a statement that active euthanasia was a violation of the right-to-life in November of 1985. Morally the painless or easy death of mercy killing still results in a death. The question of whether or not active euthanasia is killing or not is the central issue. In 1940, the Sacred Congregation of the Holy Office of the Catholic Church issued a statement that mercy-killing was unlawful and immoral. This statement was based upon the principle of right-to-life [12]. The basis of the moral decision regarding euthanasia is the value of human life. If human life had no special value, then euthanasia decisions would be easier.

The Declaration on Euthanasia prepared by the Sacred Congregation for the Doctrine of Faith [13] suggests that the controversy is more than simply allowing those in their final agony to die in order to end their suffering. For this type of passive euthanasia, there seems to be considerable consensus. What is not approved is the killing of an innocent human being whether a fetus, a retarded person, an infant, or an adult even if requested or otherwise rationalized as an action. When the sick seemingly request to die, what they are often asking is not to die, but rather not to continue to live in the manner in which they are now living. Whether it is pain, loneliness, or lack of love, the ill need to live with dignity. To die with dignity, one must not allow events or other persons to take command of himself or herself. To maintain dignity, each person should master the situation as must as possible. Each should conduct himself or herself according to his or her standards, setting his or her own goals and deciding how to achieve them. Dignity not only means self-command, but also not giving in emotionally or intellectually to cowardice. To die with dignity is to die calmly with all passions spent [2].

Four principles articulated from the Catholic tradition might assist one regarding dying with dignity. First, the principle of doing good and avoiding evil [14]. Evil must be avoided. One does good by attempting to act out of the authentic concern for the well-being of others rather than selfish personal interest. One can do only so much in the care of another. Obviously, there is a time to allow another to die. Can causing them to die before their time be in their self-interest? If one views another's death as relieving them from pain and suffering, one might ague that it was for their benefit. Perhaps, it was to relieve the person of the duty of caring for the person whose life was no longer as meaningful or pain-free as it once was.

Secondly, a good end does not justify an evil means [15]. The end does not justify the means. Though one may no longer be suffering, it is still an evil act to kill them.

Thirdly, the principle of double effect also applies. This is the principle that suggests that a single act has two or more effects [14]. Certainly, to end one's suffering by administering pain-killers is a good effect. The bad effect might be that the person lapses into a coma and dies sooner. Is the aim, then, to cause death sooner or to relieve pain? A second consideration is whether or not the dying person will be deprived of satisfying his or her obligations to the family and the moral duties involved in facing one's death [13]. Individuals who are dying may need to satisfy such moral duties as making peace with their relatives with whom they have been feuding or whatever. They may need to deal with "unfinished business" such as bills, insurance policies, disposition of goods, etc.

Fourthly, the principle of proportionality applies to the moral decision and euthanasia. Like the principle of double effect, proportionality is based upon the idea of the relationship of good and evil. Since many moral decisions are often not clearly right or wrong, the principle of proportionality suggests that one needs to weigh whether or not the evil of the act is offset by the good of the act [14]. For example, if one gives drugs to ease pain and the patient dies sooner because of the drugs, is the good of easing the pain proportional to the death that is caused by easing the pain? A drug can be given to a terminally ill patient that may cause his or her death if there is no reasonable hope for recovery and the patient can be better able to prepare for death without constant or excruciating pain. The effect of allowing the patient to die pain-free and to have the state of mind to focus upon his or her relationships rather than pain is proportionate to the evil effect of causing the patient to die sooner. Basically, this principle is that sometimes good things may have bad consequences, and one must decide if the good consequences outweigh the bad consequences.

Morally, one must base the decision as to whether or not euthanasia is acceptable or not by also considering what is being called for in treating the dying person. The Catholic tradition suggests that ordinary and extraordinary means must be looked at in different ways. Ordinary treatment is looked upon as morally necessary. This would normally mean that all treatments, medicines, and operations which offer a reasonable hope of recovery of the patient without excessive pain, expense, or other unusual inconvenience is considered to be ordinary [15]. Extraordinary means would be all treatment, medicines, and operations which cannot be given without causing excessive pain, expense, and other inconvenience or else offer little reasonable hope of recovery [15]. While what is considered to be routine has certainly changed in medicine, the basis for decision-making has not changed. The distinction is not necessarily all that clear. The basic necessities are generally considered ordinary. It is not necessary to connect a brain-dead, comatose patient to life-support machines. That would be considered to be extraordinary. Certainly, however, one would need to provide nourishment to a patient with a broken leg.

Morally, one must then decide to practice or not practice euthanasia based upon the well-being of the patient and not his or her own convenience. A framework to make the moral decision does exist. Certainly, one cannot knowingly take an innocent life. Yet, one can allow an innocent life to end naturally. A substantial remaining gray area is the use of drugs to ease pain. One needs to decide as to whether or not the drugs are greater in benefit to the patient than the shortening of the life that occurs.

SUMMARY

The medical profession has made great strides in life-saving technology. One aspect of this progress is that one can now be kept "alive" indefinitely through the use of machines and devices. Clearly, it is not in the best interest of the patient or the society to have life unnecessarily prolonged. At the same time, it is not necessarily in the best interest of the patient to have his or her life ended prior to the natural time of their death. To decide whether or not to use euthanasia cannot be absolutely decided prior to facing the decision involving a human life. Little controversy exists in cases involving passive euthanasia. Active euthanasia is clearly controversial and legally prohibited. Moral guidelines do exist that can facilitate the decision-making process; however, these guidelines do not make the particular life-ending decision any less difficult.

APPENDIX I.
SAMPLE LEGAL EFFORTS AT DEATH DEFINITION

1971: KANSAS-INSPIRED STATUTES

Contain dual standards of heart-lung functions and brain functions.

A person will be considered medically and legally dead if, in the opinion of the physician, based on ordinary standards of medical practice, there is the absence of spontaneous respiratory and cardiac function and, because of the disease or condition which caused, directly or indirectly, these functions to cease, or because of the passage of time since these functions ceased, attempts at resuscitation are considered hopeless; and, in this event, death will have occurred at the time these functions ceased; or

A person will be considered medically and legally dead if, in the opinion of a physician, based on ordinary standards of medical practice, there is the absence of spontaneous brain functions; and if based on ordinary standards of medical practice, during reasonable attempts to either maintain or restore spontaneous circulatory or respiratory function in the absence of aforesaid brain function, it appears that further attempts at resuscitation or supportive maintenance will not succeed, death will have occurred at the time when these conditions first coincide. Death is to be pronounced before artificial means of supporting respiratory and circulatory function are terminated before any vital organ is removed for purposes of transplantation.

These alternative definitions of death are to be utilized for all purposes in this state, including the trials of civil and criminal cases, any laws to the contrary notwithstanding.*

---

*Kansas Statutes Annotated, articles 77-202, 1971.

1972: The Capron-Kass Proposal attempts to overcome the difficulties of the Kansas-type statutes.

A person will be considered dead if in the announced opinion of a physician, based on ordinary standards of medical practice, he has experienced an irreversible cessation of respiratory and circulatory functions, or in the event that artificial means of support preclude a determination that these functions have ceased, he has experienced an irreversible cessation of total brain functions. Death will have occurred at the time when the relevant functions ceased.*

---

*Alexander M. Capron and Leon Kass, University of Pennsylvania Law Review, Volume 121, pp. 87-118, 1972.

Alexander Capron, "Legal Definition of Death," 315 Annals of New York Academy of Science, 349, 356, 1978.

1975: The American Bar Association Model Statute Proposal attempts to simplify even more:

For all legal purposes, a human body, with irreversible cessation of total brain function, according to usual and customary standards of medical practice, shall be considered dead.*

---

*100 American Bar Association Annual Report, pp. 231-232, 1978 (February Midyear Meeting).

1978: The Uniform Brain Death Act states:

For legal and medical purposes, an individual who has sustained irreversible cessation of all functioning of the brain, including the brain stem, is dead. A determination under this section must be made in accordance with reasonable medical standards.*

---

*12 Uniform Laws Annotated, 15 (1981 Supplement)

CANADA

1976: Law Reform Commission of Canada in its report "Criteria for the Determination of Death" (Working Paper No. 23) recommended amendments to the Interpretation Act of 1970:

(1) A person is dead when an irreversible cessation of all that person's brain functions has occurred.

(2) The cessation of brain functions can be determined by the prolonged absence of spontaneous cardiac and respiratory functions.

(3) When the determination of the absence of cardiac and respiratory functions is made impossible by the use of artificial means of support, the cessation of the brain functions may be determined by any means recognized by the ordinary standards of current medical practice.

In drafting the statute, the Commission noted the following series of objectives:

(1) The proposed legislation must avoid arbitrariness and give greater guidance to doctors, lawyers, and the public, while remaining flexible enough to adapt to medical changes.

(2) The proposed legislation must not attempt to solve all the problems created by death, but only the problems of establishing criteria for its determination.

(3) The one proposed piece of legislation must apply equally in all circumstances where a determination of death is at issue.

(4) The proposed legislation must recognize only the standards and criteria of death; it must not define the medical procedure to be used, nor the instruments or procedures by which death is to be determined.

(5) The proposed legislation must recognize standards and criteria generally accepted by the Canadian public.

(6) To remain faithful to the popular concept, the proposed legislation must recognize that death is the death of an individual person, not of an organ or cells.

(7) The proposed legislation must not in practice lead to wrong or unacceptable situations.

(8) The proposed legislation must not determine the criteria of death by reference only or mainly to the practice of organ transplantation.

For a comprehensive listing of state and selected country statutes, see *Defining Death: Medical, Legal, and Ethical Issues in the Determining of Death*. President's Commission for the Study of Ethical Problems in Medicine and Biomedical and Behavioral Research, 1981.

APPENDIX II: SAMPLE MURDER STATUTES

Kansas:

Article 34.—CRIMES AGAINST PERSONS

21-3401. Murder in the first degree. Murder in the first degree is the killing of a human being committed maliciously, willfully, deliberately and with premeditation or committed in the perpetration or attempt to perpetrate any felony.
Murder in the first degree is a class A felony.

21-3402. Murder in the second degree. Murder in the second degree is the malicious killing of a human being, committed without deliberation or premeditation and without the perpetration or attempt to perpetrate a felony.
Murder in the second degree is a class B felony.

21-3403. Voluntary manslaughter. Voluntary manslaughter is the unlawful killing of a human being, without malice, which is done intentionally upon a sudden quarrel or in the heat of passion.
Voluntary manslaughter is a class C felony.

21-3404. Involuntary manslaughter. Involuntary manslaughter is the unlawful killing of a human being, without malice, which is done unintentionally in the wanton commission of an unlawful act not amounting to felony, or in the commission of a lawful act in an unlawful or wanton manner. As used in this section, an "unlawful act" is any act which is prohibited by a statute of the United States or the state of Kansas or an ordinance of any city within the state which statute or ordinance is enacted for the protection of human life or safety.
Involuntary manslaughter is a class E felony.

21-3405. Vehicular homicide, (1) Vehicular homicide is the killing of a human being by the operation of an automobile, airplane, motor boat, or other motor vehicle in a manner which creates an unreasonable risk of injury to the person or property of another and which constitutes a material deviation from the standard of care which a reasonable person would observe under the same circumstances. (2) This section shall be applicable only when the death of the injured person ensues with one

(1) year as the proximate result of the operation of a vehicle in the manner described in subsection (1) of this section.

(3) Vehicular homicide is a class A misdemeanor.

21-3406. Assisting suicide. Assisting suicide intentionally advising, encouraging, or assisting another in taking of his own life.

Assist suicide is a class E felony.

Source: Kansas Statutes Annotated, 1981.

REFERENCES

1. J. Ladd, *Ethical Issues Relating to Life and Death*, Oxford University Press, New York, 1979.
2. M. Kohl, *Beneficent Euthanasia*, Prometheus, Buffalo, New York, 1975.
3. R. M. Veatch, *Case Studies in Medical Ethics*, Harvard University Press, Cambridge, Massachusetts, 1977.
4. President's Commission for the Study of Ethical Problems in Medicine and Biomedical and Behavioral Research, *Deciding to Forego Life-Sustaining Treatment: Ethical, Medical, and Legal Issues in Treatment Decisions*, United States Government Printing Office, 1983.
5. R. Turbo, *An Act of Mercy*, Nash, Los Angeles, 1973.
6. A. E. Weiss, *Bioethics: Dilemmas in Modern Medicine*, Enslow, Hillside, New Jersey, 1985.
7. A. B. Downing, *Euthanasia and the Right to Die: A Case for Voluntary Euthanasia*, Humanities Press, New York, 1971.
8. G. A. Larue, *Euthanasia and Religion: A Survey of the Attitudes of World Religions to the Right-To-Die*, Hemlock Society, Los Angeles, 1985.
9. J. B. Wilson, *Death by Decision: The Medical, Moral, and Legal Dilemmas of Euthanasia*, Westminster, Philadelphia, 1975.
10. B. A. Backer, N. Hannon, and N. A. Russell, *Death and Dying: Individuals and Institutions*, John Wiley, New York, 1982.
11. F. Rosner and D. Bleich, (eds.), *Jewish Bioethics*, Sanhedrin Press, New York, 1979.
12. J. P. Kenny *Principles of Medical Ethics*, Newman Press, Westminster, Maryland, 1952.
13. *Sacred Congregation for the Doctrine of the Faith*, Daughters of St. Paul, Boston, 1980.
14. T. E. O'Connell, *Principles for a Catholic Morality*, Harper and Row, San Francisco, 1978.
15. G. Kelly, *Medical-Moral Problems*, Catholic Hospital Association, St. Louis, 1958.

CHAPTER 22

Informed Consent in Relation to Transplants

Abbyann Lynch

Consideration of the general ethical concerns surrounding organ transplantation in human beings—the donation and receipt of appropriate tissue in the quest for health and life—will not be out of place in a volume dedicated to discussion of death, dying and bereavement. We know that each year many individuals die as the need for heart, lung, kidney replacement outstrips their supply. At the same time, many individuals who are dying choose to be organ donors. Some families may choose to make donations after relatives' death. This latter activity is one response to the challenge of bereavement.

Any discussion of transplantation will entail discussion of consent—certainly of donor and recipient, or of those providing permission for this procedure. In these cases, consent marks respect for donor and recipient. It expresses choice and self-direction; it limits the activity of any other person with respect to the patient; and it defines what may and may not be done so that the possibility of harm is limited by the choice of the one who receives or the one who gives. This ethical understanding of consent is well-delineated in Canadian law (Human Tissue Gift Act [1]) and in American legislation (Uniform Anatomical Gift Act [2]). Briefly, lacking consent, transplantation—donation/receipt—is legally and ethically unacceptable.

The main emphasis in this chapter is to consider consent and transplantation in a quite different, but related context: to explore with you informed *community* consent—the public ethic—in this area, pressing consideration of several social questions arising here. These considerations exceed the limit of individual consent—that of a patient as donor or recipient—or of those acting in their place—or even those who perform or assist in transplantation procedures—physicians, nurses, transplant coordinators, government officials. The concern is with the consent we all give—implicitly/explicitly—to transplantation activity generally by way of support for it via legislation, finance, ongoing donation of organs, creation of that public opinion in which transplantation as human activity can begin and thrive. And, thus, I turn to the public sense of right/wrong as basis for what is done in this area. The issue then is the direction to be given by *us* about newer developments arising in this context.

As with any issue of consent—expressed, implied, tacit—*public* consent rests on understanding and choice. In this case, public consent, public direction, must be given, clearly and forcefully, within the four following areas.

1. OUGHT AN INDIVIDUAL'S DONATION OF ORGANS CONTINUE TO BE TOTALLY VOLUNTARY?

We can now *choose* to be donors of kidney, heart, lung, bone marrow, etc., by way of a form signed before death, to be effective after death (leaving aside consideration of donation of organs by a donor from whom organs are taken while the donor is still living.) We opt to be givers; we need not do so. The title of the legislation indicates the common sense here—Human Tissue *Gift* Act, Uniform Anatomical *Gift* Act. Ethically, this legislation recognized donor choice—and gives it priority over the need of the sick would-be recipient. In this understanding, those who 'require' the cadaver kidney, for example, have no legal claim against the choice of any possible donor who might not wish to make such a donation.

This North American legal support for donor choice does not prevail in numerous European countries: e.g., Scandinavia and France. In those countries one must *opt out*—one is assumed to be willing to be a donor, unless one says 'No.' Is this an appeal to another facet of humanness, i.e., generosity, interdependence, care for others? Is it that in these jurisdictions the claim of those who need the cadaver's organs so that they can live is recognized to be greater than the claim of those who can no longer use these organs but who choose to say they shall not be taken? Is the basis for such thinking and legislation in countries outside North America a response to the social need for organs in a time of shortage, a utilitarian response to an ethical dilemma? Is this a *better* response, ethically speaking?

The situation in terms of public ethic, then is *here* (North America), the donor gives or *opts in*. *There* (outside North America), the non-donor *opts out*. In non-North American countries, all individuals are *presumed* to opt in unless notice to the contrary is given. But, as the song says, "The times, they are a-changing . . ."—at least here.

And so, in the United States, for example, more than fifteen states now have legislation in terms of which the dying patient, or the dead patient's family, must be asked whether an organ donation *might* be given. The legislation is titled "routine request—routine inquiry." Many perceive this as coercive, as threatening free choice of patient or family, as somehow making a gift of an organ under these circumstances less than a gift. Others perceive this step as the right one, as a partial answer towards alleviating the organ shortage, as an encouragement to generosity, not coercive but an invitation to 'good action.' Understand, of course, that this is a *legislative* request. Those asked to donate organs in these circumstances may refuse, but they *must be asked* by physician or staff, and that request must be noted.

Here, in the more local community, the matter is still at the stage of "recorded consideration." Physician-staff must have given attention to the possibility of donation by a patient who is dying. Again, the question of coercion, this time of physicians-staff, is raised. The justification for "recorded consideration": public need as superseding individual claim on privacy in this matter. However, there is also some legitimate concern here about possible conflict of interest on the part of the physician. Is the physician's appropriate concern the present or the future patient?

The problem of organ shortage is real enough. Without organs being made available, many persons will die. To refuse to be an organ donor may well result—indirectly—in another's death. That being said, is it the public will that the present priority given individual choice here be shifted? Should physicians be requested to ask—should patients be required to hear requests—concerning the possibility of organ donation? What is the public ethic in this area to be? What is informed *community* consent re: assumed individual consent (opting out) and assumed individual non-consent (opting in) now; what should it be?

2. HOW 'DEAD' OUGHT THE ORGAN DONOR BE?

Of course, in the strict sense, dead is 'dead'—there is no more or less 'dead.' The legal and medical standard for death, prior to removal of organs of donation, has been recognized to be brain death—particularly brain stem death, a condition from which no return to life has been seen to be possible.

But, in recent experience, there have been questions raised in this regard. For example, some would declare newborn infants who lack so-called upper brain—anencephalic infants—dead—for purposes of obtaining their organs for transplant purposes. How can this be, at least for those anencephalic infants who breathe, and who have beating hears—even for those whose brain stem still functions though mechanical devices may be used to assist breathing and heartbeat? The argument, of course, is that these infants will never be able to socialize or develop intellectually, even if they survive for some little time. They lack the capacity for this human developing since they lack the necessary brain-formation. For some individuals, lack of this capability is lack of human-ness. Further, since these babies lack upper brain formation, they can never meet the criterion for death of the brain as a whole—they have never had a 'whole brain.' The attempt to identify such infants as dead on arrival—by law—was attempted in California. It has been suggested elsewhere, again—partially as a means to alleviate the organ shortage. Perhaps there should be recognition of these infants as dead, since it appears they will inevitably die, sooner rather than later. Whatever the rationale, if these infants are identified as dead on arrival—then even if breathing, even if with hearts which beat without assistance, they cannot be killed. They are already dead.

And thus, the issue of informed public consent arises. What is the attitude of the community to be here? What value will attach to these young infants? Are they to be seen as useful to others only? Are they to be allowed to die—*Not* hastened in that dying—as is now the case, for example here in London in the case of Baby Gabriel? Will, should, the definition of death be changed in these cases?

The problem is not so different for those individuals who have suffered irreversible brain damage—victims of disease or trauma, presuming they cannot regain their socializing ability or their cognitive ability. Are they as good as dead—thus dead—even if brain stem function remains? Should those patients like Miss Quinlan be identified as 'dead'—and thus be useful as organ donors, perhaps? Or is the public view that life of this kind is to be protected, sustained, without violation for organ retrieval so long as this life persists?

When considering the public choice to be made here, it is well to remember that the original (Harvard) delineation of irreversible coma, later designated as criteria for death, was drafted in the context of the need for organs for transplantation and concern about the demand for care posed by the growing number of patients in a comatose state. The question, then: ought a need for organs set the parameters for determination of death? Or, is determination of death a quite separate, separable matter? What should the public consent be in this matter? Why?

3. OUGHT THE HUMAN FETUS BE
GROWN FOR USE AS ORGAN DONOR?
WHAT ABOUT THE FETAL FARM?

Recently, public attention has been drawn to the possibility that transplantation of certain fetal tissue might prove useful in the treatment of Parkinson's disease—perhaps of other human brain disorders as well. Further, there have been numerous claims concerning the potential usefulness to others of the fetal thymus gland and fetal pancreatic tissue. There are published reports of the larger fetus being a useful source for various organs needed by infants and children.

At a time when, in both Canada and the United States, there are no— or few—restrictions regarding pregnancy termination, ought fetuses be grown for these purposes?

If it might be argued that the fetus spontaneously aborted poses less of an ethical dilemma, it must still be noted that these fetuses might not be useful for transplantation purposes. The anomaly which causes their spontaneous displacement could well render them useless as organ or tissue donor.

An so the issue turns to the public sense of *right* about the fetus. What is its moral status? When is it properly called alive? When is it dead? How is the public sense of protection of life to be exercised here— priority given to the older, needy recipient? Priority given to the newer, developing life? Or is there any ethical issue at all—the fetus is not yet 'human' (for some) and before it becomes so (at birth, in Canadian law), it can be utilized for the purposes of other presently-recognized human beings?

This issue too, is one for public consent. The matter of fetal tissue use is under very real consideration in Canadian medical groups. Committee approval for such use has already been formally granted in several U.S. locations.

4. A LAST TRANSPLANT-CONSENT ISSUE.
TO WHAT EXTENT OUGHT TRANSPLANTATION
ACTIVITY BE GOVERNMENT-FUNDED?
WHAT PLACE IN THE THERAPEUTIC MENAGE
SHOULD THESE PROCEDURES BE ASSIGNED—
FINANCIALLY SPEAKING?

In fact, of course, transplantation procedures are in some competition within any institutional budget and any governmental health budget. Thus the questions: ought more money be allocated to neonatal

intensive care? More money to community health? More to transplantation? More to genetic counseling? and so forth.

Again, and in fact, at least one of the American states has ceased
public funding for transplantation activity. The Governor of Oregon,
announcing that decision, identified grave concern for other social
needs as rationale: the fact that many individuals lack access to
primary care, the fact that many school children lacked adequate
nutrition, were cited as examples.

The United States and the Canadian systems for health care
funding differ, of course. To speak specifically to Canadian concerns
for a moment, and to quote from a September article [3, pp. 433-434]:
"Can Canada afford an expanded organ transplantation program
and, if so, what will be expanded at the expense of other health care
services?"

The question is under formal study by the CMA Council on
Economics, particularly as there is growing activity to obtain more
organs for transplant. Organ transplantation is expensive: $121,000
the given figure for heart-lung or lung transplant; $84,000 for a liver
transplant. But other procedures are also costly—care in the ICU, e.g.
And these costs must also be weighed against costs for education,
certain types of publicly-sponsored recreation, welfare housing and the
like—all largely publicly funded in the Canadian context.

Now, even though Canadians need not pay the full cost for these
transplantation procedures as individuals (since they are covered
under the provincial pre-paid insurance plans to which they
contribute), transplantation is still not an inexpensive health
care procedure when considered in the overall federal or provincial
expenditures.

To be fair, the cost of such activity should be weighed against alternatives—dialysis, for example, is more expensive in aggregate years than
the kidney transplant operation, but the cost of maintenance drugs
following transplantation must be added in the latter case. And how is
the extension of quality life, aided by the successful transplant operation to be measured in dollars and cents? To respond to the question of
relative expenditures here is to query first the rates of success in such
procedures—to define that, value it, enhance it—if possible.

As the Council report, earlier mentioned concluded:

> There must be a concerted effort by health policy—makers
> to decide on the amount of resources that society will be willing
> to expand pursuing such procedures . . . the public must be
> made more conscious of the sacrifices involved due to scarcity of
> resources.

Again, there is need for public consent in this aspect of transplantation work.

These public questions could be multiplied, of course. The need to determine whether use of animal donors in transplantation is appropriate, the need to consider availability of transplantation services to non-Americans or non-Canadians, the need to delineate appropriate criteria in the selection of candidates as recipients in organ transplantation. These are areas of concern and there are others as well beyond these few examples. In each of these, there is more than the individual concern of the individuals directly involved: donors, recipients, physicians, other staff, and administrators.

What is true in terms of general discussion is true in setting out legal rules as well. In the case of moving towards any 'opt out' mechanism of consent for organ donation, the public sense of 'right' will be the basis for any new legislation, or retention of that legislation which is already in hand. Similar argument will prevail in the case of criteria for donor death—at least, insofar as that will be a legal matter.

On consideration of the use of the fetal donor, where there is no present legislative sanction regarding abortion, it will be the public ethos—or public consent—which will dictate action. If the question is one of funding for transplantation activity, or the setting of criteria for selection of candidates for receipt of organs, again these will be matters of public consent.

The case made does not demote or ignore the expertise of health care personnel, nor does it set aside the rights and responsibilities of individual patients to determine actions appropriate for their choice. What is emphasized here is that the activities of *individuals* in this area take place within a broader context—one which allows, gives, the very possibility for such action. With particular reference to health care personnel and government officials, the case made identifies them as decision-makers, yes, but decision-makers who are stewards of the public consent. The decision-makers influence and lead public consent, perhaps—but they do not *own* these decisions. The decisions are taken *in trust* for all of us.

And so, the role of public consent in the area of transplantation is one of the most critical of the many ethical components here. It calls for what others have identified as the "grassroots public ethics movement." Impetus to such a movement was given by way of the Oregon 1987 decision to limit public funding of transplantation. Such a movement now has extended to eleven or more states in the United States. It is the means many find acceptable and helpful for stimulating public thinking, and for delineating the public context so necessary for informed public consent in these matters of contemporary ethical decision-making, particularly in the area of transplantation.

It might be argued that decisions here are best left to legislators— and, indeed, many of these decisions will be incorporated in statute, eventually. The law is a slow instrument, however, and blunt. It is a coarse sieve of public viewpoint, picking out only the lowest common area of agreement, leaving the rest to develop by way of practice and some policy until the need for law is (again) demonstrated.

Thus, as shaping the formulation of law, as offering more immediate response to the questions raised here, and more generally around the serious emergency ethical issues in the transplantation context, informed public opinion—then public consent—the right and good public and community ethos—is imperative.

I trust these few remarks may be a beginning—or a further impetus—towards public discussion and the much-needed public consent concerning transplantation ethics.

REFERENCES

1. *The Human Tissue Gift Act*, S.O. 1971 Vol. 2, c. 83, III, 11.
2. *Uniform Anatomical Gift Act, Uniform Laws Annotated*, Master ws. Vol. 8: Estate, Probate and Related Laws, St. Paul, Minnesota, West Publishing Co., 1972, pp. 15-44, Approved by the National Conference of Commissioners on Uniform State Laws and the American Bar Association in August 1968.
3. P. Sullivan, Report Raised Questions about Cost of Organ Transplantation, *CMAJ, 139*, pp. 433-434, September, 1, 1988.

Epilogue

Decisions are a part of the practical life of every individual. The decisions of professional care providers take on special significance because they tend to confront the limits of knowledge and the degree of societal consensus. Ethical decisions are those grounded in a collective sense of the proper and the appropriate; however, higher standards are also brought to bear especially when the decision at hand involves human life and an interruption or intervention in the natural life course. Terms such as negligence, responsibility, duty, blame, honor, criminality, disgrace are often attached to one's ethical decisions or become labels on the consequences that follow such decisions.

Ethical decisions are related to institutions and the socialization content and processes that they promulgate. Individuals are taught what is right and wrong and are then under certain pressures to conform to the rules of one's institutional arrangements. Ideally, institutions would be expected to develop and promote clear and relatively consistent guidelines upon which the individual could build one's own ethical base. The reality in which most of us operates, however, is filled with mixed messages, confused signals, uncertainties, conflicts between ethics and law, and a lack of consensus about how we/they should live, should/should not intervene (or at what level), should/should/not be allowed to suffer, should/should not allow passive/active euthanasia, etc.

Different cultures offer distinctive perspectives for making and evaluating ethical decisions. The chapters in this volume offer a substantial contribution in assisting caregivers in arriving at acceptable ethical positions in their pastoral, counseling, medical, and mortician roles. The difficult task is, of course, for the individual to decide which and under what circumstances a particular ethical framework applies, to whom does one's ethical obligations apply, and then, in fact, to do what one decides is ethical.

Contributors

TADINI BACIGALUPI. Ph.D. Department of Sociology, Metropolitan State College, Denver, Colorado. Formerly active in two hospices in Colorado.

MICHAEL BULL, M.S.W., C.S.W. Lecturer, Social Administration, The Flinders University of South Australia, Bedford Park, South Australia.

GERRY R. COX, Ph.D. Professor of Sociology, Fort Hays State University, Hays, Kansas.

JEAN M. CRABTREE. Director of Pastoral Care at Women's College Hospital in Toronto.

TED CREEN, B.A., M. Div. St. Andrews Presbyterian Church, Owen Sound, Ontario.

BRIAN C. DOAN, Ph.D. Psychologist at Sunnybrook Medical Centre and the Toronto-Bayview Regional Cancer Centre in North York, Ontario.

RONALD J. FUNDIS, M. Phil. Professor of Sociology, Director of The Docking Institute of Public Affairs, and Executive Assistant to the President, Fort Hays State University, Hays, Kansas.

DELTON J. GLEBE, M.A., Th.D., D.D. Professor of Pastoral Care and Counseling, Waterloo Lutheran Seminary and Wilfrid Laurier University, Waterloo, Ontario.

ROSS E. GRAY, Ph.D. Clinical Psychologist at Sunnybrook Medical Centre and the Toronto-Bayview Regional Cancer Centre in North York, Ontario.

CONNIE GUIST, M.S., R.N.C. Graduate Student in Nursing at the University of Wisconsin-Milwaukee.

VERNON F. GUNCKEL, Ph.D. Clergyman.

CAROL IRIZARRY, Ph.D. Professor of Social Administration, Flinders University of South Australia, Bedford Park, South Australia.

MARY K. KACHOYEANOS, R.N., Ed.D. Associate Professor of Nursing at the University of Wisconsin-Milwaukee.

KALLENBERTG, KJELL. Th.D. Department of Hospital Chaplaincy, Orebro General Hospital, Orebro, Sweden.

DOROTHY LEY, M.D., Physician.

ABBYANN LYNCH, Ph.D. Director, Bioethics Department, The Hospital for Sick Children, Toronto, Ontario, Canada.

LYNN MARTINS. Bereavement Counselor in Los Angeles.

DAVID K. MEAGHER, Ph.D. Associate Professor of Education, Brooklyn College of the City of New York, New York.

GREG MORGENSON, M.A. Psychologist in Clinton, Ontario.

PAUL SAKALAUSKAS. Funeral director at Cresmount Funeral Home in Hamilton, Ontario.

CRAIG E. SEATON, Ph.D. Associate Professor of Psychology and Sociology, Trinity Western University, Langley, British Columbia.

FLORENCE E. SELDER, R.N., Ph.D. Associate Professor of Nursing at the University of Wisconsin-Milwaukee.

DOROTHY SOUTHALL, B.A., M.A. Bereavement counselor, LaFayette, Kentucky.

BRIAN E. WOODROW, C.D., S.T.M. Department of Pastoral Care, Alberta Children's Hospital, Calgary, Alberta.

The editors extend their gratitude to Ms. Dee M. Hand for her professional secretarial assistance in the preparation of this manuscript.

Bibliography

Adams, E., Reminiscence and Life Review in the Aged: A Guide for the Elderly, Their Families, Friends, and Service Providers, *Center for Studies in Aging*, North Texas State University, Denton, Texas, 1979.

Aden, L. H., The Challenge of Becker: A New Approach to Pastoral Care, *LCA Partners*, pp. 16-30, Aug./Sept., 1984.

Anderson, R. S., *On Being Human*, William B. Eerdmans, Grand Rapids, Michigan, 1982.

Anderson, R. S., Theological Anthropology and Revelation, Reconciliation and Healing of Persons; and Theology of Christian Community, *Class Notes*, Pasadena, California, Fuller Theological Seminary, 1985-1986.

Anderson, R. S., *Theology, Death and Dying*, Basil Blackwell, New York, 1986.

Annis, A., The Autobiography: Its Uses and Values in Professional Psychology, *Journal of Counseling Psychology, 14*, pp. 9-17, 1967.

Becker, E., *Denial of Death*, Macmillan, New York, 1973.

Berghorn, F. and D. Schafer, Reminiscence Intervention in Nursing Homes: What and Who Changes?, *International Journal of Aging and Human Development, 24*:2, pp. 113-127, 1987.

Boeck, M. A., Don't Let Death Education Backfire, *USA Today*, March 19, 1987.

Bordewich, F. M., Mortal Fears, *Atlantic, 261*:2, pp. 30-33, February 1988.

Campbell, P., and E. McMahon, *Bio-Spirituality*, Loyola University, Chicago, 1985.

Cassem, N. H., Pastoral Care of the Dying Patient, *The Journal of Pastoral Care*, pp. 52-61, June 1972.

Childress, J. F., The Gift of Life: Ethical Problems and Policies in Obtaining and Distributing Organs for Transplantation, *Ethical Principles and Practices*, J. Howie (ed.), Southern Illinois University Press, Carbondale and Edwardsvilles, Illinois, 1987.

Congram, J., A Time to Mourn, *Presbyterian Record*, Don Mills, Ontario, February 1989.

Dawes, T., Multicultural Nursing, *International Nursing Review, 33*:5, pp. 148-150, 1986.

Doka, K. J., and M. Jendreski, *Spiritual Support for Suffering: Clergy Attitudes Toward Bereavement, Loss, Grief, and Care*, Hayworth, pp. 155-160, 1986.

R. Donley, Beyond Umbrellas: Health Care Delivery in Kenya, *Image, 13*:2, pp. 40-42, 1981.

Ebersole, P., Problems of Group Reminiscing with Institutionalized Aged, *Journal of Gerontological Nursing, 2,* pp. 23-27, 1976.

Fox, B. H., Current Theory on Psychogenic Effects on Cancer Incidence and Prognosis, *Journal of Psychosocial Oncology, 1*:1, pp. 17-31, 1983.

Georgemiller, R. and H. N. Maloney, Group Life Review and Denial of Death, *Clinical Gerontologist, 2*:4, pp. 37-49, 1984.

Griffin, G. M., Grieving and the 1980s, *The Journal of Pastoral Care,* pp. 155-162, June, 1984.

Gould, J. and L. Craigmyle (eds.), *Your Death Warrant?: The Implications of Euthanasia,* Arlyington House, New Rochelle, New York, 1971.

Hala, M., Reminiscence Group Therapy Project, *Journal of Gerontological Nursing, 1*:3, pp. 35-41, 1975.

Hansel, T., *You Gotta Keep Dancin',* Word Books, Waco, Texas, 1984.

Harris, R., and S. Harris, Therapeutic Uses of Oral History Techniques in Medicine, *International Journal of Aging and Human Development, 12*:1, pp. 27-34, 1980-1981.

Havighurst, R. J. and R. Glasser, An Exploratory Study of Reminiscence, *Journal of Gerontology, 27*:2, pp. 245-253, 1972.

Hicks, A., Euthanasia: A Personal View, *Kenya Nursing Journal, 11*:1, pp. 24-25, 1983.

Hoelter, J. W. and R. J. Epley, Death Education and Death Related Attitudes, *Death Education, 3,* pp. 67-76, 1979.

Huasman, C., Life Review Therapy, *Journal of Gerontological Social Work, 3*:2, pp. 31-37, 1980.

Hughston, G. and S. Merriam, Reminiscence: A Nonformal Technique for Improving Cognitive Functioning in the Aged, *International Journal of Aging and Human Development, 15*:2, pp. 139-149, 1982.

Ingersol, B. and L. Goodman, History Comes Alive: Facilitating Reminiscence in a Group of Institutionalized Elderly, *Journal of Gerontological Social Work, 2*:4, pp. 303-319, 1980.

Jernigan, H. L., Bringing Together Psychology and Theology: Reflections on Ministry to the Bereaved, *The Journal of Pastoral Care,* pp. 88-102, June 1976.

Kalish, R. and D. Reynolds, *Death and Ethnicity: A Psychocultural Study,* University of Southern California, Los Angeles, 1976.

Kaminsky, K., Pictures from the Past: The Uses of Reminiscence in Casework with the Elderly, *Journal of Gerontological Social Work, 1*:1, pp. 19-31, 1978.

Kastenbaum, R. and R. Aisenberg, Death as a Thought, *Death: Current Perspectives,* E. S. Schneidman (ed.), Mayfield, Palo Alto, California, 1980.

Kiecolt-Glaser, J. K. and R. Glaser, Psychosocial Mediators of Immune Function, *Annals of Behavioural Medicine, 2,* pp. 16-20, 1987.

Kiereini, E. M., Evolution on Health Care in Developing Countries: The Challenge for the Nurse, *Kenya Nursing Journal, 11*:1, pp. 15-21, 1983.

Kiernat, J., The Use of Life Review Activity with Confused Nursing Home Residents, *American Journal of Occupational Therapy, 33*:5, pp. 306-310, 1979.

Knapp, R., *Beyond Endurance: When a Child Dies,* Schoeken Press, New York, 1986.

Lang, G., A Method for Doing Grief Work with Families Who Have Had a Child Die with Cancer, *The Journal of Pastoral Care,* pp. 209-215, Sept., 1984.

Lewis, C. N., The Adaptive Value of Reminiscing in Old Age, *Journal of Geriatric Psychiatry, 6*:1, pp. 117-121, 1973.

Lewis, M. I. and R. N. Butler, Life Review Therapy: Putting Memories to Work om Omdovodia; and Group Psychotherapy, *Geriatrics, 29*:11, pp. 165-173, 1974.

Lind, A. J., High Tech Dying: Reflections on the Death of a Patient in ICU, *The Journal of Pastoral Care,* pp. 65-67, Spring, 1989.

Liton, J. and S. C. Olstein, Therapeutic Aspects of Reminiscence, *Social Casework,* pp. 263-268, 1969.

LoGergo, M., Three Ways of Reminiscence in Theory and Practice, *International Journal of Aging and Human Development, 12*:1, pp. 39-48, 1980-1981.

Marks, A. S. and B. J. Calder, *Attitudes Toward Death and Funerals,* The Center for Marketing Sciences, Northwestern University, Chicago, 1982.

Mburu, F. M., Implications of the Ideology and Implementation of Health Policy of a Developing Country, *Social Science and Medicine, 15A*:1, pp. 17-24, 1981.

McMahon, A. W. and P. J. Rhudick, Reminiscing: Adaptational Significance in the Aged, *Archives of General Psychiatry, 10,* pp. 292-298, 1963.

Merriam, S., The Concept and Function of Reminiscence: A Review of the Research, *Gerontologist, 20*:5, pp. 604-609, 1980.

Miller, J., *You Can Become Whole Again: A Guide to Healing for Christians in Grief,* John Knox, Atlanta, 1981.

Minear, M., A. Therapeutic Funeral, *The Journal of Pastoral Care,* pp. 252-253, December 1979.

Mitchell, K. R., Ritual in Pastoral Care, *The Journal of Pastoral Care,* pp. 68-77, Spring, 1989.

Muhuhu, P. W., The Role of the Public Health Nurse in Provision of Mental Health Care in Kenya as I Envision It, *Kenya Nursing Journal, 8*:2, pp. 39-43, 1979.

Nighswonger, C. S., Ministry to the Dying as a Learning Encounter, *The Journal of Pastoral Care,* pp. 86-92, June, 1972.

Nyce, D. Y., Grieving People, *The Journal of Pastoral Care,* pp. 36-45, March 1982.

Oates, W. E., Pastoral Care and Counseling in Grief and Separation, *Fortress,* 1976.

Oglesby, W. B., Jr., Biblical Perspectives on Caring for Carers, *The Journal of Pastoral Care,* pp. 85-90, June 1984.

Ostheimer, N. C. and J. M. Ostheimer (eds.), *Life or Death: Who Controls,* Springer, New York, 1976.

Paylor, N. R., The Patient as Care Giver, *The Journal of Pastoral Care,* pp. 91-97, June, 1984.

Pearson, C. S., *The Hero Within,* Harper and Row, San Francisco, 1986.

Perrotta, P. and J. Meacham, Can a Reminiscing Intervention Alter Depression and Self-Esteem?, *International Journal of Aging and Human Development, 14*:1, pp. 23-29, 1981-1982.

Phillips, J. B., *Your God Is Too Small,* Macmillan, New York, 1961.

Pincus, A., Reminiscence in Aging and Its Implications for Social Work Practice, *Social Work, 15*:3, pp. 47-53, 1970.

Pollack, G., Mourning and Adaptation, *International Journal of Psycho-Analysis, 45*:4-5, pp. 341-361, 1961.

B. Rafheal, *The Anatomy of Bereavement,* Basic Books, New York, 1983.

T. Rando, *Parental Loss of a Child,* Research Press, Champaign, Illinois, 1986.

Redd, W. H. and P. B. Jacobsen, Emotions and Cancer, *Cancer, 62,* pp. 1871-1879, 1988.

Renner, P., Pastoral Accompaniment of the Cancer Patient, *Journal of Religion and Health,* pp. 138-148, Summer, 1984.

Revere, V. and S. Tobin, Myth and Reality: Older Person's Relationship to His Past, *International Journal of Aging and Development, 12*:1, pp. 15-26, 1980-1981.

Reynolds, D. K. and R. A. Kalish, Death Rates, Attitudes, and the Ethnic Press, *Ethnicity, 3,* pp. 305-316, 1976.

Romaniuk, M., Review: Reminiscence and the Second Half of Life, *Experimental Aging Research, 7,* pp. 315-335, 1981.

Romaniuk, M. and J. G. Romaniuk, Looking Back: An Analysis of Reminiscence Functions and Triggers, *Experimental Aging Research, 7,* pp. 477-489, 1981.

Ryden, M., Nursing Intervention in Support of Reminiscence, *Journal of Gerontological Nursing, 7*:8, pp. 461-463, 1981.

Schlafly, P., Death Education Comes into Open, *The Brooklyn Spectator,* April 18, 1988.

Sempebwa, J. W., Religiosity and Health Behavior in Africa, *Social Science and Medicine, 17,* pp. 2033-2036, 1983.

Sklar, L. S. and H. Anisman, Stress and Cancer, *Psychological Bulletin, 89*:3, pp. 369-406, 1981.

Slater, R. C., A Cross-cultural Study of the Death of a Child, *Director, 54,* pp. 21-29, 1984.

Smith, E. A., *A Spiritual Exercise for the Grieving,* Fortress, Philadelphia, 1984.

Spero, M. H., Confronting Death and the Concept of Life Review: The Talmudic Approach, *Omega, 12*:1, pp. 37-43, 1981-1982.

Volpe, J. J., Brain Death Determination in the Newborn, *Pediatrics, 80*:2, pp. 293-297, August, 1987.

Wahl, W., Helping the Dying Patient and His Family, *The Journal of Pastoral Care,* pp. 93-98, June, 1972.

Weber, O., *Foundations of Dogmatics,* Vol. I, Erdmans, Grand Rapids, Michigan, 1981.

Weisman, A. D., On the Value of Denying Death, *The Journal of Pastoral Care,* pp. 24-33, June 1972.

Weizman, S. and P. Kamm, About Mourning: Support and Guidance for the Bereaved, *Human Science,* 1985.

Wells, R. V., Dignity and Integrity in Dying, *The Journal of Pastoral Care,* pp. 99-107, June 1972.

Willenfield, L., *When Children Die,* Kendall/Hunt, Dubuque, Iowa, 1977.

Wolf, M. A., The Meaning of Education in Late Life: An Exploration of Life Review, *Gerontology and Geriatrics Education,* 5:3, pp. 51-59, 1985.

Worden, J. W. and W. Proctor, *PDA,* Prentice-Hall, Englewood Cliffs, New Jersey, 1976.

Wrye, H. and J. Churilla, Looking Inward, Looking Backward: Reminiscence and the Life Review, *Frontiers: A Journal of Women's Studies,* 2:2, pp. 77-84, 1979.

Yancey, P., *Where Is God When It Hurts?* Zondervon, Grand Rapids, Michigan, 1977.

Index

DATE DUE